The World
in 2050

The World in 2020: Power, Culture and Prosperity
Capital City: London as a Financial Centre
(with Frances Cairncross)
What Works: Success in Stressful Times

The World in 2050

How to Think About the Future

Hamish McRae

BLOOMSBURY PUBLISHING
LONDON · OXFORD · NEW YORK · NEW DELHI · SYDNEY

BLOOMSBURY PUBLISHING
Bloomsbury Publishing Plc
50 Bedford Square, London, WC1B 3DP, UK
29 Earlsfort Terrace, Dublin 2, Ireland

BLOOMSBURY, BLOOMSBURY PUBLISHING and the Diana logo are trademarks of
Bloomsbury Publishing Plc

First published in Great Britain 2022

A catalogue record for this book is available from the British Library

ISBN: HB: 978-1-5266-0007-3; TPB: 978-1-5266-0008-0; EBOOK: 978-1-4088-9997-7;
EPDF: 978-1-5266-5250-8

2 4 6 8 10 9 7 5 3 1

Typeset by Newgen KnowledgeWorks Pvt. Ltd., Chennai, India
Printed and bound in Great Britain by CPI Group (UK) Ltd, Croydon CRO 4YY

To find out more about our authors and books visit www.bloomsbury.com
and sign up for our newsletters

Contents

For my grandchildren, Magnus, Sebastian, Grace, Leonard and Frankie, and in memory of little James

Where the World Is Now

Introduction:
The Journey from 2020

HOW TO THINK ABOUT THE FUTURE

Why should anyone take predictions about the future seriously when so many in the past have turned out to be not just wrong, but absurdly so? That is the core challenge that this book faces. I believe it is worth tackling that challenge for three reasons.

First, if one is looking one generation ahead, twenty-five or thirty years, many of the broad economic trends that will dominate this period are already evident. Beyond that we move into science fiction. Thus we already know roughly how many people will be alive in 2050 and more or less where they will live. We can judge which countries and regions are likely to grow swiftly and which are likely to lose pace. We can see in broad outline the technologies that will drive economic development, though their details and the pace at which those technologies will be adopted are both hard to predict. And we can make some judgements about political and social developments, though turning points are always hard to catch. After all, we are helped by the intergenerational mathematics. The key decision-makers of the next thirty years are alive now, perhaps still studying in schools or universities, or maybe starting out on their chosen careers. Their ideas will shape the world.

Second, all of us make assumptions about the way the world will develop, certainly implicit and often explicit. For example, the careers we choose are shaped to some extent by our vision of the future. We don't choose jobs that look like being replaced by robots. Most of us are aware that we may have to retrain several times during our working careers. So to paint a picture of the future is to try to help people clarify their own ideas and expectations. Even if people disagree with some of the predictions, as of course they will, at least they will have tested their ideas against an alternative vision. One of the humbling experiences I have had a few times over the past quarter-century is that people have come up to me and said that my book *The World in 2020*, published in 1994, changed their life. They made choices they would not otherwise have made, and the fact that they were prepared to acknowledge this suggests that they thought those decisions were good ones. At least I hope so. If this book can help people put their expectations into some sort of order, then it will be doing something useful.

That leads to the third point: I have done this before. We are now beyond 2020 and can see to what extent that sketch of what the world might look like does indeed resemble the reality. I have tried to learn from the bull's-eyes – always satisfying to have a few of those – but even more from my mistakes.

That book envisaged a world that was more prosperous, healthier, better educated and informed, and more peaceful than in the early 1990s or indeed in any previous period of recorded history. This has proved broadly correct. None of the unbearable catastrophes that might have made all predictions meaningless, such as a nuclear war, have occurred. Even the Covid-19 pandemic seems likely to eventually be brought under control, albeit at massive economic and human costs. There was indeed a warning of a pandemic in that book, though in the context of the AIDS epidemic still raging in the early 1990s. But the book also warned that it would be difficult for the advanced countries to continue to raise the living standards of their citizens, and that the West's liberal democracies would be under pressure as a result. That, too, has been the case, though I suspect that the economists are at fault in their measurement of living standards, and fail to take into account the benefits of the communications revolution. As for the emerging world, the book if anything underestimated the progress it would make. That China would boom was obvious, though it has done even better than I had expected. Less obvious was India's emergence as a more buoyant economy, albeit an uneven success story, and I quite failed to appreciate how it would leap forward and by 2020 be growing even faster than China.

Economics has a powerful impact on politics and one of the great themes of this book is that China will pass the US to become the world's largest economy and that that shift of economic power will generate massive political tension between these two great nations. But there are other forces beyond economics that drive political change, and these include identity, religion and nationalism. The long hand of history hangs over everything, and politicians have to try to manage the conflicting wishes and aspirations of citizens in that context.

So it was possible back in the early 1990s to see that the UK would feel increasingly uncomfortable with its relationship with Europe, and that it might leave the European Union and seek to negotiate a free trade deal instead. I did acknowledge it might be very difficult to do so. But sometimes the outcome of a known tension flips the other way. I felt there was an even chance that Scotland would have become independent by 2020. As it turned out its electorate has chosen not to follow that path, at least not on the timescale envisaged. I feel it remains an even chance, maybe a little less than that.

As far as the EU is concerned, it has so far proved more cohesive that I had expected, for I had envisaged it would be more of a multi-speed Europe, with an inner core of founder states and an outer ring around it. But there will never be a final form for Europe, and it may be that the pressures against greater integration will dominate the next thirty years. Political structures have to evolve to meet the aspirations of each generation, and those aspirations change.

You can see this in the US. It was clear even in the early 1990s that there would be some sort of populist challenge to the vested

interest groups, against what I wrote was the power 'of the medical
and legal establishments, of the National Rifle Association, of the
Hollywood moguls, even of the liberal press'. I was lucky in my
timing, for I expected it to be in the second decade of this century,
but as I acknowledged it was impossible to see what form this
radical shift in political attitudes would take. Put it this way: it was
impossible to predict that Donald Trump would be president, but
it was not difficult to identify the forces that led to his election.

What about the other forces that drive change? First and
foremost, what about the pressure on the environment? It was easy
to predict that concern about the environment would be greater in
2020 than it was in 1990. Population pressure and the explosion of
growth in the emerging world would see to that. It was easy, too,
to see that local pollution would be tackled with some success in
the developed world, but that worries about climate change would
climb. One of the great questions now is how grave is the threat of
global warming, and this book seeks to make some judgements on
that. If the climate outlook appears more serious now than it did
a quarter of a century ago, other fears such as a shortage of oil and
gas seem less pressing. We remain a global economy driven mainly
by fossil fuels, but renewable sources of energy are building fast.
By and large, however, the concerns of 1990 remain the concerns
of 2020. The world is just rather more frightened now than it was
then – and, I judge, rightly so.

The hardest area to predict has proved to be technology, and
in particular the social implications of technological change. That
was my most serious 'miss'. I could see that the world would
be transformed by computers being linked together. That was
what we were doing already as journalists in news gathering and
reporting. But I could not see the mechanism by which this would
happen. My excuse is that at the beginning of the 1990s, while
the internet existed as an academic and defence tool, it had yet
to have widespread general application. The key innovations that
transformed it were developed progressively through the 1990s.
Thus the World Wide Web was not made available to the public
until 1991. Mosaic, the first popular browser, was launched in 1993,

and the first effective search engines, WebCrawler, Lycos, AltaVista and Yahoo!, came through in 1994–5. Google, the search engine that came to dominate the world, was launched in 1998.[1]

This phenomenon is not new. It was noted by the economist Alfred Marshall, in 1920, when he wrote: 'The full importance of an epoch-making idea is often not perceived in the generation in which it is made. A new discovery is seldom effective for practical purposes till many minor improvements and subsidiary discoveries have gathered themselves around it.'

And so it has been with the motor car, which needed a raft of minor improvements such as the windscreen wiper and the self-starter, and some major ones such as higher quality roads; or the supermarket, which needed Sylvan Goldman, owner of a supermarket chain in Oklahoma, to invent the supermarket trolley in 1936. I'm not sure one could call the iPhone a 'minor improvement', but by bringing together mobile telephony and the internet it made possible the array of services that we now take for granted. One could, back in the middle 1990s, have envisaged a superior mobile phone that would do what the iPhone does, but Steve Jobs had to work out how to make the vision reality.

That brings us on to the challenge of forecasting what technology might make possible by 2050. Projecting incremental advance is easy. Fly across the Atlantic now and you may well be in an aircraft built in the early 1990s. The newest generation of aircraft are more efficient and the next generation will be more efficient still. But people will still be flying in today's aircraft in 2050, and the laws of physics don't change. The global car fleet will be largely electric and self-driving will be the norm. But vehicles won't travel significantly faster in 2050 than they do in 2020. Falling costs and greater access to cars will have social impacts, but we can have some feeling for what those might be.

Projecting the next great leaps of technology is much harder. We simply don't know what advances currently at the frontiers of the possible will truly change the world, and which ones will prove blind alleys. Just because something can be done does not mean it is of any practical use. Or it may simply be too expensive for widespread application. There are, however, many areas where there are social or economic issues that are crying out for a technical fix. Take something very simple: security scans at airports. Technology should be able to make that seamless. You should be able to walk through a scanner with your belongings, and with none of the stuff about putting your toothpaste in a little plastic bag. Technology will identify who you are, as well as what you are bringing with you. But – and this is the harder thing to see – technologies that identify and track everyone may not be socially or politically acceptable. Imagine a world where every immigrant is tracked every moment of the day, or every person on earth is on a DNA database.

This leads to ideas about how societies may develop everything from the job contract, through family organisation, through inequality, to the future of the nation state itself. It was possible in the early 1990s to see that self-employment would grow, which it has in many advanced economies. It was harder to see what would happen to that most basic element of family life, the marriage contract. As it has turned out divorce rates have levelled out in the US and much of the developed world, but they have not fallen as fast as I expected. It was harder, too, to make a judgement as to whether inequality would rise in the developed world, and the data there is not conclusive anyway. But it was easy to see that, globally, inequality would fall as the emerging world's living standards caught up with those of the advanced countries. As for the nation state – well, it has made rather a comeback. As the weight of China and India, both strongly nationalistic entities, grows, it seems reasonable to expect that comeback to persist. Indeed, one of the major themes of this book is that the social and political ideas of the two Asian giants will have a massive impact on Europe and North America. Economic success is not everything, but it is a hugely important driver of ideas about society.

THE ECONOMIC CORE

In two important ways it is easier now to predict about the future of the world economy than it was in the 1990s. One, paradoxically,

is that we know more about the past. The other is that a lot of work
has been done trying to model future growth, and this has – with
some qualifications – proved quite accurate.

For the past, our debt is to the late Angus Maddison, a British
economic historian who did much of his work at the Organisation
for Economic Co-operation and Development (OECD) in Paris
and the University of Groningen in the Netherlands.[2] He looked
back over the past 2,000 years and calculated the GDP of the
various regions and countries of the world, together with GDP per
head. There is a snapshot of the world at the time of Christ, then
increasingly detailed calculations of what happened since the year
1000. His core findings were published by the OECD in a series of
booklets, notably in *The World Economy: A Millennial Perspective* in
2001. He died in 2010, but his work has been carried on by a group
of academic friends and followers.

This long view of history shows what for many people will be huge
surprises – as you can see from the graph here, drawn from his work.

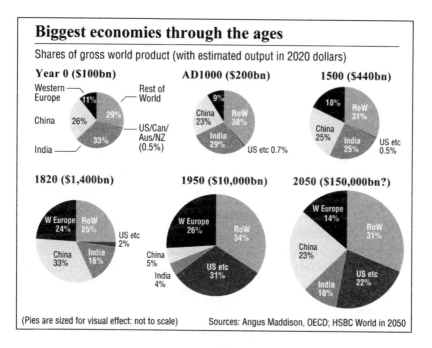

Biggest economies through the ages

Shares of gross world product (with estimated output in 2020 dollars)

Year 0 ($100bn)
Western Europe 11%
Rest of World
China 26%
29%
US/Can/Aus/NZ (0.5%)
India 33%

AD1000 ($200bn)
9%
China 23%
RoW 38%
India 29%
US etc 0.7%

1500 ($440bn)
18%
RoW 31%
China 25%
India 25%
US etc 0.5%

1820 ($1,400bn)
W Europe 24%
RoW 25%
US etc 2%
China 33%
India 16%

1950 ($10,000bn)
W Europe 26%
RoW 34%
China 5%
India 4%
US etc 31%

2050 ($150,000bn?)
W Europe 14%
RoW 31%
China 23%
US etc 22%
India 10%

(Pies are sized for visual effect: not to scale)   Sources: Angus Maddison, OECD; HSBC World in 2050

Back in the year AD 1 the Roman Empire was only the third largest economic region. Both India and China were much larger, with China nearly double its size and India larger still. They were still by far the largest economies in 1000 and 1500, dwarfing the European countries – indeed, right through to 1820, when the Industrial Revolution began to enable Europe to pull ahead. Then, through the nineteenth century, Europe grew rapidly and the US began its rise to global stardom, though it was not until the 1880s that the US passed China to become the world's largest economy. By 1950 what Angus Maddison dubbed 'Western Offshoots', the US, Canada, Australia and New Zealand, had become one-third of the world economy. China and India had fallen far behind.

Now look forward to the projection for the world in 2050. Sometime around 2030, China again takes its place as number one, and India surges forward. The US will have had a mere 150 years in pole position. We will come to the economic modelling behind this projection in a moment. You can understand why many people in China feel the country is simply resuming its natural position in the world.

As for India, it had a larger economy than that of the UK until the 1890s, when it was number three after China and the US. It looks as though it will pass the UK in the early 2020s, and if by 2050 it has again become the world's third largest, it, too, will be resuming what many Indians feel is its natural position.

There is one further example of the pull of history that is both intriguing and troubling. It is the changing position of Russia. On the eve of the First World War, and just before the Russian Revolution, its economy was second only to Germany among the European nations. It was larger than the UK, France or Italy. It retained that position through to the 1960s, and in 1990 on the eve of the breakup of the Soviet Union, what soon was to become the Russian Federation had a larger economy than any European nation. Then came, in economic and also in social terms, a catastrophe. You can argue that Russia's command economy was unsustainable and that what happened when the Soviet Union broke up demonstrated that. But there can be no argument about the scale of the collapse. By 2020 its economy was not only smaller than those of Germany, the UK, France or Italy. It was smaller in relative terms – relative that is to its European neighbours – than at any stage in the past 2,000 years. You can begin to understand Russian resentment at its diminished status.

Angus Maddison's work gives us perspective on where we are now. For perspective on the likely future, the best place to start is the work of Robert Solow.[3] He is an American economist who won a Nobel Prize in 1987 for his development of a model that sought to explain how economic growth took place. He distinguishes between two different forms of growth. One is frontier or cutting-edge growth, where growth comes from developing and applying new ideas. This encompasses everything from more efficient factories to using new technologies to improve the quality of services – think how satnav cuts delivery times. This is the main driver in the most advanced economies. The other is catch-up or copy-and-paste growth, where a less-developed country applies the technologies invented elsewhere, and this is the main driver of the emerging economies. Put bluntly, this form of growth is why China will pass the US to become the world's largest economy.

An economic model is just a model: you have to decide what variables to put into it. The most famous application of the Solow approach was by Goldman Sachs with its BRICs report. The first mention of the acronym that brought together the four largest emerging economies was in a modest paper by Jim O'Neill, Goldman's chief economist, in 2001.[4] It noted that these four countries, Brazil, Russia, India and China, were contributing more growth to the world economy than the Group of Seven (G7), the seven largest developed countries, the US, Japan, Germany, the UK, France, Italy and Canada. And it pointed out that China was already a larger economy than Italy, and that the BRICs as a group would grow much more quickly than the G7. A couple of years later O'Neill returned to the theme, using economic modelling to quantify this out-performance, with his paper *Dreaming with BRICs: The Path to 2050.*[5]

The results were stunning. It projected that China would pass Japan to become the second largest economy by 2015 and the US, to become the largest, around 2040. India would pass Japan in the 2030s to become third after the US. Russia and Brazil would also prosper, both taking a much larger place in the world economy than they had back in the early 2000s. O'Neill did qualify these projections by saying that they were optimistic in the sense that they assumed reasonably successful development, and that there was a good chance that the right conditions for such growth would not fall into place in one or more of these countries. We now know that while China and India have, if anything, beaten these projections, both Russia and Brazil have for different reasons started to fall short.

This paper struck a chord that resonated around the world. It is surely the best current example of the aphorism attributed to Victor Hugo that 'nothing is as powerful as an idea whose time has come'. It caught the shift of power that is taking place and will by 2050 have reshaped the world. So now there is an annual BRICS economic summit and a development bank based in Shanghai. (The S stands for South Africa, Africa's largest economy until it was passed by Nigeria in 2012. It was invited to join the group so that the continent would be represented.)

However, the BRIC countries are very different. Both China and India are huge, rapidly growing developing economies, with China far further advanced along the path than India. Brazil is a middle-income economy, having developed much earlier – really from the 1930s onward – but one that is struggling to advance further. Russia is still coping with the disruption following the breakup of the Soviet Union, and while it has huge natural resources it also, unlike India and Brazil, has a sharply falling population. As a general way of viewing the world, the BRIC work is wonderful. It caught the mood of the moment, and Jim O'Neill, now Lord O'Neill, deserves great credit for promoting it. But the concept of the BRICs has proved misleading. To oversimplify a bit, the economies of the developed world are broadly the same, whereas those of the developing and emerging world are very different.

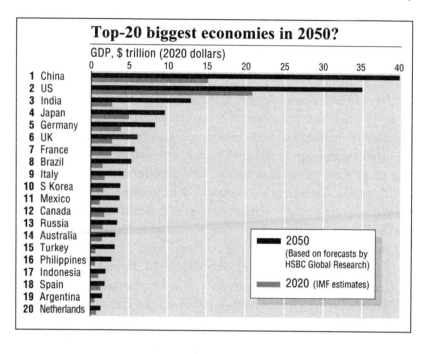

Another version of the model, developed by Harvard Professor Robert Barro, was used by the bank HSBC, and its projections were published in 2011 and 2012. That is where those projections in the graph above come from. As the main author of this report, Karen Ward, notes, whatever happens in the frontier nations, there are many years of catch-up growth left for the rest of the world. However, she also adds: 'As economies become wealthier and technology more sophisticated, they will gradually lose the advantages of "starting from behind".'[6]

Whether a country manages to catch up depends on a number of things, but most important are its levels of education and the quality of its institutional infrastructure, such as property rights and the rule of law. Intriguingly, democracy may not matter that much, at least not in the short and medium term. A good example of a high-income, non-democratic economy, but one with good education and until 2020 the rule of law, is Hong Kong. It will in the years ahead become something of a test case of the relationship between the rule of law and growth. Will its performance falter now that China has imposed tighter control over the territory's legal system? To some extent at least, the answer is almost certainly yes.

The HSBC team re-ran their model with some different assumptions, for example the faster-than-forecast decline in population in Russia. Their work was also broadened to cover a hundred countries. A rather different set of projections resulted, and these have been the starting point for the economic forecasts of this book. The largest economies – China, the US, India, Japan, Germany and the UK – remain in the same position as they were in the Goldman work, but Russia in particular is much further down the league table. Indeed, based on these projections, it will have a smaller economy than Turkey or Spain.

These are just projections and need to be seen as such. They are not what will inevitably happen. Rather, they are the best basis we have for thinking about what may well happen. They raise obvious questions. For the frontier nations – the US of course but also all other sophisticated economies – the great question is whether productivity and hence living standards are indeed stuck. That is something dealt with at length in the sections of the book devoted to technology. If the next generation in the developed world does not have a higher standard of living than its parents and grandparents, then the social glue that holds societies together would be much weakened. If on the other hand living standards are actually rising and will continue to do so, and much of the problem is mis-measurement, then it is possible to be much more optimistic. I shall try to demonstrate that to be the case.

For the emerging world, the questions come in two groups. First there are a string of issues about the ability of countries to sustain catch-up growth. How good is a country at developing its human capital? Is there enough investment in both physical infrastructure (its roads, ports and so on), and legal and regulatory infrastructure (its national finances, its civil service, its currency, its trade relationships, etc.)? Second, once an emerging economy starts to approach full developed status and the gains from cut-and-copy growth diminish, can it then become a true frontier nation? If not, why not? There are some harsh lessons from history here. Japan made that transition; Argentina failed to do so. I shall try and make some judgements there, acknowledging that I will inevitably sometimes be over-optimistic and sometimes the reverse. The big judgement is that the world will indeed continue to become more prosperous, as well as healthier, better educated and I hope more peaceful. But there are enormous challenges, of which perhaps the most important will be those of the environment.

THE ENVIRONMENTAL CHALLENGES

Our perspective on the environmental challenges the world faces has shifted over the past thirty years. Some concerns remain the same. Water stress was, is, and will continue to be one of the grave pressure points. The loss of habitat, which has continued, should alarm anybody who wants their children and grandchildren to be able to experience the great variety of different creatures on our planet. But some of the great worries of the 1990s have receded.

One then was that the world would reach 'peak oil', the point at which global oil production would start to decline because the big established oilfields would run dry and we would not discover new supplies fast enough to meet demand. That has not proved the case. Not only has a lot more conventional oil been discovered, but hydraulic fracturing of oil-bearing rocks, fracking, has opened up vast new supplies. Instead, there is the prospect that the peak in oil production will come not from a shortfall of supply but, rather, from a decline in demand. Greater efficiency, general efforts at energy conservation, and above all the switch of the world's vehicle fleet from the internal combustion engine to electric power, will start to reduce oil demand. The two other fossil fuels, gas and coal, will remain important. Though the world economy will still depend on fossil fuels in 2050, alternative sources of energy will steadily be replacing them.

Another concern was whether the world could adequately feed 7.5 billion people – in 1990 it was 5.3 billion. It seemed then it would be a close-run thing. As it has turned out, not only is the world better fed in the sense that calorie consumption per person has risen, but there are fewer malnourished people both in absolute numbers and proportionate to the increased world population. In 1990, nearly a quarter of the world was malnourished, while by 2017 it was close to 10 per cent – still too many, but real progress.

Yet another concern was the impact of urbanisation. Would the mega-cities of the developing world be able to cope with their burgeoning populations? The answer there seems that broadly they have. Urban incomes are almost always higher and health outcomes better than in the country. Local pollution remains a grave concern, but the worst fears of thirty years ago seem unfounded.

If these specific issues seem in many cases more manageable than they might have done, there is a general worry of such huge scale that it overshadows much of the environmental progress that has been made. It is climate change. It is hard to write dispassionately about climate change partly because the science is complex, but more because any discussion provokes a strong politicised response. What is beyond dispute is that whereas thirty years ago there were real concerns about global warming and rising carbon dioxide emissions, there was less certainty about the link between them, and less widespread concern about the danger and consequences of climate change. Now this issue is centre stage.

How the debate will shape over the next generation will depend on a number of things. These start with the science, for we will gradually improve our understanding of what is happening. That will bring clarity and help shape the world's response. As we know more, the scope for political debate will narrow. It will be more 'what should we do to cope?' and less 'do we need to do anything?'. All that is for later in this book. The point to recognise now is that ideas and concerns change as evidence becomes available. The world is as worried about what human beings are doing to their planet as they were thirty years ago. But some worries have retreated and one very big one has advanced.

THE TECHNOLOGY CONUNDRUM

The past thirty years have seen rapid technological advance, some would argue the fastest ever in such a period, though that is less clear. Yet for most people in the developed world, this cornucopia of new products and services – initially the internet, then the iPhone, Google, Facebook, and the millions of apps – have not increased living standards in the advanced economies to any significant extent. Can that be right?

Intuitively, it can't be. Every previous period of rapid technological change has seen increased living standards for the majority of people throughout the developed world, since the Industrial Revolution set the whole process in motion. There have, sadly, been groups of people who have had their jobs displaced and have lost out, and there been environmental and health costs of technical advance. But overall, in the advanced countries living standards have risen steadily since the early 1800s. You would expect, given the explosion of new technologies that have been developed over the past thirty years, that this would have continued. But this is not what the figures show. Median earnings in the US have barely risen in real terms since the 1970s, while in Europe the picture is more varied, but certainly since 2007 they have at best been flat. In general, people at the top of the income range have done well, while in most developed countries those at the bottom have seen their living standards protected. But for the great mass in the middle it has been a dispiriting time.

There are two views about this. One, argued among others by Robert J. Gordon, a professor at Northwestern University in Evanston, Illinois, is that the great burst of American prosperity is over. Productivity, which had slowed to a crawl, will be held back by rising inequality, stagnating education, an ageing population and the rising debt of college students and the federal government. His book *The Rise and Fall of American Growth*[7] suggests that the next generation of Americans may be the first to have a lower standard of living than their parents.

The other view, argued by Professor Hal Varian, an emeritus professor from the University of California at Berkeley, now chief economist at Google, is that there isn't a productivity problem. Rather, there is a measurement problem: we are undercounting the benefits that the communications revolution has brought.[8] One of his examples is photography. He notes that between 2000 and 2016 the number of photographs taken worldwide increased twentyfold. But because the shift from film and printing to digital and online cut the cost of each one from some fifty cents to zero, this shows up as a reduction in GDP. The living standards of the world have risen in the sense that people take many more photographs, but living standards as shown by GDP per head have fallen because once you have a smartphone, the cost of taking and sharing a photo is free.

When there is a known product such as a photograph, or a service such as a telephone call, and the cost falls dramatically, you can make some sort of adjustment to take this into account. But there are many other examples of new products and services made possible by the communications revolution where it is almost impossible to do so. What price should we put on social media? As of 2021 approximately 60 per cent of the world's population share their data on some social media platform. For nearly all of them the service is free to the user, and the advertisements that pay for it are funded largely by diverting money from other media. So this great revolution does not show up at all in higher living standards.

This creates a huge challenge for anyone trying to see how technology might change the world over the next generation. What I think we can see is that the combination of two technologies, big data and artificial intelligence, has huge potential for increasing the efficiency of service industries. Data is accumulating on a scale that would be unimaginable a generation ago. But there is too much for human beings to be able to use, learn from or deploy effectively. That is where AI, which has been around since the 1960s, comes in. This matters because it is vital to increase the efficiency of the service industries, but it has proved extremely hard to do so. Services make up some 80 per cent of the US and UK economies. Yet while manufacturing has become steadily more efficient, service industry productivity has barely risen.

It is easy to see why. You can automate a factory, but you cannot automate a hospital. Mass manufacturing was the great driver of increased living standards during the twentieth century. Manufacturers produce near-identical products in a carefully controlled single location. Services, by contrast, must be crafted for the individual at multiple locations. A doctor's appointment, a child's music lesson or a retiree's pension plan all require human attention to make sure that the service fits the need. So somehow we have to find ways of applying the extraordinary technological advances in IT to do for services what the moving production line did for manufacturing.

In one sense this is wonderful, because we can be confident that living standards will continue to advance. But like all changes it will be disruptive, and deeply so. It is easy to be negative about such disruption because it is easy to put a negative interpretation on what has happened over previous periods of disruption. For example, when looking at the implications for AI, it is easy to focus on the jobs being lost to it, as many will be, rather than try to imagine how people released from repetitive tasks will find more creative and fulfilling careers. Just as it was impossible to imagine the boom jobs of 2020 in 1990, it is impossible now to imagine what jobs many people will be doing in 2050. But we can have a feeling for some of the social and educational skills that will be in demand. They will include 'hard' skills such as numeracy and literacy, but also 'soft' ones, including flexibility and empathy for other human beings. How you teach, encourage or nudge young people to build these is another matter.

That leads to a troubling question. Will inequality in the developed world rise over the next generation as a result of technological change? Viewed globally, inequality will almost certainly narrow rapidly over the years to 2050. That is a result of catch-up economic growth, driven by the transfer of technology. If the economic projections noted above are anything like correct, China, India, much of Africa and so on will narrow the gap in living standards between them and the developed world. There will be the greatest explosion of the number of middle-class people that has ever happened in human history. In that sense, the world in 2050 will be a middle-class world.

But a narrowing of differentials between countries can take place alongside a widening of differentials within them. That has happened since the early 1990s in most of the developed world, to some extent in incomes, but more markedly in wealth. Indeed, within most emerging countries wealth gaps have risen, too. Is this a result of technology? In part it must be, for it is pretty clear that large swathes of production-line and middle-management jobs are no longer needed. Meanwhile, demand has increased at the top and bottom end of the skill range.

There are, however, other forces at work. The West has had a long period of peace in the sense that there have been no major wars. Wars destroy wealth. Thus there was a sharp narrowing of wealth differentials in Europe and to some extent in the US as a result of two world wars. Put crudely, those who have wealth, the rich, pay for war. There have also been no financial catastrophes over the past thirty years on the scale of the crash of 1929, or the great inflation of the 1970s. The two economic crises of the twenty-first century, those triggered by the banking crash of 2008 and by the Covid-19 pandemic, have certainly destroyed some wealth, but nothing like on the scale of a major war. The world economy recovered quite swiftly from the banking crash, and while writing in 2021 it is too early to make a judgement, it does look as though the economic scars of the pandemic will heal reasonably swiftly. Put simply, these two crises have not narrowed wealth and income differentials. If anything, they may have increased them.

What both of these crises have done, however, is make people across the developed world become more concerned about unfairness – the way in which market economies distribute their rewards. Those families that are doing well seem to be doing better, while those that are struggling find the struggle harder.

There is a further twist to the story of increasing inequalities in the developed world: a change in dating and mating, which seems to have been brought about in part at least by technology. There has been a tendency since the 1980s, particularly in America, for young people to choose their life partners from similar education and income groups rather than from different ones. But this phenomenon, clumsily called assortative mating, seems to have increased as a result of online dating.[9] When people meet each other randomly, in a bar or at a workplace, at least some sorting has taken place: lower-paid workers go to the pub along with high-paid ones. When people specify precisely the sort of person they want to meet, it seems that they choose people similar to themselves in terms of education, interests and so on. If high-earners mate with other high-earners, the result is that inequality increases still further.

The point here is simply that technology has complex social and economic consequences, consequences far beyond the creation and destruction of certain types of jobs. At the moment, the focus is on how technology changes people's access to and understanding of news: the 'fake news' issue. It may well be that the shift from paper to online has encouraged people to choose the news and commentary they receive more specifically than before. As a result, technology may have hardened political divisions. But it may well turn out that the more important impact of the communications revolution on human behaviour is not how people shop or vote, but how they choose their life partners!

THE SHIFTING IDEAS ABOUT HOW SOCIETY SHOULD BE ORGANISED

Predicting social change is always difficult, but in some ways it is even more difficult now than it was in the early 1990s. It was reasonable then to assume that Western democratic values would spread more widely through the world. Francis Fukuyama's essay arguing this, *The End of History?*, was published in 1989; it was expanded into a book in 1992.[10] For much of the past thirty years, that is indeed what has happened. The fall of the Berlin Wall and the expansion eastwards of the European Union, the dissolution of the

USSR, the economic reforms started by Deng Xiaoping in China, the relaxation of bureaucratic controls on the Indian economy, the gradual adoption of market economics in much of Africa and Latin America – all these reflected an acceptance that the West had won the intellectual battle as to how economies should be organised. If your country wanted to become rich it had to follow the Western model. There was no alternative.

This seemed to be a triumph of consumerism over communism, in the sense that the people of the emerging world relished their ability to acquire the trappings of a Western lifestyle. China, which produced less than a million passenger cars in 1990, was by 2017 making a peak of some twenty-five million.[11] It is an extraordinary industrial and economic story, but also a tangible illustration of an extraordinary social story. The people who had endured a brand of communism for some forty years that repressed individualism and personal consumption have now become just as eager to 'keep up with the Joneses' as American consumers did from the 1950s onwards. Chinese citizens show their status by the car they drive just as enthusiastically as their American and European counterparts did a couple of generations earlier. It is a reasonable assumption that, as India grows richer, its people will move along a similar path – actually, it is already pretty evident that they will.

This leads to a key question: will the values of the new middle class of China, India and the emerging world more generally be broadly similar to those of the middle class of the developed world?

I think the answer will be: broadly, yes. But neither sets of values are static. Look at the changes in family structure across most of the developed world since the Second World War, with the decline of marriage, the loosening of the ties of extended family and the increase in the proportion of people living alone. Attitudes to the role of women in the workforce have changed radically, too, though many women feel they have not changed nearly enough. It seems sensible to expect parallel swings in social attitudes among the new global middle class, which in any case is far from a common entity. Not only is the spectrum of social values across the emerging world surely much greater than the spectrum across the developed world;

there is even greater tension than in the West between longstanding cultural values and those of modernity.

Yet there does seem to be a commonality of what might be called 'middle-class life', in the sense that a family home in the suburbs of Bangalore is not so different from a family home in the suburbs of any large city anywhere in the world. Or take that most basic family decision of how many children to have: as incomes rise and women and girls gain more access to education, families become smaller everywhere in the world. If there is to be a big shift in what the middle class aspires to, it will probably be a global one. It is easy to foresee a world dominated by middle-class values, simply because that income group will dominate the world's population – a state of affairs that has never occurred before in human history. But it is harder to see whether and how those values will themselves change, when they are no longer shaped principally by people in Europe and America. That is part of the great shift in power that will continue to take place, a shift that will affect global politics for generations to come.

POLITICS, RELIGION, CONFLICT

Economic power and political power are inevitably intertwined, but as we have learned over the past half-century, the link is tenuous. For obvious reasons neither Japan nor Germany have sought to rebuild their military power, but they have not really attempted to create overseas economic empires either. Where their companies have established overseas plants it is because of commercial necessity: German cars are built in the US and China to enable them to serve those markets, rather than for some greater national purpose. Russia, by contrast, has certainly sought to deploy power globally but it has been hampered by the weakness of its economy. Its outrageous invasion of Ukraine began as this book went to press. While it is impossible to make any judgement of the full implications of its action, it seems quite clear Russia will emerge even weaker in the years ahead.

China, conversely, has been more cautious, and much more effective, in making the world take it seriously, not only as an economic superpower but also as a commercial and political one. So it builds roads in Africa not simply to enable it to extract minerals and agricultural products, but also to forcibly expand its political influence. Inevitably, China's economic success story carries the explicit message for the rest of the developing world that its political system delivers the goods. There is also an implicit message that China has provided economic support more effectively and less intrusively than the aid programmes of Western democracies and the activities of NGOs. There has naturally been criticism of the way Chinese investment has taken place, for example the use of Chinese rather than local labour. But anyone driving around sub-Saharan Africa will be impressed by the quality of the roads and other infrastructure that China has provided.[12]

Chinese investment in the West has also had a strategic focus: to gain access to technology or natural resources. Investment, initially welcomed, has been subjected to greater scrutiny in both the US and Europe, partly because of a lack of reciprocity but also because of a wider sense, even a fear, that Western openness is somehow being exploited. This tension will not go away, and it will have to be managed as China's clout within the world economy increases.

The link between economic relationships and political relationships is one of the central themes of this book. Political tension between the US and Europe on the one hand, and Russia on the other, has been the dominant feature of the world since the Second World War. Sadly, that will continue – sadly, because there is no underlying reason why it needs to. Russia and Europe are natural economic partners, while the US has won the economic war with Russia. With China it is all too easy to see how what should be a cooperative relationship may break down. China's relations with its East Asia neighbours are difficult. Its aspirations to control the South China Sea will be hard to square with maritime law, and will be a flashpoint for generations to come. Will the whole region, with the exception of Japan, become China's accepted sphere of influence, rather as Latin America became subsumed by the power of the United States at the beginning of the twentieth century? Would the US accept that?

Similar pressures will continue between China and India. This is not new at all, for they have been evident for the past half-century. But as both countries become more important in the world order, containing these pressures, essentially nationalism, may become harder. In 2020 China's economy was five times as big as India's and its GDP per head nearly five times bigger, too. But this disparity is quite recent. In the first half of the twentieth century India actually had a higher GDP per head than China, and even given China's larger population, China had only a slightly larger economy than India in the early 1960s. In the 2020s India will pass China in population and will almost certainly continue to grow more swiftly. So if China is the great rising power now, by 2050 India will be in that position.

There are other potential flashpoints and it is worth noting two further ones here, regions where the balance of power has shifted and will continue to shift. One is the frontier between Siberian Russia and China. It will become progressively harder for Russia's ageing and shrinking population to run the economies of its Far East. By contrast, China needs access to the region's natural resources and has ample human resources to do so. From a practical point of view, large numbers of Chinese people already live and work in eastern Siberia. There is also a legal issue. Parts of what was Chinese territory, including Outer Manchuria, were ceded by China in the Convention of Peking in 1860 and other late nineteenth-century treaties, and so have only been under Russian control for some 150 years. These treaties, including the 1842 Treaty of Nanjing, which gave control of Hong Kong island to the British, are regarded as unequal by China, with some justification.[13] At some stage it is easy to see China seeking to reclaim those lost territories, too. In the early 1990s the relative positions of Russia and China were quite different and this sort of action would not have been conceivable. Now both in population and in economic power China is much stronger than Russia. By 2050 that gulf will have become wider still.

The other region where big global forces have shifted is in the Middle East. There was until the early 1990s a measure of stability there. There had been wars, including the Six Day War in 1967, the Iraq–Iran conflict from 1980 to 1988, and the First Gulf War following the invasion of Kuwait in 1990. But however troubling these conflicts have been – and no one should try to play down the misery they have caused – they were largely contained. Since then the region has become even less stable, with the Second Gulf War and particularly since the so-called Arab Spring, the series of political upheavals across the Middle East and North Africa that began at the end of 2010.

It is too early to be able to put much perspective on this unrest, but it is important to recognise one striking feature of the region: its demography. Population growth is very rapid and the median age very young. For example, Egypt's population in 1990 was 57 million, in 2020 it had risen to 102 million, and in 2050 it is projected to rise to 160 million. The median age is currently twenty-five. For Iraq the corresponding figures are 17 million, 40 million, and 80 million, and the median age just twenty. It will inevitably be hard to manage this rate of population growth in any stable and sustainable manner, and still harder to fulfil the hopes and aspirations of these millions of young people. Why, they quite reasonably ask, should young Europeans have so much better life chances?

Then there is religion. It is difficult to discuss the rising religious tensions, obviously within the Middle East but actually everywhere, in a way that does not cause offence. Writing in the early 1990s I avoided the subject largely because I failed to foresee that rising religious feelings would have a material importance in shaping the world over the years to 2020. That was clearly wrong. It is impossible to ignore them now, but extremely difficult to predict how they will affect different societies over the period to 2050. Looking back over the past two millennia there have been periods of religious conflict, sometimes of a particularly horrible kind. But there have also been long periods of tolerance, with different communities living together in harmony and mutual respect.

So I suggest looking forward to 2050 the question is: when does the world next move back into a period of religious harmony? Do we have to wait for another generation, or will there be some sort of turning point in the immediate future? That is one of the issues explored in the pages to come.

And then there is war. The nightmare that hangs over all Europeans, and indeed anyone with any sensitivity to history, is the horror of the First World War and the catastrophic first half of the twentieth century. A century of extraordinary progress, with its flaws, of course, was blown to bits by the arrogance and stupidity of European leaders. Writing in the 1990s, I felt that the folk memory of that stupidity would preserve stability for another generation. But I was much more worried about the years from 2020 to 2050 and beyond once that memory faded. Russia's behaviour proves my fears were justified.

It is impossible not to be worried now, but for some perspective I find it helpful to read the work of Stephen Pinker, the Canadian professor of cognitive psychology, who has spent most of his career at MIT and Harvard. In particular his 2011 book, *The Better Angels of Our Nature*,[14] demonstrated that violence has declined both in the long and the shorter terms. That is true even factoring in the chaos of the first half of the twentieth century. We may feel that the world is full of conflict, as we see and read evidence of it every day. But actually we are as human beings behaving better to each other – more kindly, more cooperatively – than ever before in the history of our species. If it does not feel like that, perhaps that has something to do with our access to and consumption of the news media. As a journalist I am very aware that good news is not news, whereas bad news is. People buy pessimism. Those of us who do sometimes focus on success stories get mocked for our supposedly Panglossian view of the world. I suspect, too, that it has something to do with the growth of NGOs, which highlight disasters, for it is their job to respond to them. Indeed, that is the principal pitch they make when raising funds. But it may also be because we have a lower tolerance towards violence than earlier generations. We expect more of people, and of ourselves. If that is right, then it is really encouraging – and provides hope for the next thirty years.

A BETTER-BALANCED WORLD, OR A MORE CHAOTIC ONE?

There is a clash between reason and emotion. Reason says that a world where power is more widely spread should be a saner and safer one. But emotion for many people says it isn't. Why does the world, after a long period of success, feel more fragile than it did thirty years ago? Or, rather, why does it feel so in the old developed nations of Europe and North America, for in India, China and elsewhere in the emerging world optimism is much more prevalent?

Part of the answer comes from the work of Hans Rosling, the Swedish professor of international health, who sadly died in 2017. He became famous for his presentation of health and wellbeing statistics in a TED Talk – as well as for ending some of his lectures by his party trick of swallowing a sword.[15] In his book *Factfulness*, completed by his son and daughter-in-law and published after his death, he set out thirteen questions about the world that people generally get wrong. Few people realised, for example, that over the twenty years to 2017 the proportion of the world's population in extreme poverty almost halved. Or that the average life expectancy was now seventy-two. Or that the vast majority of people lived in middle-income countries rather than poor ones. Not only did most people give incorrect (and overly pessimistic) answers to his questions – they were also more incorrect than you would expect from a random choice. He notes that chimpanzees, picking bananas for each answer, would do better. More alarming, the better educated people were, the more pessimistic they were, and hence the worse their performance. On two of three questions he put to the attendees at the World Economic Forum in Davos, they were still worse than the chimps. Nobel laureates and young scientists who were meeting at the Swedish city of Lindau in 2014 were worse still, while a meeting of Norwegian teachers he spoke to were worst of all.

But it cannot just be that people don't know the facts, or that people who are experts in one field are particularly bad when trying to assess what is happening in an area outside their competence. It cannot just be the effect of negative news in the media, or the fund-raising activities of the NGOs. There must be something deeper. Hans Rosling describes it as a negativity instinct, Steven Pinker as a negativity bias, or 'progressophobia'.

It is complex. Rosling attributes it partly to a misremembered past. People fail to remember the unpleasant aspects of earlier periods and therefore fail to appreciate how much progress has been made. It may be partly because assuring everyone that the world is in general getting better, when there are obvious specific examples where it is not, seems heartless. Pinker notes that it is a form of intellectual one-upmanship, in that complaining about modern society is a backhanded way of putting down rivals. And it may simply be intellectual fashion. Say things are getting worse and you are seen as a sage. Say they are getting better and you are classed at best as naïve and at worst as a fool. Pinker observes that there has been a stream of optimistic books about human progress but not one has won a major literary prize. By contrast non-fiction Pulitzers have gone to 'four books on genocide, three on terrorism, two on cancer, two on racism, and one on extinction'. But it is the pessimists who have in general been wrong, and the optimists (broadly at least) who have been right.

There is, however, an important qualification. Blind optimism, of course, is as irrational as blind pessimism. There is no good way of expressing the thought that we should feed an element of caution into any generally positive view of the future – an awareness that humankind is capable of making catastrophic mistakes. What is really needed is a judgement as to where the most serious risks lie. Hans Rosling calls for a fact-based world view, that 'the world is not as bad as it seems', and that is surely the most helpful base on which to make projections of the future. Unless we are clear about where we are, we cannot hope to know where we might be going.

THE NEXT STAGE OF THE JOURNEY

The next section of this book sets out where the different parts of the world are now – the base that we start from. It acknowledges the embedded qualities and advantages of the developed world, noting the differences between its different regions as much as the similarities. It is more optimistic about the strengths of the United States than many of that country's own citizens, scarred by the political turmoil of the Trump presidency and the many divisions that remain. It looks at the emerging nations, including, of course, the two giants, China and India, and in particular recognising the inadequacy of the concept of an emerging world to capture the extraordinary diversity of middle-income and lower-income countries. This is a snapshot of a world that is racing ahead, 'emerging' indeed, but in many cases already making that transition to developed country status. But advance will take place at different rates. The challenge for a world of nation states is for the leadership of those states to make the most of the advantages, and to tackle the disadvantages, of the regions for which they have responsibility. It is a challenge for the citizens of the advanced and emerging nations, too.

After that, the book looks at five forces for change, starting with demography, which is massively important in determining both the potential for economic growth and the 'feel' of a society, in particular its vibrancy or otherwise. It looks at the pressure on resources and the environment, and in particular the humungous challenge of climate change. It next looks at the changing nature of international trade and finance, and whether globalisation will continue to shape all our lives. Then technology, of course: where to look for the transformative technologies that will reshape our lives. The final chapter of this section looks at how ideas about the role of government and how the governance of societies will shift in different parts of the world.

Then we come to my judgements as to how the different parts of the world might look a generation from now – how those five forces will help shape the countries and regions sketched in Chapter 1. I have taken the five traditional continents of the Americas, Europe, Asia, Africa and Oceania as a framework, accepting the anomalies that this structure involves. For example, most of Russia's land area is in Asia, but the majority of its people live in Europe. There are some regions which are inevitably dealt with more briskly, too briskly I am afraid, than others. For that I ask forbearance. There will be some judgements that for some readers will jar. There will be some that will turn out to be very wrong. But all of us who are trying to peer into the future are making a journey. We all have views that will change as new evidence comes along – as the roadmap we are following must be redrawn. I do believe that is better to have a roadmap and change it than not to have one at all.

Then there is the final section of this book, 'How the World Will Look in 2050'. This is my best effort to wrap up all the information, the projections, the judgements, the fears and the hopes into a coherent whole. I acknowledge the ten things I am most worried about, and I pick out what seem to me to be the ten biggest ideas that have, for me, emerged from this book.

Overarching everything, however, is a thought – I would say a truth – that has been best expressed by Barack Obama. It reflects the views of Hans Rosling and Steven Pinker, and Barack Obama has made the point several times. But the version[16] I like most was when he was talking to a group of young people in Laos in September 2016. This is the key passage:

If you had a choice of when to be born, and you didn't know ahead of time who you were going to be, what nationality, whether you were male or female, what religion, but you said when in human history would be the best time to be born? The time would be now. The world has never been healthier. It's never been wealthier. It's never been better educated. It's never been less violent, more tolerant, than it is today.

He went on to explain that we did not always see that, because there are terrible tragedies and injustices. But the opportunity for young people to tackle those tragedies and injustices was greater than ever before. Finishing this book while war rages in Ukraine, the global pandemic continues and with the background of wider fractious international relations, it is really important to see the world now in this long historical context. The best time to be born must be now. So let's set off on the next stage of the journey to the world that will be run by our children and grandchildren, and do so with a spring in our step.

I

The World We Live in Now

THE AMERICAS – STILL THE FUTURE

The United States and Canada

The United States is extraordinary. It remains the world's only superpower; we all know that. But to many people it seems troubled: a giant, certainly, but a giant in retreat. That is wrong – though this may come as a surprise to many Americans accustomed to hearing their country talked down. On many measures the United States is actually increasing its weight in the world, not just in economic heft but also in its influence over the daily lives of people just about everywhere.

Let's start with the economics. On share of global GDP, the United States is indeed in retreat. But that is because of the rapid advance of the emerging nations, notably China. Within the advanced world, the US economy is growing faster than almost all the other developed economies. In 1990 the US economy was smaller than the EU (even adding in the soon-to-become EU members in Eastern Europe). Yet since then, the United States has grown a lot faster than the EU, and by 2020 it was significantly larger. And if US wealth and importance compared to Europe is rising, its place relative to Russia is soaring. In 1990 the US economy was roughly three times the size of that of the Soviet Union. By 2020 it was more than ten times the size of Russia and the other USSR successor states, and some fifteen times that of Russia itself.

So the United States has been a huge economic success story. Why? And why are many Americans apparently unaware of that?

The answer lies in its people, and how it has both tapped – and sometimes squandered – its richest resource: human talent. The United States has a relatively youthful population compared with that of Europe, and particularly compared with Japan. It has had higher fertility rates than Europe or Japan for most of the past thirty years, with mothers having an average of more than two children, though there is evidence that this may have shaded down a little after 2015. Immigration has further boosted its population, as well as bringing in ambitious young people from all over the world. More of that in a moment.

It has also seen a renaissance as an energy producer. Thanks to the fracking revolution, since the mid-2010s the United States has been the world's largest oil producer, regaining the position it held for the whole of the twentieth century until the early 1970s.[1] Oil, and in particular cheap gas, have helped drive a manufacturing revival – along with rising labour efficiency.

But the most powerful force behind American dominance is its mastery of human capital. Take higher education. It depends on which ranking you take, but on every tally in 2017/18 the United States was home to more than half the top twenty universities in the world, and on the Shanghai Jiao Tong league it had sixteen of them.[2] The only country able to mount any challenge is the UK, with Oxford and Cambridge ranking in the top ten. Knowledge drives frontier growth, and US institutions attract the world's most talented students. So this advantage will ensure the United States remains top dog in the global league for some years to come. Other countries, notably China, will eventually challenge it, but their efforts will take a generation to be effective.

That leads to the most important aspect of US economic might, and the reason to be confident that it will be hard to dislodge: its high-tech behemoths.[3] Something extraordinary has happened on the West Coast of America. This region has created companies that have changed the world, their names so familiar that one hardly need mention them. They include the five giants – Apple,

Alphabet (the parent company of Google), Amazon, Microsoft and Facebook – but there are hundreds of others chasing along behind. No other country in the world has ever achieved this level of power. There is nothing on this scale in the UK or Europe, nothing much in Japan, nothing significant yet in India – though there may well be soon. Only in China, with Tencent, Alibaba and a few others, are there enterprises of similar scale. And the Chinese ventures were, at least in their early stages, clones of US ones, and were able to grow because the Chinese authorities were for various reasons able to keep America out.

How did it happen? Well, go back to the year 2000. The world of computers was indeed the duopoly of two American companies, Microsoft and Apple. But other countries had high-tech champions. The world's largest mobile phone company was Vodafone, based in the UK; the world's largest mobile handset manufacturer was Nokia in Finland; Research in Motion in Canada introduced the BlackBerry smartphone. Japan was producing more sophisticated handsets than anything in Europe or the United States. But over the first two decades of this century, high-tech America shot ahead. It introduced the iPhone, which gave the internet mobility. It developed the concept of social networks. It invented platforms such as Uber and Airbnb that transformed two service industries, taxis and holiday accommodation. And so on. Nowhere else in the world could come up with the idea of a Facebook, born in a dorm at Harvard University in Cambridge, Massachusetts, devised by the nineteen-year-old Mark Zuckerberg. As of 2021 there were 2.9 billion people on the platform – more than one-third of humankind.

This was not a rags-to-riches story. Zuckerberg's parents were successful New York professionals. He was sent to Phillips Exeter Academy, one of the most prestigious (and expensive) independent schools in the land. It was investment in the education of a clever and ambitious young American.[4]

America has invested – relentlessly yet unevenly – in human talent, and this is one reason for its power. There is another. It is the magnet of immigration, the magnet that attracts many of the cleverest and most ambitious people in the world, and then develops their human capital, too. More than half of the most highly valued tech companies in the United States are founded by first-generation or second-generation immigrants. Other countries strive to emulate America but nowhere else has really managed to do so, at least not on anything like that scale.

Education, culture and immigration are the huge, defining strengths of the United States for the next generation, the reasons to be hopeful that for the first half of this century the giant will not be in retreat. Yet there are inevitably dark sides to the success story, and we need to deal with those now.

Any society as vibrant and competitive as the United States will have tensions. After simmering for years, those tensions burst to the surface in 2016 with the election of Donald Trump as president. The questions today are whether the economic and social forces that led to this disruption can be contained and channelled. Other questions concern inequality and education. America's treasure – human talent – is too often wasted through mismanagement and scant opportunities. The best US universities are wonderful, but according to the OECD's PISA study, its schools are only in the middle-band of attainment worldwide.[5]

The difficulty is to put all this in perspective. The United States has relatively poor health outcomes: relative, that is, not only to the rest of the developed world but also to the amount of money spent on healthcare. On the other hand it has no serious secessionist movement, unlike Canada, the United Kingdom and Spain. Its people don't want to break it up. It has severe racial injustice, though it has begun to work harder to address this. But so do many countries in Europe, some of which have been less prepared to face their demons. In any case, the United States has a long history of acknowledging aspects of its society that need to be corrected. There is indeed a dark side, but there has always been a dark side, and there has always been the energy and will to bring light to it.

One of the great issues for the United States over the next thirty years will be how well it copes with these tensions and finds ways to channel its boundless energy and drive so that everyone benefits. On the scale of challenges faced by the country in the past, this is surely manageable. There is a temptation, having witnessed the chaos of the presidency of Donald Trump and the storming of the Capitol by his supporters, to emphasise the searing divisions in America. But these divisions had been there since the nation was founded. They are just more in the open today than they have been for much of the period since the Civil War. Acknowledging that they exist is a necessary step towards figuring out how to tackle them.

Tackle them America will. It has done so in the past and there is little reason to suppose it won't in the future. There will be a huge challenge for global leadership when China becomes the world's largest economy. Who will run the world? That will be discussed at length later in this book. But if you make a pile of the United States' strengths, it is a tall stack indeed.

One of those strengths is its position as leader of the English-speaking world, the Anglosphere, as will be argued later. Next, a word about its neighbour to the north, Canada.

Canada is an easy nation to love. No enemies; welcoming to immigrants; huge land area; and massive natural resources, including the third largest oil reserves in the world. A calmer, kinder, less extreme version of the United States. All this makes Canada extraordinarily attractive. It has so many of the positive characteristics of the United States, plus some. Its secondary education is outstanding, scoring higher than the UK and much higher than the United States in the OECD's PISA study of fifteen-year-olds. It has solid higher education, and though it has no universities in the world's top twenty, there are strong performers just outside that band. It has well-run banks and insurance companies. Indeed, it came through the 2008 financial crash with its financial system in better shape than that of any other G7 country.[6]

In business, however, Canada's track record is more mixed – and it still plays second fiddle to the United States. Its attempts to challenge US hegemony in the high-tech world have largely failed. Nortel Networks, the once-giant telecommunications group, became Canada's largest bankruptcy in 2009. BlackBerry revolutionised the world with mobile email, but while its famous devotees included Barack Obama and Hillary Clinton, it lost out to

Apple's iPhone and Google's Android, and is now simply a software company.

Firms rise and fall, and a secure financial system enables new ones to sprout and grow. Canada has its share of high-tech start-ups and indeed regular ones. But the future of its economy is inevitably aligned to that of the United States. Anyone seeking to think through its competitive advantages has to start with one central fact, its location.

Canada has the second largest land area of any country on earth, but nearly all of that great expanse is barely populated. Some 90 per cent of its people live within 100 miles of the US border. Its largest city, Toronto, is 80 miles from the border. Its second largest, Montreal, is 40 miles. Its third largest, Vancouver, is 30 miles. In fact, there is only one sizeable Canadian city more than 200 miles from the US border: Edmonton. This leads to economic dependence, for the Canadian economy is essentially an extension of the US one that happens to be under a separate constitutional jurisdiction. One statistic: three-quarters of Canadian exports go to the United States. Canada's future is intimately bound up with that of its boisterous neighbour, and its prosperity turns on that.

Geography won't change, but two other things might: one is the language and nationalism fissure; the other its assimilation of immigrants.

Canada came within a whisker of splitting into two countries. French-speaking Quebec deciding not to separate from the rest of Canada in the 1995 referendum by 50.58 per cent versus 49.42 per cent. Since then, support for independence has waned, but it will not have gone away. It may well lie dormant for a generation or more, but the world's experience of nationalist movements suggests that they can burst out at any time.[7]

Canada is, of course, like the United States in that it is a nation of immigrants. Its indigenous peoples account for a little over two million of its thirty-seven million people. It is also a country that remains hugely attractive for new immigrants and one that continues to welcome them. As of 2018, it is receiving more than 300,000 immigrants a year, and there are suggestions this could go higher. So Canada will, like the United States, become a more fluid and open society.

On past form, Canada will cope well with the language and identity issues of Quebec, and it will successfully surf the opportunities and tensions that large-scale immigration generates. If it does, it will remain one of the most admired nations on earth. But it must also nurture its relationship with the United States, and that, depending on how each society develops, may become trickier over the next thirty years.

Latin America

Why has South America performed so much worse than North America? That is the challenging question that anyone assessing its economic prospects must explain. If the forces that drove this past century are any guide, South America will continue to disappoint.

It is far behind not just on basic economic measures such as GDP per head, but also on social yardsticks – most shockingly, its murder rates. In 2018 the *Wall Street Journal* headlined a story that 'Latin America Is the Murder Capital of the World'.[8] Latin America, the wider definition that conventionally includes Mexico, the clutch of smaller countries to its south and the Caribbean, has 8 per cent of the world's population, but 38 per cent of its murders.

It was not always so. A century ago, Latin American economies were much more on a par with their European counterparts. In fact, in terms of wealth per head, Argentina in the 1890s was one of the world's richest countries – on some calculations *the* richest.[9] Brazil, though the largest South American economy and the 'B' of Goldman Sachs' BRICs, has always been poorer per head than Argentina. But in the 1950s it had a standard of living that was not far behind that of Portugal, whereas by 2017 it was less than half that of its former colonial master. The most extreme example in Latin America of past wealth and current failure has been Venezuela. In 1960 it was richer in income per head than Canada, Australia or any Western European country bar Switzerland – and not far behind the United States. By 2018 its thirty-two million people had a standard of living one-tenth that of Western Europeans, and lower still vis-à-vis Americans.

There are some success stories. Chile is one, with living standards similar to an Eastern European country such as Poland. But that success is relative, for back in the 1890s it was richer than Spain or Italy.

So the question really is whether Latin America can regain the relatively affluent position it had at the end of the nineteenth century, or whether its disastrous second half of the twentieth century will be the norm. The basic point is that it has huge natural and human resources, but for some reason – education, culture, politics? – Latin America plays below its game.

EUROPE – THE OLDEST CONTINENT

The thirty years up to 2020 have seen European nations gradually become more cohesive politically, and their economies become more integrated. The two huge changes have been the then European Community's expansion from twelve members in 1993 to the European Union's twenty-seven in 2020, and the creation of the euro in 1999. It is an oversimplification, but I hope helpful shorthand, to say that expansion has been a success – but the euro has been a failure.

Encompassing most of the countries of the former Soviet bloc has paid huge economic dividends to the whole region. Eastern Europe benefited from EU subsidies and investment by its established members, and from an open door to the wealthy markets of prosperous Western Europe. In return, the 'old' EU members got access to cheaper labour and new fast-growing markets. There have inevitably been downsides. The loss of young, skilled people has troubled several countries, notably Poland and Bulgaria, and the whole region's adverse demography has been made worse. Social tensions have risen, and political support for the EU has weakened. Nevertheless, for Central and Eastern Europe, this has been a period of widespread economic success.

For Western Europe, the outcome has been patchier. For some countries, notably Germany, the UK and much of Scandinavia, this has been a period of reasonable economic growth, and until the financial crash of 2008 some increase in overall living standards. For others it has been two decades of stagnation or worse, marred by the highest unemployment in the developed world and the emigration of many of its best-qualified young people. In the case of Italy, overall living standards in 2018 were lower than they were in 1999, when the euro was founded. In the case of Greece, between 2008 and 2018 it experienced the greatest fall in both GDP and living standards that any advanced economy has endured since the Second World War.

Why this mixed record? There are lots of explanations, most of them deeply politicised. But it is hard not to acknowledge that many of the problems have stemmed from the introduction of the euro. Whether you criticise the design of the single currency or the entire concept is open to debate. But the results are not. The harsh truth is that European countries that did not adopt the euro grew faster, as a group, than those that did.[10] Among those non-euro European economies that have performed relatively well have been the UK and Ireland.

The United Kingdom and Ireland

Step back for a moment from politics. Whatever constitutional arrangements the UK has within its borders, with the Republic of Ireland, and with the European Union, the English-speaking economies of the European time zone will continue to thrive. There are a number of reasons for this. One is that there seems to be a growing competitive advantage to countries where English is widely spoken. It is easier for Facebook or Google to run their European operations from Britain or Ireland than it would be from a continental base. There may also be a competitive advantage in having common law, which non-nationals find easier to navigate, making the UK and Ireland the legal base of choice for many cross-border contracts. There is a clear advantage in higher education, in which the UK is the United States' only significant competitor. Now the UK has left the EU, the highest-ranked EU university on the three major league tables – the Times, QS and Shanghai – is not even in the top thirty. Aside from the British institutions, there is a star European university in the top twenty: ETH Zurich. But it is in Switzerland, which has never been an EU member.[11]

There is probably some cultural advantage in entrepreneurship. In terms of managerial competence, it would be hard to argue that the UK and Ireland have any advantage at all. Indeed, the reverse is probably true. Foreign-owned and -managed enterprises in the UK have higher productivity than domestic ones.[12] But business start-up rates in the UK and Ireland are higher than in most of Western Europe – much higher than in France, Germany, Italy or Spain.[13]

There are two further features that distinguish the UK economy, one broadly positive, the other clearly negative. The positive one is the relative size of services, and in particular of financial services, vis-à-vis everything else. Although services have been hammered by the Covid-19 pandemic, most will eventually adapt and bounce back. Some 80 per cent of the UK economy is in services, similar to that of the United States but higher than the rest of Europe or Japan, while 12 per cent is in finance.[14] This is largely a function of the falling share of manufacturing as a proportion of output, which has sunk further in the UK and United States than in most of continental Europe and Japan. If people choose to spend more of their income (either through taxes or directly) on healthcare, education and entertainment, and less on cars, washing machines and so on, that is their choice. It is a choice that the people in all developed countries are making, and, as we will see later, fast-growing emerging nations, notably China, are actively planning to make this shift.

So in a sense the UK is a pioneer economy. It is the second largest exporter of services in the world after the US. It uses that surplus to offset its deficit in goods. Some see the reliance of a services surplus to offset a goods deficit as a handicap, but actually that pattern runs back to the early nineteenth century. Even when Britain was the workshop of the world, exporting steamships to America and railway engines to Argentina, it still bought more goods from abroad than it sold. It relied on revenue from its international investments – including those in its growing empire – to cover its trade deficit. So there is a durable track record. The question really is: where does the UK's competitive advantage lie? The market says it is in services.

There are three caveats. One is that the UK excels in high-end manufacturing: aircraft engines, racing cars, pharmaceuticals, etc. Another is that manufacturing supports services, in the sense that the two are inextricably bound up. Rolls-Royce makes an aircraft engine, but it also maintains it for the next twenty years of its life. Much of the profit, maybe all, comes during those years rather than at the moment when it is actually produced. And the third is that the shift from manufacturing to services is potentially destructive if managed badly. The UK has not done this well.

That leads to the huge negative aspect to the UK economy. It is extraordinarily uneven. It is uneven geographically: the Western part of inner London is the richest region in Northern Europe, but five of the poorest regions are also in the UK, including West Wales, Cornwall and Lincolnshire.[15]

It is uneven in health. Life expectancy in central Glasgow is five years lower than in the city's wealthy northern suburbs of East Dunbartonshire.[16]

It is uneven in education. UK schools score a bit higher than the average for the developed world on the OECD's PISA study, but schools in Wales are poor, while the best British private schools are as good as or better than any in the world.[17]

And it is uneven in corporate performance. The UK has a productivity problem: output per employee is between 10 and 25 per cent lower than the other G7 economies. The best UK companies (often foreign-owned) are right up there with global leaders. But the problem is the long tail of indifferent firms.[18]

Ireland is uneven in a quite different way. It has been one of the great economic success stories of the world over the past fifty years. It has transformed itself from an economy overly dependent on one form of exports, agricultural products, and one principal market, the UK, into an exporting powerhouse. It is the European base for a raft of US technology giants, including Apple, Google, Twitter and Facebook. In 1970, food accounted for half the country's exports. In 2017 that had fallen to just over 10 per cent. Manufactured goods – and, crucially, intellectual property – had shot up to replace them. Why? It was partly tax, for Ireland brought in the lowest rate of corporation tax for any sizeable economy, but it was also other incentives and the availability of a well-educated, English-speaking workforce. Ireland became the 'Celtic Tiger',[19] the fastest-growing economy of the developed world, before the property and banking crash of 2008/9 put a temporary, if severe, brake on its progress.

This policy has been controversial. Ireland was called the biggest corporate tax haven in the world in a study carried out by the University of Copenhagen and the University of California at Berkeley.[20] But countries are free to set their own tax rates and Ireland has cleverly exploited that freedom. The policy has, however, created a two-tier economy, with a booming foreign-owned sector and a more restrained home-grown economic base. Looking forward, the country is vulnerable to changes in global taxation and regulation.

The common theme running through the British and Irish economies is that they share not just the English language, but many features of other parts of the Anglosphere, including, of course, the US but also Canada, Australia and New Zealand. They are open to foreign investment; they have a common legal system; similar banking and financial market structures; broadly similar labour-market legislation; inventive consumers eager and happy to buy foreign goods; and common business practices.

The English-speaking economies share a further characteristic: favourable demographic outlooks by the standards of the developed world, particularly continental Europe and Japan. The UK and Ireland will grow faster than the rest of developed Western Europe, simply on the grounds that they will have a younger (or rather less old) population, which is growing rather than declining. This does not guarantee economic success, but it will make it easier to cope with challenges, especially the unevenness noted above, in the years ahead.

Continental Europe

It would be neat to write of the European Union as an integrated economic entity. That has indeed been the aim of the supporters of its single market, founded in 1993 to allow free movement of goods, capital services and labour. But it isn't. If anything, the region has become less integrated since the early 1990s, not more. Take German exports. At the beginning of the 1990s neighbouring France was Germany's largest market, buying 13 per cent of its exports, while Italy was number two, taking more than 9 per cent. The US took only 7 per cent. By 2020[21] the positions had reversed. The US had displaced France as Germany's largest market, taking nearly 9 per cent of its exports, with France under 8 per cent, while Italy took only 5 per cent.

There is a straightforward reason for this. The US grew faster over this period than France, and much faster than Italy, so it became a better market for German exports. However, what the single market, and the single currency, the euro, have failed to do, is to narrow the gap in economic performance between the different parts of the EU. If anything, the gap has widened, with Italy in particular failing to keep up with Germany. So it is best to write about European countries as separate economic entities, each with different strengths and weaknesses, rather than any sort of single unit. Start with the largest, Germany, and the three countries – Belgium, the Netherlands and Luxembourg – whose economies are most closely integrated with it.

Germany and the Benelux countries

Germany is better at top-end manufacturing than any other place on earth. There are many ways of grading this success. Germany has the world's largest trade surplus. It is the world's largest exporter of cars by a huge margin: $142 billion in 2019[22] compared with Japan, number two, at $98 billion, and the largest exporter of drugs and medicines.[23] In other sectors it is at or near the top, inciting the admiration and envy of the rest of the world. The particular genius of the country for much of the post-war period has been to push upmarket every time a currency revaluation threatened to make its products uncompetitive. So whenever the Deutsche Mark was periodically revalued there was a temporary lull, but then German industry managed every time to cut costs and improve quality to justify the higher prices. The last time they performed that trick was in the early 2000s, after the country joined the euro at what was initially an uncompetitive rate. Growth was slow and unemployment soared to double digits. People talked of Germany as 'the sick man of Europe' at that time, for it was carrying the additional burden of funding the rebuilding of the former East Germany. But then thanks in part to labour reforms, but especially to the competence and adaptability of its industry, it recovered its competitiveness to become the powerhouse of Europe. The fact that the euro exchange rate reflected the less competent other members of the currency zone has meant that Germany has become super-competitive. Something will change this, but, until it does, Germany's success will unbalance the rest of Europe.

There is, however, another side to the German economy. It is a brilliant exporter, but the quality of services at home is less impressive. There are weaknesses in financial services, in higher education (no university in the top forty-five in any ranking), and in some infrastructure projects. But perhaps the greatest concern is whether engineering excellence will remain a key competitive area. As manufacturing shrinks as a proportion of total global output, and services grow, maybe excellence in services will come to matter more. It is possible, though it is contentious to argue this, that Germany has too large a manufacturing sector. It was 19 per cent of GDP in 2019 versus 11 per cent in the US, 10 per cent in France and 9 per cent in the UK.[24] There is a bigger point here: maybe Germany is very good at producing things that people will be less eager to buy? Cars are the obvious example. Younger people throughout the developed world are using cars less. A smaller proportion of the young have driving licences than older generations. Electric cars are much easier to make than internal combustion ones. Battery technology is being developed in the US and Asia, rather than Europe.

None of this should be taken to suggest that Germany will cease to be a most successful economy. Every time over the past seventy years it has risen to the challenges it faces. But maybe other skills will become relatively more important, for example the ability to produce luxury goods, a field in which its neighbour France is the global leader.

As for the Benelux countries, their prosperity depends on Germany. Belgium has benefited massively from its role as the administrative capital of Europe, with the largest single net contributor being Germany. The Dutch economy has become almost an offshoot of the German, with the latter taking a quarter of all its exports. Perhaps surprisingly, given its dense population (seventeen million people in an area not much larger than Maryland) the Netherlands is a very successful agricultural exporter. In fact, it is second only to the United States, and vies with Mexico to be the second largest exporter of tomatoes in the world.[25]

Tiny Luxembourg – with a population of 600,000, roughly that of Bristol or Baltimore – has a different claim to fame. It is extraordinarily rich. With the possible exception of the oil state Qatar and teeny Liechtenstein, it is the world's richest country in terms of GDP per head. It has done that by cleverly creating an offshore financial centre, mostly run by German banks, which allows them to work around German tax and other restrictions. It has also crafted tax deals that attract US multinationals, such as Amazon, to use it as their European hub. If that sounds harsh, it is not intended to be. Luxembourg has few natural resources but has been very astute and deserves credit for that.

France

France is tantalising. The country is in many ways an extraordinary economic success story. Luxury is a good place to start, for of the world's top ten luxury brands France has six, including the top three, Louis Vuitton, Chanel and Hermès.[26] It is extraordinary that any single country should dominate the luxury business in this way, but even more extraordinary that this dominance should date back to the seventeenth century. Louis XIV's minister of finance, Jean-Baptiste Colbert, is best known for his quip: 'The art of taxation consists in so plucking the goose as to procure the largest quantity of feathers with the least possible amount of hissing.'

But he also observed in 1665: 'Fashion is to France what the gold mines of Peru are to Spain', a reflection on the way the country generated its wealth. The French Revolution put a temporary block on luxury industries, but they recovered during the nineteenth century so that by the 1900 Paris Exposition Universelle,[27] France represented the highest pinnacle of civilisation on earth.

There are other less glamorous sectors where the country is also exceptional. Before the pandemic curbed international travel, more people visited France from abroad than any other nation, nearly ninety million a year. It is the third largest exporter of armaments in the world, after the US and Russia. Airbus, a European project but headquartered in France, shares with Boeing the global market for civil aircraft. Its healthcare services deliver very good outcomes: for example, it has the second lowest infant mortality (after Sweden) in Europe.

All this is impressive. Add in France's diverse natural beauty – the Alps, the Mediterranean and Atlantic coastlines – and it would seem like a paradise on earth. But there lies a puzzle: its people appear to be relatively unhappy, less happy than those of Germany or the UK, for example. One reason is that unemployment has been persistently high for a generation, averaging around 9 per cent since the middle 1990s. Unemployment, we know, makes people miserable. Another is that French taxes are the highest as a proportion of GDP of any major economy in the world; only Denmark is higher. Public spending is high, too, and that spending does deliver good public services. But the tax burden is, well, a burden, and is resented.

There is a further twist: outsiders and insiders. France's labour market divides into two broad groups: older, well-paid workers with high job security and the promise of early retirement on a decent pension, and younger workers who have temporary jobs, very little security and sometimes have to cobble together full-time work with a series of part-time gigs. This is the result of strict labour market controls, which protect those in jobs at the expense of those seeking work. Under-qualified young people, including many from immigrant families, are hardest hit. There have been several attempts to reform this, but governments have been unable to sustain sufficient political support to do so. At some stage change will happen, but until then the country puts itself at a disadvantage. France is in many ways a success story, but that success is fragile. Its two-tier job market is part of a two-tier society. Bringing together the disparate parts is a huge challenge.

The weakest links – Italy and Greece

Italy, too, is intriguing. Like France it has so many strengths, including a lifestyle that many would consider to be the most enviable on earth. It has the second longest life expectancy, after Japan, of any large country. But it has a very low birthrate, large-scale emigration by its young people, and, since 2000, economic stagnation. Young Italians are leaving in droves, and those who stay are not having babies or making much money.

This raises troubling questions about Italy's competitiveness now and its role in the future. Objectively Italy has great gifts. These include high-end craft manufacturing – it is second only to France in luxury goods – and top-quality engineering. It has heritage (of course), which with its lifestyle attractions helps to drive a booming tourism industry. It is also the largest wine producer in the world. All these are activities that are quite difficult to excel at. It is not just that no other country can ever have a Rome, or a Florence, or a Venice. It is hard for other countries to imitate, or match, Italian excellence, for example to build up a fashion industry, or at least one with a stellar global reputation.

But something has gone wrong. In the late 1980s Italy's economy passed the UK in size, an achievement celebrated as '*il sorpasso*', the overtaking. But by 1997 the UK was bigger again, and for the first fifteen years of the twenty-first century the Italian economy barely grew at all. There is a simple explanation, which is that until it adopted the euro in 1999 Italy had been able to retain its competitiveness by periodic devaluations. Once in the euro it could no longer do that, so it gradually lost ground. But this is only a partial answer, for there are other weaknesses in Italian governance – its labour laws, its tax evasion, its illegal activities associated with the Mafia – that have progressively weakened the economy. Northern Italy, with its long history of successful city states, is much more successful than southern Italy, with its tradition of princely rulers. The classic work on this divide is *Making Democracy Work*, by the American political scientist Robert D. Putnam, published in 1993.[28] Alas, the economic stagnation of the past thirty years has underlined the difficulties facing Italy in escaping from its history. While its judiciary and police forces have been courageous and determined in tackling organised crime, its politicians have been less ambitious in pressing through reforms. The balance of probability is that Italy will muddle through, as it always has. But the country is fragile – not in its culture or competence, but, rather, in its political and social cohesion. Managing that fragility is the test for its leaders over the next thirty years.

Greece failed to manage its fragilities. It was unable to pay its debts and was bailed out by the EU with a series of loans starting in 2010. After eight years it emerged from EU control, but with an economy 25 per cent smaller than before the crisis. In 2013 unemployment reached 27 per cent, with youth unemployment 58 per cent. More than 400,000 people emigrated. Yet the debts remain huge, and the outcome uncertain. What we know already is that Greece has experienced the most serious depression faced by any developed country since the 1930s.[29]

Spain and Portugal

Spain and Portugal were also hard hit by recession. But they have options not available to the other members of the EU, for both share a language and cultural ties with Latin America. By themselves they are reasonably prosperous European nations, though Spain is more so than Portugal. Latin America and the Latin American population of North America give them an alternative focus, one that will become more important in the years ahead.

Spain has many natural strengths. It is a big country, the second largest in the EU, with double the land area of the UK for its smaller population. Its long Mediterranean coastline has helped it become the second largest destination for international tourists after France. It is the third largest wine producer in the world, after Italy and France. It has good universities and many well-educated young people. It has the glamorous port city of Barcelona, with its thriving industries and lively culture – that is, as long as Spain remains a single country and Catalonia does not secede.

There is, however, a darker side. Since the early 1980s, Spain has had on average the worst unemployment rate in the developed world. For most of this period unemployment has been above 10 per cent and for quite a lot of it more than 20 per cent. Only Greece, since 2012, has had slightly higher rates. Inevitably, many young people work in non-documented activities, while others leave the country. This outflow is offset by mostly older Northern Europeans who move to Spain to retire, and increasingly Latin Americans. As a result, Spain has some five million foreign-born residents, the highest proportion in any large European country. However, Spain also has among the lowest fertility rates in the world, an average of just 1.3 babies per mother, and while this is projected to rise a little, the country still faces the prospect of a falling population. Indeed, the country's National Statistics Office projects that the population will fall by 11 per cent by 2050.[30]

Things change. Economic success could woo back many young people who have left. But on purely economic grounds, the strongest suit in Spain's hand is its relationship with the rest of the Spanish-speaking world. Put crudely, Spain will become relatively less important; Spanish-speaking people, mostly in the Americas, will become more important. If the world is to be linked more by language and culture rather than physical proximity, that suggests a brighter future.

For Portugal the key relationship is, naturally, with Brazil. The imbalance – in terms of population and economic might – between

Spain and the rest of the Spanish-speaking world is magnified in the case of Portugal and Brazil. Spain is currently a larger economy than Mexico or Argentina, though it will be passed by Mexico sometime in the 2020s. Brazil's economy is already ten times the size of that of Portugal and that differential will widen. By Western European standards, Portugal is poor. Its government has heavy debts – it was one of the countries bailed out by the EU in 2011 – and the confidence of its middle class was shattered by the squeeze on their living standards. Since then it has achieved a modest revival, but it remains very dependent on the European market, with some three-quarters of its exports going there. Like Spain it has suffered from the emigration of many of its young. It will do better over the next thirty years, but how much better will be determined by its ability to leverage its relationship with Brazil. There are eleven million Portuguese. There are 211 million Brazilians. Brazil could be a huge boost to Portugal's economic prospects. But how to harness that potential depends more on the big offspring than the elderly parent.

The Nordic countries and Switzerland – the social and economic leaders

The five Nordic countries, Denmark, Finland, Iceland, Norway and Sweden, are among the most prosperous on earth, while Switzerland is the richest 'real' country, real in the sense that with more than eight million people it is not a tiny oil state or a tax haven.

All are held up as examples of social cohesion: successful and relatively egalitarian societies that offer impressive healthcare and welfare support as well as a covetable standard of living. For many the Nordic countries are model societies, proof that high public spending, financed by high taxes, delivers the best opportunities for their people. Critics would argue that it is easier for small countries to achieve that balance, with Denmark, Finland and Norway having between five and six million inhabitants and Sweden just over ten million. Iceland has only 340,000. Trust is high; wealth and income differentials relatively small; opportunities for women plentiful – a key aspect of equality.

Switzerland, with its tradition of direct democracy, is slightly different, in that populist options drive policy. The result is a more traditional society. The common theme, however, is that these countries seem, at least to outsiders, to be havens of calm and contentment in a turbulent world.

The Nordic countries are inevitably compared with each other, and they do share many broad social features. Their prosperity, however, comes from different sources. Norway is Europe's largest oil producer. Though its output peaked in 2001, its decision to save much of the money it received from oil revenues means that it has the largest sovereign wealth fund in the world,[31] ahead of China and the United Arab Emirates. It has in effect no national debt.

Sweden's economy is more broadly based. Its wealth derives from competent, long-established engineering enterprises, and increasingly from service exports. For example, it ranks with Canada as the largest exporter of music, relative to its size. The country combines fiscal conservatism with innovative drive, creating many high-tech start-ups. Its most extraordinary feature, though, is the way the wealth is evenly spread. It is the only country in Europe where the income of every region is higher than the EU average. There are shadows, notably the extent to which relatively large-scale immigration will test the Swedish social model, but in economic terms the country is a considerable success story.

Denmark is, too. The balance of the economy is slightly different – more revenue from oil, gas and food production, less from industry. The land border with Germany means that it is more closely integrated with core Europe. But the thing that stands out about Denmark is that it is the happiest country on earth. It repeatedly scores at or near the top of global league tables.[32] It has a word, 'hygge', that captures the sense of comfort, harmony, community and cosiness that Danes feel characterises their lifestyles. Denmark faces similar challenges to Sweden, but for the moment the prospects are bright.

Finland, and particularly Iceland, have had bumpier rides. Finland is home to what was once the world's largest mobile phone manufacturer and Europe's most valuable company, Nokia. When

Nokia soared, Finland boomed, but when it went into decline the effect was felt throughout the country. As for Iceland, it experienced a stronger boom in the run-up to the 2008 banking crash, and then a more spectacular bust, than any other nation in the world. Both countries have recovered, but their bruises are a reminder that small countries are vulnerable to economic shocks, whereas larger ones are inherently more resilient.

The bigger question for the Nordic region is whether its social model is sustainable. A high-spending, high-tax society requires a strong sense of identity and trust – trust, that is, that people will not abuse the system. This has become harder to sustain with the numbers of immigrants from outside Europe that have moved to the region. Stresses are evident despite the huge efforts made to integrate them. It is an issue for all of Europe, but the Nordic countries will be a key testbed in the years ahead.

As for Switzerland, it too is a testbed. It is for direct, as opposed to representative, democracy. Whenever a significant government decision is to be made – anything from cycle paths to financial regulation – if citizens can gather enough votes, they can put it to the people in a referendum. Typically, Switzerland has ten a year. But referendums are cumbersome. Suppose technologies were developed so that many more political decisions could be taken by direct popular votes rather than having elected representatives make those decisions? Populism is already changing democracy in the US and Europe. Switzerland shows that in economic terms it can be very successful, indeed astoundingly so. Four languages, landlocked, few natural resources, yet it has the strongest currency in the world and is the richest nation. That is an extraordinary achievement. As people in the West come to question democracy itself, Switzerland shows that more democracy, not less, can deliver the goods.

Central and Eastern Europe

It is inevitably misleading to lump together such a vast variety of countries, ranging from the Baltic through to the Adriatic and across to the Black Sea, with all their differences of history, culture and economic development. Most have become members of the European Union, giving a certain glue to the region. However, much of the former Yugoslavia remains outside the EU, as do Ukraine and Belarus, raising the question as to whether the EU has reached its natural boundaries.

From an economic perspective the key transformation for these countries came with the end of Comecon in 1991, the Soviet Union's economic union that kept much of the region under its control. The legacy has been long: countries that were part of the Western European economic system, such as Austria, are still much wealthier than even the richer former Comecon members, such as the Czech Republic. In other words, catch-up has taken more than thirty years. Despite huge subsidies, the former East Germany remains poorer than West Germany. As a rule of thumb, the further east the country, the lower the level of economic development. The closer a country lies to the Western European market, the easier it has found it to generate wealth itself.

There are exceptions. Estonia, right up on the Russian border, has created the most 'online' state, with its 1.3 million citizens able to access almost all government services digitally. And, as a whole, the region has made massive progress. Poland was the only large developed country to come through the 2009 downturn without going into recession. Slovakia, the eastern half of the former Czechoslovakia, has become the main car producer of Central and Eastern Europe, making more than a million cars a year. Romania and Bulgaria have both grown strongly, though Bulgaria remains the poorest member of the EU. It is, however, richer than Albania and Serbia, two countries that have yet to join.

Their accession means there is now a land route through EU member states to Greece. Geographically the next natural member would have been Ukraine. Here economics has been pushed aside by politics and military action, with Russia annexing the Crimean peninsula in 2014, and mounting a vicious invasion in 2022. So it is impossible to make a measured assessment of its potential, except to note that since it is much poorer than its neighbours to the west it has great potential to close the gap. That leads to a tantalising possibility: might Russia catch up, too?

Russia

Step aside from the dreadful politics, because those will change, and focus on Russia's underlying competitiveness as an economy. There are three obvious positive factors and three troubling negative ones.

First, there are the massive natural resources of the world's largest country: oil, gas, minerals, rare earths, timber. Demand for some may weaken, but as global population and living standards rise, access to such resources will become more important, not less.

Second, the human capital of Russia is extraordinary: talented, well-educated, entrepreneurial, energetic and risk-taking people.[33] It is uneven, as are so many aspects of Russia, and many of the best-qualified citizens have chosen to work abroad. But that fact gives the country a pool of workers who have foreign experience and connections, another positive factor.

Third, Russia has a land border with two of the three largest economic entities in the world, the European Union and China.

Set against this are three headwinds. One is demography. Russia's population is relatively old and projected to decline from 143 million to 116 million by 2050. Longevity for men is among the lowest of any middle-income country with an average life expectancy of sixty-six years, though for women it is much higher at seventy-seven.

Second, Russia has found it hard to establish the legal and regulatory stability that is standard in high-income countries. Business practice is unpredictable, making it a hard place for foreign capital to be invested and for knowhow to be transferred.

Third, the country is overly reliant on energy and raw material exports, which account for some two-thirds of the total. Not only does it have to cope with swings in oil and gas prices; emphasis on primary production means it has not shored up other ways of creating wealth.

Russia has failed to cope with these challenges, with the result that it has steadily lost ground not only vis-à-vis the US, but against the rest of the developed world. As a result, it is in world terms only a moderately sized economy, around number fifteen – smaller than Spain or Australia, and little larger than Turkey. Rationally, Russia ought to be doing much better. Can it? Will it? And if not, what happens in its relations with its giant neighbour to the east, China?

THE GREAT RISING GIANTS OF ASIA: CHINA AND INDIA

China, Hong Kong, Taiwan – and Singapore

The transformation of China from a subsistence economy, ravaged by famines that killed millions of its citizens, to the powerhouse it is today is one of the two great economic stories of this age, the other being the information revolution. In 1978, the year Deng Xiaoping came to power,[34] Chinese people were on average poorer than those in India and much of sub-Saharan Africa. By 2020 they had, again on average, higher living standards than people in Brazil, and similar to those in the poorer European nations, such as Romania. In forty years this enormous country has gone from one of the poorest in the world to the middle of the global pack. Hundreds of millions of people have risen out of poverty and achieved middle-class status. If you take car ownership as a measure of that, with some 300 vehicles per 1,000 population China is at the same level as the UK in the 1970s. But not only have living standards risen. Health has been transformed. Life expectancy is seventy-six years, the same as Sweden's in the 1980s.

The statistics about the growth of China's economy are stunning: running more high-speed trains than the rest of the world put together, making more cars than the US, Japan and Germany and so on. But the fact that the world's most populous country has lifted so many of its people out of poverty is surely in human terms the most important, and wonderful, story of all. How has it done it?

There are two ways of answering that, each of which raises questions about the model's sustainability.

One is to look at the policy changes that China has made since 1978, in particular how it cautiously loosened the planned economy that had been established since the communists took over in 1948.

Controls were dismantled step by step, slowly allowing market signals to replace bureaucratic targets. The structure of the mixed economies of the West was copied, but, thanks to the gradual nature of change, China avoided disruption of the catastrophic scale the former Soviet Union endured. Even forty years later large parts of the economy are still state-owned, the currency is not fully convertible, and while there has been considerable foreign investment, this has been tightly controlled. All in all, the transition from a command to a market economy has been a triumph. Inevitably there have been mistakes, and the onward rush to invest more, produce more and consume more has led to distortions in the economy. For example, a lot of new housing is substandard and may never be occupied. The debt burden from unwise investment overhangs the country. And the damage to the environment will at best take decades to repair, and at worst is irreparable.

The other way of analysing China's growth has been to note that it has copied the West, bringing in established technology, sometimes by inward investment and sometimes simply by stealing it. Any visitor to China will see clones of Western cars driving in the streets, though not quite the same: everything from a Rolls-Royce Phantom or a Porsche Cayman to a little Indian Maruti. But it is not just physical objects that China copies; it is services, too. So China is the only country in the world where the giant social media and search engine corporations are not American. US social media companies have been kept out, and have broadly accepted that exclusion, while Chinese clones have thrived.[35]

Catch-up will drive Chinese growth for many years, but there is a danger that it will reach a certain level of development and get stuck. The expression is 'the middle-income trap'. To avoid that China has to do more than apply the technology of the West. How might it do so? There is a clue in the performance of two city states, both in different ways very successful, both of whose economies have been driven by the acumen of their Chinese population. One is now part of China; the other is an independent country. The cities are Hong Kong and Singapore.

Both had extraordinary bursts of growth through the second half of the twentieth century. In 1950 in both Hong Kong and Singapore the GDP per head was roughly one-third that of the UK, their colonial ruler. By 1997, when Hong Kong was returned to China under the 'one country, two systems' agreement, it was substantially richer.[36] So, too, was Singapore. Yet by 2019, while both still outpaced the UK, Singapore had started to pull ahead of Hong Kong. Indeed, it is number three in the world ranked by GDP per head. Hong Kong has done remarkably well, and continued to do well under the mainland umbrella. But Singapore's performance has been quite outstanding. It ranks at or near the top of the various league tables: ease of doing business, economic freedom, competitiveness, human development, global education and so on. Nowhere is perfect, but to have achieved what it has is a great tribute to its leadership, and it stands as a beacon to China.

So, too, does Taiwan. It is not helpful here to get into the debate about the relationship between the two countries, though reason would suggest that the present tensions will be resolved without armed conflict. When the nationalist government of China fled to Formosa in 1949 the wealth per head there was only slightly higher than that of the mainland. But from the 1950s and particularly 1960s onwards Taiwan pulled far ahead. Now it is secure as a high-income country – poorer than Hong Kong or Singapore, but far ahead of the mainland. It is especially strong in consumer electronics, and is closely integrated with the Chinese economy. More than 40 per cent of its exports go either to the mainland or to Hong Kong.

However, over its success hangs a question mark. For some reason it has failed to push itself up the value chain in the same way as Singapore or Hong Kong, and unlike Korea has failed to create global brands. Is it stuck as a reasonably wealthy country, richer than Portugal but poorer than Spain? Or is it a frontier economy, pushing forward? This is a dilemma that China will face soon, too.

The scale, of course, is utterly different. Taiwan has a population of 24 million, Hong Kong 7.5 million and Singapore less than 6 million, against China's 1.4 billion. Scale gives China an enormous advantage, but it also means it cannot rely on catch-up. It must push forward frontiers itself. Actually, there are already many signs that it is doing just this. For example, it is the world pioneer in solar energy and in electric car production, using the size of its market to establish leadership in what it expects to be key fields. Perhaps the greatest single question overhanging China's advance is whether it becomes a true innovator or whether it ticks along in relative comfort, devoting resources to easing internal pressures rather than looking out to the world.

The Indian subcontinent

India will pass China to become the world's most populous nation some time around 2022. If you were to add the two other countries, Pakistan and Bangladesh, that were part of colonial India before independence and partition in 1947, the subcontinent is already way past China in population, and closing in on Germany to become the world's fourth largest economy. By 2030 India alone will have moved past both Germany and Japan to become number three.[37]

Like China, India experienced a sudden reawakening in the final quarter of the twentieth century. In the immediate post-independence years it bumbled along, its economy growing only a little ahead of its rising population. Living standards climbed only slowly, too, though in 1977 just before the Chinese take-off began it had a slightly higher GDP per head than China. Then China leapt ahead. Indeed, the Indian subcontinent, taken as a whole, was slightly richer than China during the early part of the twentieth century, as the graph below indicates.

In the 1990s, inspired perhaps by Chinese experience, it started to push through business-friendly reforms. These gathered pace in the early years of this century, and by 2017 Indian growth exceeded that of China. It became the fastest-growing large economy in the world.

Yet India is so huge and so diverse that comparing its national wealth to others conceals massive differences within its borders. For example, India's richest state, Goa, has similar living standards to

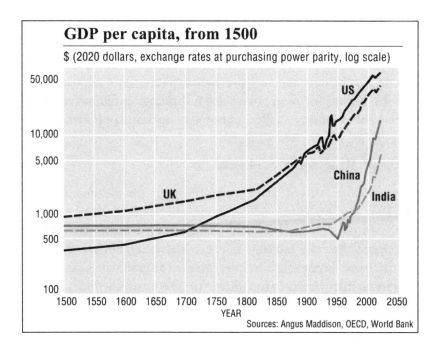

GDP per capita, from 1500

$ (2020 dollars, exchange rates at purchasing power parity, log scale)

Sources: Angus Maddison, OECD, World Bank

a poor European country such as Bulgaria. By contrast its poorest state, Bihar, ranks alongside Mali in sub-Saharan Africa. So the key to progress is lifting the states, and people, left behind. Rapid growth seems likely to persist for many years to come. That is partly because, relative to China, there is more room to catch up. India's GDP per head is a quarter of that of China. The scope and need for infrastructural investment will drive growth; so, too, will the supply of labour from the land and the still-growing population.

India has so many gifts. It has a well-educated, self-confident and ambitious elite – ambitious, that is, not just for themselves and their families but also for the country they are driving forward. It has a huge supply of skilled young people leaving higher education each year and pouring into its high-technology industries. It has great strength in its service industries as well as manufacturing. In that regard it outstrips China, which is more adept at making goods than producing services. So growth is not the issue. The questions that India faces are really about managing that growth for the good of the entire population as well as its rapidly growing middle class. The speed at which India closes the gap with China will be determined by its quality of governance, its environmental controls and the breadth of access to a good education. India has so much to play for: daunting challenges but also stunning opportunities.

Pakistan, Bangladesh, Sri Lanka

Because India so dominates the subcontinent, people tend to forget that Pakistan, with more than 200 million people, is the sixth most populous country in the world. Bangladesh, with 160 million, is the eighth. But the tensions between these neighbours stunt the region from becoming an integrated economic area, and suck resources into defence spending. In the case of Pakistan, the contrast with India is stark. According to World Bank calculations[38] it was slightly richer than India in GDP per head until 2010. But by 2017, Indians had become on average one-third richer than Pakistanis.

Bottom of the subcontinent's wealth league is Bangladesh, with per capita incomes of half those of India, while the twenty-two million people of Sri Lanka far outpace everyone else. Thanks in part to its successful tourist industry, Sri Lanka is really a middle-income country with a GDP per head not far short of that of Brazil. So Sri Lanka will be fine, at least in economic terms. What about Pakistan and Bangladesh? Are they likely to achieve a take-off?

Rationally, both should have a boom ahead. They have seen what India has achieved: a model for faster economic development is on their doorstep. Indeed, the HSBC projections suggest that Bangladesh will be the fastest-growing economy in the world through to 2030, India the second fastest and Pakistan the fourth. But both face political challenges – how to improve their standards of governance – and they face environmental pressures, too. The largest city in Pakistan, Karachi, will struggle to meet its water needs. The population of Pakistan is projected to balloon to about 275 million by 2050, with Karachi having perhaps more than 30 million people. Dhaka, capital of Bangladesh, could reach 35 million to become the third largest city in the world. Population growth stimulates economic growth – provided education, healthcare and other social services can keep up. But both countries have structural weaknesses. For example, Pakistan is the world's third largest exporter of rice – most impressive, except that growing rice demands a lot of water. Some 90 per cent of Bangladesh's export earnings come from clothing, also impressive, but dangerous to be so dependent on a single industry. In general terms, however, the future of each country will be determined by the way they accommodate their millions of new citizens. Yes, they will grow rapidly. What matters is whether that growth will be sustainable, and, if not, in what way things might go wrong.

JAPAN AND THE KOREAS

Japan

If the Indian subcontinent's principal challenge is coping with youth, Japan's is coping with age. Japan is the oldest society on earth, the oldest that has ever existed on our planet. In that sense it is the frontier nation for the rest of humankind. The past half-century has seen Japan experience an extraordinary roller-coaster ride. It was, from the 1950s through to the early 1990s, the fastest growing economy in the world, becoming the second largest after the US. In 1995 its GDP at market exchange rates was $5.45 trillion, compared with that of the US, at $7.66 trillion. National income per head was one-third higher than the US. But then it stopped growing. By 2018 its GDP was actually smaller than it had been twenty-three years earlier, and its citizens were much poorer than Americans. Instead of challenging the US for global economic leadership, as some had predicted, it turned inwards and focused on caring for its own people. While it remains an orderly and admirable society, it does not influence the world in the way it did a generation ago. Some of its household-name companies, for example Toyota, remain global leaders in their fields. But others, such as Sony, Toshiba and Panasonic, have struggled to maintain the dominance they enjoyed twenty years earlier.

That is troubling, because the world has so much to learn from Japan. Take two hard facts: crime rates are the lowest in the world, and Japanese people live the longest.[39] Add in its efficient, cooperative and harmonious human relations, the quality of services and the cleanliness of its cities, and you can see that Japan has created a society that is quite special. But the thing that Japan can teach the world is more than this. It is coping with its elderly population. The rest of the world will have to do it, too.

The Korean peninsula

North and South Korea represent two extreme examples of an economic and political experiment. The North is a command economy that struggles to feed its people; the South is one of the most energetic market economies in the world. There are other extreme instances of successful and unsuccessful economic management: the way that Singapore has overcome its lack of natural resources, while Venezuela has squandered its oil wealth. But since the reunification of Germany, there is no other instance of a single people experiencing completely different outcomes because they happened to live on one side or the other of an ideological divide. So the obvious questions are how long this can persist and the way in which convergence might happen.

There is no conclusive answer to these questions. What is clear is that the competence and drive of the people of Korea have, in the south, created a great success story. Hyundai-Kia is the fourth largest car producer in the world, and Samsung is the largest smartphone manufacturer. There is an argument that the country has become too dependent on these two industries and that it is weak in services. But there is no doubt that, like Japan, it has escaped the middle-income trap. Unlike Japan it avoided the worst of the financial excesses of the 1980s and 1990s. But it does share one other characteristic with Japan, in an even more extreme form: very few babies.

In 2019 its total fertility rate – the number of babies the average woman will have in her lifetime – was estimated by the World Bank to be 0.92, the lowest in the world.[40] As it happens, fertility rates in North Korea are much higher, at just under two, not that far from replacement rate. Quite why people in the economically successful country should choose to have much smaller families than those in the poverty-stricken one is a puzzle. But unless something radical changes, South Korea's population will dwindle and it will face the pressures of coping with rising numbers of elderly people. For all its evident success, South Korea does face a huge challenge.

THE SOUTH-EAST ASIAN 'TIGERS'

Anyone thinking about South East Asia should start by acknowledging that it has been one of the most vibrant areas of the world over the past twenty years, growing slower than China or India but faster than just about everywhere else.[41] The conventional way to look at the region is to take its kaleidoscope of countries together under the heading of the Association of Southeast Asian Nations. ASEAN was founded in 1967, partly to encourage regional trade rather in the same way that the European Economic Community sought to foster European trade, but also to link the non-communist countries of the region. There were five original members: Indonesia, Malaysia, the Philippines, Singapore and Thailand. Next to sign up were Brunei, Vietnam, Laos, Myanmar (Burma) and Cambodia.

There are obvious parallels with Europe: a market-economy group of countries, joined later by former planned-economy ones. But there are also sharp differences. There is no aim of creating an ever-closer union. There is no single currency, no common travel area and no significant central budget. Instead, this is a group of countries that cooperate where it is mutually helpful to do so. ASEAN uses the slogan 'One Vision, One Identity, One Community', but this is more a statement of aspiration than the current reality. Yet, unlike Europe, which despite its strengths may add up to less than the sum of its parts, South East Asia's energy and combined work ethic may lead to a stunning regional success story – if it is not destabilised by Chinese expansion.

There are enormous differences in the ASEAN members' size, ranging from Brunei with less than 500,000 people, to Indonesia with more than 270 million. There are gulfs in wealth, for Singapore has a per capita GDP of more than $60,000 and Myanmar of less than $1,500. One is a class leader in economic development, the other has hardly begun. The ASEAN countries have their own histories, cultures and identities, and they face different pressures. They also – and it is important to acknowledge this – have great differences in economic potential. Thus Singapore is 'frontier land', while Indonesia is a classic 'catch-up' case. Indonesia looks like becoming one of the fifteen largest economies in the world, with growth driven by rising population as well as increases in productivity. It is less easy to be optimistic about Myanmar.

The challenges will vary from country to country. For example, Indonesia will have to learn to cope with the booming population of its capital Jakarta, which may pass Tokyo to become the largest city in the world. It is plausible that Indonesia will then have a population of nearly 300 million by 2030, which would make it the fourth most populous country. The question for this vast, sprawling country is how to ride this tiger: how to increase productivity, improve environmental standards, and crucially, satisfy the ambitions of its young people.

The Philippines, the next most populous ASEAN member, is also the only country in Asia that is predominantly Christian – more than 90 per cent of its population of 110 million. It has relatively strong demographics, and excellent growth prospects. But it faces environmental and governance challenges, and like several other countries in the region could also face the middle-income trap – never quite achieving developed-country status. Vietnam, Thailand, Myanmar and smaller (in terms of population) Cambodia and Laos must all in different ways make that leap. Malaysia, the wealthiest country in the region in terms of GDP per head – bar Singapore and oil-rich Brunei – is probably far enough along the path to wealth that it will pull clear. Thailand is, too. It is famed for the success of its tourist industry, as it is consistently among the top ten tourist destinations in the world, but it is also a successful manufacturing exporter.

The main point to make about the ASEAN nations is that they have a powerful following wind. Their location, their range of competences, their natural vigour and their collective determination to advance economically puts them in a strong position to benefit from global growth. The fact that they are at very different stages of development should be a strength. It has been an exciting ride in recent years and things bode well for the future.

AFRICA AND THE MIDDLE EAST — THE WORLD'S YOUNGEST REGIONS

Africa is becoming a success story. That is a huge, sweeping statement about a continent that has many cultures, many problems, many tensions and many uncertainties. Sub-Saharan Africa remains the world's poorest region in terms of income per head, and it has overall the shortest life expectancy, so it might be more precise to say that there are many success stories within Africa. But because so many images of Africa in the West are negative – with charities featuring malnourished children in their advertisements – it is important to recognise success where it is happening, and it would be unwise to underestimate the continent. Consider this. Africa has in the present century been the fastest growing region of the world in terms of rising GDP – faster even than China. That is in itself fascinating because it has been Chinese investment that has, in part at least, become a major driver of African growth. But it also gives a clue to the future, for the continent will continue to grow rapidly thanks to its youthful population and high fertility rates. So the big challenge will be to invest in infrastructure certainly, but also in human capital. Africa needs to improve governance, education and training, so that it creates a stable framework for growth, and prepares its young people for the complex opportunities that rocketing economies inevitably bring.

This is a common theme, but it is particularly relevant to the four most populous countries of sub-Saharan Africa: Nigeria, Ethiopia, the Democratic Republic of the Congo and South Africa. Each acts as an economic anchor for its region. If they do well, they will pull other countries along with them. If not, the region suffers.

Some thoughts about each.

Nigeria is a giant, but it is overly reliant on oil production to pay its way in the world. Its 207 million people vie with South Africa's 58 million as the largest economies of sub-Saharan Africa, with their relative positions shifting largely as a result of changes in the oil price and Nigeria's production levels. Since petroleum products, mostly crude oil, account for 95 per cent of its export revenues, the dependence is stark. Oil enables the country to generate a GDP of some $400 billion a year, which works out at $2,500 per head. At purchasing power parity exchange rates it is roughly double that, so it is not poor – it is at the bottom band of middle-income countries. But to put that in perspective, Nigeria's GDP in 2020 was not much larger than that of the Republic of Ireland, which has fewer than five million people.

Like other oil-dependent countries, Nigeria must diversify. But that will be extremely difficult. It is not just a question of building other industries with a potential to export, though that needs to be done. It is also finding employment for the two-thirds of Nigerians who currently earn their livings through agriculture,[42] and who will, as the country develops further, tend to leave the land. Yet there is huge entrepreneurial drive in Nigeria, and the question is how that might be harnessed to the national good. That requires good governance.

It is not for foreign authors to tell any country how it should choose to govern itself. What is worth noting is that Ghana, 150 miles to the west, has become a beacon in West Africa as a country that has much improved the management of its economy in recent years, so that in 2017 it was the second fastest-growing economy[43] in Africa – the fastest being Ethiopia. Ghana is also very dependent on raw material exports, in its case gold as well as petroleum. It has half its workforce in agriculture, which will remain the backbone of the economy. But it has made more progress in diversifying into manufacturing and service industries.

Ghana is much smaller than Nigeria, with a population of twenty-seven million and a GDP of some $50 billion a year. But it is the second largest of the whole coastal belt of countries, some Francophone, some Anglophone, from Mauritania through to Nigeria. The different colonial legacies, as well as the differences in local culture, religion and resources, have made it difficult for the region to function as an economic unit. One of the complaints of the late Kofi Annan, the Ghanaian diplomat who became secretary-general of the United Nations, was that communications between Africa and Europe were better than those between different African countries.[44] Yet a decade of infrastructural investment by China has started to rectify some aspects of this problem. As communications improve, and Ghana and most importantly Nigeria become more successful, then West Africa as a whole will do very well.

Ethiopia, Africa's second most populous country with more than 100 million people, has been one of the world's fastest-growing economies throughout this century. In several years it has been the fastest of all: in the ten years between 2007/8 and 2017/18 annual growth averaged more than 10 per cent.[45] This is a stunning achievement and deserves to be celebrated. But that growth, however, did start from a very low base. In the early years of this century Ethiopia was one of the poorest countries in Africa, and you have to see its progress in that light. It was the third poorest country in the world.[46] Despite this run of growth, its GDP per head is only about a quarter that of Nigeria, or, to look at it another way, the level of India and China in the 1970s. There is a long way to go. The challenge is to be able to push on, lifting the country to middle-income levels in another thirty years.

Since Ethiopia has been the recipient of a large amount of aid funds from the developed world, considerable analysis has gone into its competitiveness, its problems and its opportunities. The conventional prognosis is positive[47] with the proviso that the country must continue to wrangle with its social and ethnic tensions. It has a competitive advantage in tourism and related services, but there should equally be opportunities in manufacturing. A huge population – projected to be close to 200 million by 2050 – with relatively low wage levels should be a big enough base to build an industrialised economy. The path to prosperity has been trodden by many other countries, so the question is whether Ethiopia can continue to march along it.

The vast Democratic Republic of the Congo (DRC, known as Zaire between 1971 and 1997) has different, but equally tough challenges. It is the largest country in sub-Saharan Africa, and one of the wealthiest in mineral resources, with copper and cobalt accounting for 80 per cent of its exports. But it is also among the poorest countries in the world in both income per head and human development. The core reasons for this sad juxtaposition of potential wealth and current poverty are government mismanagement and political instability. The troubling outcome has been that over the thirty years to 2010 wealth per head plunged to about one-third of the level of 1960s and 1970s. It has only recovered a little since then.

It is unhelpful to dwell on the details of this sorry tale, except perhaps to note that some of that instability has stemmed from the discord in neighbouring countries, notably the war in Rwanda. What is worth underlining is that given reasonable governance and stability the DRC should be able to prosper. The more it does so, the more central Africa will flourish, too. There are pockets of wealth in the region. For example, oil-rich Gabon has a GDP per head of more than $7,000. But it has a population of only two million. Just to the north and thanks also to oil, Equatorial Guinea is the richest country in Africa. But its population of 1.4 million is the most unequal on earth, with less than half its population having access to clean drinking water. There are obvious specific issues here, but the most populous countries must lead for the region to prosper as a whole.

The powerhouse of sub-Saharan Africa has long been South Africa, the continent's richest big economy, with its most developed industries, its best-educated workforce and home to the largest Black African middle class. It also has a mass of natural resources, strong service industries of tourism and finance, and Africa's biggest manufacturing economy. It has, in short, a great deal going for it. Yet its performance in recent years has been disappointing, for it has been one of the continent's slowest-growing economies. Much of the rest of Africa has been growing at around 8 per cent while South Africa has struggled to reach 2 per cent.

Growth isn't everything. But in the case of South Africa the disappointing economic performance has meant that unemployment and inequality have risen, which has put severe strains on an already tense society. Unemployment is officially around 27 per cent, while youth unemployment is close to 40 per cent.[48] Unsurprisingly, crime is a grave problem. Murder rates are lower than in Latin America, but high by the standards of everywhere else, including other countries in Africa.

South Africa inevitably suffers from the stained legacy of apartheid. But a quarter of a century on from Nelson Mandela becoming president in 1994, the negative economic effects of that should have faded. Running a successful economy requires confidence in the business community, and that seems to be quite thin. So the question really is whether economic requirements will determine policy in the years ahead, or whether future governments will continue to focus on patching social difficulties. The challenge is that of chicken and egg: sustained growth requires greater social stability, but social stability requires better job opportunities, which in turn requires economic growth.

That paradox applies to the entire continent. But there is something else holding Africa back: poor communications. There is a great arc of African countries, stretching from Kenya and Uganda in the north-east to Namibia and South Africa in the south-west, most of which are members of the Commonwealth. They range in population size from Tanzania, which has nearly 60 million people, through Kenya with 50 million, to Lesotho and Swaziland with fewer than 2 million. In land area there is Tanzania, which is the size of Western Europe, to Swaziland, which is smaller than Wales. Wealthy Botswana has a GDP per head of some $8,000 and the highest human development ranking in sub-Saharan Africa, while Malawi has less than $500 per head.

This huge area has some 250 million people – more than 300 million if you add South Africa. It has massive natural resources, sophisticated cities and a booming tourist industry. These are all elements that give it great economic potential. So why does it also encompass some of the poorest countries of the world? Poor communications start with roads. There are still no good north–south roads and internal roads are frequently bad. There are few railways. Even air transport is weak. Often it is easier to fly several thousand miles to Europe than to a neighbouring capital city. However, this is changing. Road networks are being transformed by Chinese investment. Divided-lane highways are limited, but a network of high-quality two-lane roads is spreading across Africa.

Will Chinese investment – in agriculture, infrastructure and manufacturing – support and broaden current rapid economic development? Put more bluntly, will Chinese commercial investment succeed where Western aid programmes have failed? Investment in Africa is a key element of China's so-called Belt and Road Initiative (BRI).[49] It is a natural partnership. Africa needs commercial investment. China needs natural resources. China, perhaps because it feels free of colonial guilt, finds it easier to operate in Africa than Western governments and corporations. Much of the future of the continent will turn on the success or otherwise of this relationship. But whatever happens, Africa becomes more important to the world economy.

The Middle East, by contrast, may become less so. It is hard to discuss the economic advantages and disadvantages of the Middle East without discussing its politics. In political terms it is and will remain one of the most fragile regions of the world. But it is more helpful to focus on the economy, because the more successful the region is in creating employment and opportunities for its young people, the more likely it will be that the different countries can cope with political tensions.

The Middle East is extraordinarily diverse. Take wealth. In terms of GDP per head, Qatar is the richest place in the world. Afghanistan, to the region's east, is one of the poorest. Or take population density. Libya's seven million people live in the world's sixteenth largest country by land area, whereas the northern Nile region of Egypt, with Cairo and Alexandria, is one of the most densely populated places in the world. Or take economic structure. Oil and gas dominate the Gulf and Saudi Arabia. Egypt has an unusually diversified economy, with agriculture and industry both employing about a quarter of the workforce, and services and government the rest. Turkey, on the region's north-western flank, is one of the top twenty economies of the world. Tajikistan and Kyrgyzstan, far to the east, have tiny economies – about the size of the city of Oxford in the UK. Meanwhile, Israel is a high-income 'Western' developed economy in what is basically a middle-income region.

Because it is so diverse, there are few common lessons to be drawn. Some points are easy to make. The oil-rich nations need to diversify. The large population countries must figure out a way of creating jobs for their young people. Educational standards need to be raised. And, of course, political stability is vital to support growth. But to cite this is to miss a bigger point. Potentially the Middle East could over the next generation be much more successful than it has been over the past one. A youthful, energetic Middle East is the perfect partner to ageing Europe. From a European perspective, too often this youth is seen as a threat – the threat of mass immigration, importing ideas and cultures that clash with those of older Europeans. There is reason behind such fears. But most people do not want to leave their own countries, their families and their friends, if they can get the opportunities they seek at home.

The relationship between Europe and the Middle East has been a long and difficult one over many centuries. It would be optimistic to expect it to become easier. But the fact that there is a natural economic partnership is a place to start. Europe provides the investment capital, access to skills and a more open market for the region's exports. In return it gets cheaper and higher quality goods and services than it can get from anywhere else. Viewed objectively, the region has so much to offer. It is very much in

Europe's self-interest to see that, and manage the relationship as thoughtfully and creatively as possible. It is equally in the self-interest of the Middle Eastern countries to see Europe as an ally in helping them attack their problems.

OCEANIA – WILL AUSTRALIA STILL BE LUCKY?

Two excellent books written in the 1960s capture the essence of Australia. Australia remains lucky, arguably even more so than it was in 1964 when Donald Horne published his analysis, *The Lucky Country*. He argued that the Australian people had succeeded thanks to their natural wealth and distance from the problems of the rest of the world rather than their inherent talents. Subsequent history has, however, shown that Australians have played the good hand they were dealt with skill. Australia is luckier partly because the Asian nations in its time zone have become more important globally, for Perth is in the same time zone as Beijing. But it is also luckier because the communications revolution has reduced one potential economic handicap of being far from other Western countries. The way that geographic isolation has shaped Australia was described by Geoffrey Blainey in *The Tyranny of Distance* in 1967. He pointed out that Australia's challenge was to create a new Anglophone society out of what was, to the settlers at least, virgin territory, and to become independent from its distant European roots. But distance has shrunk with the falling cost of air travel and in particular near-free telecommunications.

You can measure the way growth in its time zone has transformed Australia by looking at who buys its exports. At the turn of the century roughly half went to Asia. In 2018 it was over two-thirds; nearly one-third went to China. It is easy to see why. Australia can deliver what booming Asia needs. It is the world's largest exporter of iron ore, with nearly 60 per cent of the global market. Other main exports are coal, gold, gas and wheat – all in heavy demand from Asia.

But it would be misleading to focus just on physical exports. Australia has also built up impressive service industries: tourism obviously but also education. Only the US and UK have more universities in the world's top 100 according to the QS rankings, an astounding achievement for a country of just twenty-five million.[50] For anyone in Asia seeking an alternative education to the US or UK, and in an English-speaking environment, Australia is the credible option. In the years ahead this is a strong plus point: lots of clever young people with experience of Australia.

Put together the package – natural resources, English language and legal system, excellent education, plenty of space, location in the East Asian time zones, functioning, decent democracy – and it is extraordinarily attractive. There is, however, one serious potential negative: the environment. Australia is the driest continent and as such faces some of the most extreme threats from climate change. That is something its growing population will have to confront.

New Zealand tends to be bracketed with Australia as its smaller cousin. That is useful shorthand given their common heritage and cultural similarities, but ignores sharp differences of scale and geography. Its five million people occupy a land area slightly larger than the UK's sixty-seven million. The climate is temperate and there are no water shortages. Rather, the reverse: the west coast of the South Island is one of the wettest places on earth. This makes New Zealand an attractive location in an increasingly crowded world. Unlike Australia it does not have scale, but that may not matter. It will have to make some similar big choices, such as to what extent it wishes to grow by attracting more immigration.

That leads to a final point about both Australia and New Zealand. Like Canada, they are in an enviable position in the world, and whatever they do they face a sunny future. Many people around the world would like to move there. It is in a way flattering that this should be so, for it suggests they are doing something right. There are other parts of the developed world that would appear to have similar attractions – the Scandinavian countries, for example – but those three countries stand out as places people want to make as their homes. They are magnets for talent. It is a wonderful accolade, but it is also a tricky challenge.

THE WORLD OF TODAY SHAPES THE WORLD
OF TOMORROW

Countries have some things they cannot change: most obviously their location and their neighbours. Their populations shift over time, growing or perhaps shrinking, but do so only slowly. The education levels of the workforce can change only slowly, too, if you consider that the average working life is more than forty years. Immigration and emigration affect both the age structure and the size of a country's population, but there are social and practical limits to both immigration and emigration. A sudden discovery of natural resources can have a huge impact on GDP, but the benefits may be squandered if the political and institutional structures of the country are weak.

In considering the economic advantages and disadvantages of any country, you have to distinguish what can be changed and what cannot. A small, landlocked country surrounded by poor neighbours will struggle to overcome the disadvantages of its location. A country surrounded by prosperity is likely to be prosperous itself. It would need to have pretty catastrophic economic management not to succeed. However, many countries, large and small, have managed to impose unnecessary poverty on their people, notably China before the Deng Xiaoping reforms.

Culture and education are clearly of massive importance. Why is North America richer than South America? Or Northern Europe richer than Southern Europe? But cultures can and do change over time, and education levels certainly so. In assessing how countries might make progress over the next generation there has to be some sort of judgement as to ability and willingness to change. Long-term educational performance is a useful guide to whether countries will improve their economies. But there is a lot more to the mix of policies and social characteristics that support economic success. It is a fool's errand to expect a simple indicator to tell us whether a country will punch above or below its weight. We know that the rule of law matters a great deal and corruption destroys wealth, but some countries with unpredictable legal outcomes and serious corruption still manage to produce decent growth.

Adam Smith's observation 'there is a great deal of ruin in a nation'[51] is often quoted as a warning that countries can damage their economic prospects with poor management. He meant it ironically. He wrote it in a letter in response to a friend who had exclaimed after the loss of the Battle of Saratoga in 1777 'we shall all be ruined'. Britain did, of course, lose the American colonies, but at that moment something much more important was happening. The Industrial Revolution was gathering pace, utterly transforming living standards not just for Britain, but for America, Europe and indeed the world. The American Revolution was of great political significance, but in global economic terms it was a blip. In thirty years' time the current tensions in America will, I suggest, seem just a blip, too.

Some countries will improve their economic position radically in the years to 2050, while others will make only modest progress. But no country need be a prisoner of its past. Nor does it need to cling to past ideas about what drives economic growth, ideas that have proved to be blind alleys. Other factors, encapsulated in the five forces for change outlined in the next chapters, matter more. It is to those we now turn.

Forces for Change

2

Demography – An Ageing World and a Youthful One

Start with some numbers. How many of us will there be? In 2050, the world will have just under 10 billion people, up from 7.7 billion in the middle of 2019. This is not a precise forecast; rather, it is a projection made in the middle of 2019 by the United Nations,[1] an exercise it does every two years. But we can have some confidence in the UN's work, for back in the early 1990s it judged correctly that there would be between 7.5 billion and 8 billion people in the world in 2020. If you try to squint into the distant future to 2100 and beyond, the numbers become speculative. But look just one generation forward, and – barring some unbearable catastrophe – the numbers will be broadly right. After all, everyone who will be over the age of thirty in 2050 is already alive.

The most populous country will be India, with more than 1.6 billion people, closely followed by China, with 1.4 billion. A long way behind these two giants will be everyone else. The United States will be number three, with some 400 million, and Nigeria fourth with just under 400 million. Then will come Indonesia, Pakistan, Brazil and Bangladesh, probably in that order and all with between 200 million and 300 million people.

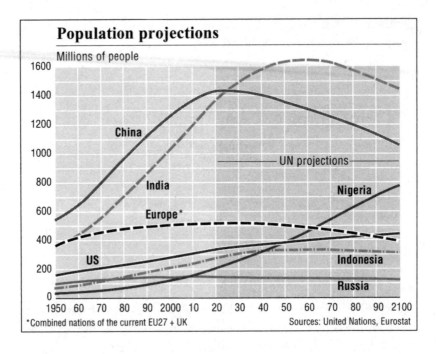

Population projections

Millions of people

China

India

UN projections

Nigeria

Europe*

US

Indonesia

Russia

1950 60 70 80 90 2000 10 20 30 40 50 60 70 80 90 2100

*Combined nations of the current EU27 + UK   Sources: United Nations, Eurostat

We can also be reasonably sure of these numbers, but only *reasonably* so. Population projections for the world as a whole have two main inputs: birth rates and longevity. But when you look at individual countries and regions you must add a third: migration. You can get the global view more or less right, for the net changes as people flow out of one country and into another are likely to cancel each other out. But the smaller the unit, the harder it is to be confident.

Migration, of course, is neutral viewed globally, but it can transform a country. For example, between 1985 and 2019 Bulgaria lost more than one-fifth of its population, which fell from a peak of just under nine million to below seven million. True, migration to the rest of Europe was not the only reason for this plunge. Death rates remained relatively high, falling more slowly than, for example, its neighbour Greece. And the birth rate stayed relatively low, with a total fertility rate of 1.4 – that is the average number of babies born to each woman during their lives. Bulgaria and Latvia are the only two countries in the world that had in 2019 a smaller population than they did in 1950.

If there are to be ten billion people in the world in 2050 that raises a string of testing and sometimes troubling questions. Some are associated with the burden on the environment: at the very least, we will need enough food, fresh water and space. Other questions concern the impact on global finance. Heavily indebted countries with shrinking populations will struggle to pay the interest on their national debt. Still others relate to human capital. Will it be possible to give a good enough education to Africa's burgeoning ranks of teenagers? Will technological advances help the developed world's ageing citizens to maintain a decent quality of life? And hanging over everything is the shift in economic power that will result from a dwindling population in Europe, India overtaking China as the world's most populous nation, and the booming number of young people in Africa.

Some of the consequences of these demographic shifts are discussed in the following chapters. What this chapter seeks to do is to highlight the main changes that will almost certainly take place in the balance of the world's population, but also to acknowledge some of the uncertainties, particularly over migration.

There are three big trends. One is the ageing of the entire developed world, with in some countries a decline in population. The second is the shift of the balance of the world's population within Asia (which accounts for 60 per cent of the total), from China to India. And third is the rising population of Africa. We look at each, and then at some of the questions these shifts raise.

AN OLDER DEVELOPED WORLD

The ageing of the developed world is a given. It is happening already and it will continue for another generation at least, as the graph overleaf shows.

And not just the developed world, for what is happening now in Japan, Europe and more slowly the United States is already spreading to China and Russia. It will eventually sweep across India

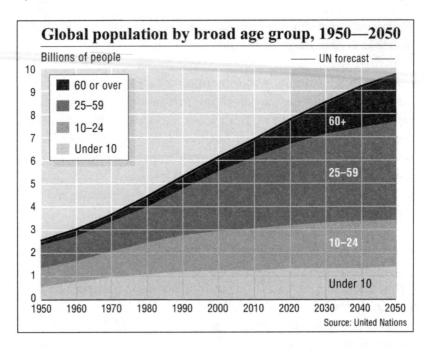

Global population by broad age group, 1950—2050

and the rest of the subcontinent, and – as far as we can be sure of anything half a century ahead – to Africa.

An older world will feel different in many ways. To catch a sense of this the place to go is Japan, with the oldest population on earth. Superficially, Japan has coped remarkably well with this demographic change. It has, of course, long been an unusually cohesive and collaborative society. Families matter, too. This social glue helps enormously, in that the 'young old' – those in late middle age and beyond – look after the 'old old' – the very elderly. Many of Japan's older people continue to do paid work well beyond normal retirement age. But there are towns where there are no children, so the schools close and the towns initially become retirement communities – and then simply have to be abandoned.[2]

A huge amount of work has gone into studying projections of the country's ageing and declining population, and what might be done about it. The main government body, the National Institute of Population and Social Security Research,[3] suggests that by 2045 a quarter of the country's workforce will be over the age of seventy-five. But what sort of work will they be doing? And what does this imply for the country's living standards? Younger workers are in general more productive than older ones. Already Japanese productivity appears to be falling, with the lowest level of output per worker in the G7 nations. While this is probably as much the result of stodgy business practices as the ageing workforce, it will be hard to shift this performance.

Japan now is calm, orderly, clean and crime-free. It offers a comfortable life experience for many of its citizens. But it is not the restlessly innovative society it was in the 1980s, and it is hard to see it ever returning to that dynamism. Japanese people talk of the lost two decades, from about 1990 to 2010, when the economy barely grew. But, actually, it will continue to face a long period of economic stagnation.

Does that matter? If the present ratio of people of working age to the elderly were to remain stable, perhaps not. But the ratio is shrinking inexorably, year by year, so that by 2045 there are projected to be only ten workers for every seven retirees. Large-scale immigration might alter the arithmetic but that seems to be rejected by the Japanese people. Thanks to Japanese traditional harmony, the present situation is manageable, but the outlook is dicey indeed.

It boils down to this. Provided young people are prepared to accept a lower standard of living than would otherwise be the case, and probably a lower standard than their parents, then ageing societies should be able to function peacefully and successfully. Japan has the most serious problem, but it also perhaps has the best shot at coping. But Europe?

Europe follows Japan in its pattern of ageing. Southern Europe tends to have lower fertility rates than Northern Europe, while Eastern Europe has lower rates still. Both Southern and Eastern Europe have seen a loss of young people, moving north and west. People talk of Europe as the next Japan, a characterisation that is not intended to be flattering. But European countries differ in two main ways from Japan. They are more fragmented societies; and there is more immigration and emigration. So it is perhaps better to see some parts of Europe as resembling Japan – at least in the mathematics of ageing – while others resemble the United States, and have a different set of challenges.

Italy shows the closest parallels to Japan. It has a similarly low fertility rate, estimated at an average of 1.35 babies per mother. In Japan the figure is 1.4, both far below the replacement rate of 2.1. Italy also has the highest public debt of any large economy bar Japan – 132 per cent of GDP, against Japan's 250 per cent – although it lacks Japan's freedom to control its own currency. And like Japan, in recent years Italy's economy has barely grown at all.

But that is where the similarities peter out. Unlike Japan, Italy has experienced large-scale immigration and emigration. In recent years its immigrants have come largely from North Africa, and while most have moved on to other European countries, Italy has a foreign-born population of more than five million, equivalent to over 8 per cent of the population. More than one million people arrived in 2015, leading to political pressure to check the flow, which has subsequently fallen sharply.

Italian immigration policy has been widely criticised,[4] but in some ways the outflow of its young people, while receiving less attention, is more troubling. Between 2008 and 2015 more than half a million of them emigrated, mostly to Northern Europe but also to North America. The reasons have been a mix of social and economic factors – fewer job opportunities, promotion by age rather than merit and so on – but the flow has far-reaching demographic consequences. Spain, and particularly Greece, face similar pressures. As a result, Southern European countries will have falling populations and rapidly ageing workforces. Northern European countries will have a much slower transition – and in some instances, notably the UK, a rising population that is expected to continue increasing through to 2050 and beyond. It is possible that by 2070 the UK will have passed Germany to become the most populous European nation.

Germany and France lie somewhere between the UK and Italy in their demographic outlook, with Germany experiencing a falling population, though at a slightly slower rate thanks to large-scale immigration between 2015 and 2017. France, with higher birth rates, will age more slowly. But the big contrast will be between a relatively vibrant north and a relatively somnolent south. That will inevitably lead to tensions that will have to be managed. Can they be managed? Well, the Robert Schuman Foundation, a European research centre created in 1991 after the fall of the Berlin Wall, has described Europe's prospects by 2050 as 'demographic suicide'.[5] That may be too brutal a way of putting it. But Europe unquestionably will be a much less muscular force in the world, particularly as the UK economy swings further from that of the Continent. The Foundation argues that Europe is failing to face up to this challenge. Sadly, it is probably right.

Europe's relative decline will lead to tensions, too, between it and the United States. The latter, along with the rest of North America, will continue to grow in population, with the United States probably passing Europe sometime in the 2070s. Add in Canada to the North American tally and subtract the UK from the European one and the tipping point is likely to come sometime in the 2040s. A United States of nearly 400 million people will remain the world's third most populous nation. But that population will feel different from that of today in three main ways. US government projections[6] suggest it will be greyer, with the proportion of people aged sixty-five or older rising from 15 to 22 per cent. It will be more diverse, with the non-Hispanic white population becoming a minority, with about 40 per cent of the total. And it will increasingly become, once again, a nation of immigrants, with the foreign-born population rising from 14 to 17 per cent: the highest proportion at any time since 1850.

The United States knows better than Europe how to integrate immigrants into its society. It has, after all, been at it for longer. Europe has for centuries been a region of net emigrants, not immigrants. For the Europeans, mass immigration is a recent phenomenon. For Americans, it is foundational. What's more, the United States has had, and still does have, the pick of the bunch. It is the country of first choice for most immigrants, many of whom are enticed initially at least by its higher education opportunities, and virtually all of whom are attracted by the powerful magnet of its job market. Immigration will take over from natural increase as the main driver of population growth, for the fertility rate of the existing population seems to be falling to below 1.8, well below replacement level.[7] Fertility rates may pick up in the United States, as they have done in some countries in Europe, but it seems unlikely that they will recover enough to alter the picture of a country that needs immigration to maintain population growth.

As a result, the US population will continue to expand through 2050, whereas Europe's will shrink. That will change the relationship between the two largest developed world blocs. Both face a challenge to turn what is potentially a negative force into positive outcomes. But this will be more difficult for Europe to pull off.

There is a further twist: what will happen to Russia. The UN projects that its population will dwindle from 146 million in 2020 to 136 million in 2050. That is still a lot of people, even if the population is shrinking and elderly. But Russia is the world's largest country by land area, and though much of it is a harsh environment for human beings, it would be a natural place for land-hungry people to move. So the great question facing Russia is whether it will be a nation of immigrants or emigrants. Perhaps surprisingly, since the breakup of the Soviet Union at the beginning of the 1990s, Russia has been a nation of immigrants. In fact, it is the second most immigrated-to country in the world after the United States,[8] with the bulk of immigrants coming from countries with sizeable Russian-speaking populations. It needs them. Indeed, given that Russia's fertility rate, like that of the United States, is just 1.8 births per woman, the Russian state statistics agency Rosstat estimates that the country needs half a million immigrants a year to steady its population.[9] But the inflow may have reversed. It is too early to be sure, but Russia may have started to experience net emigration. If that trend establishes itself and persists, the outlook for the country might be an even faster decline.

CHINA SHRINKS, INDIA RISES

The demographic fluctuations within the developed world, however, are relatively small when set against the shift of the balance towards the emerging world. It will account for almost all the global rise in population that is likely to occur. Most of that increase will be in India and the rest of South Asia, and in Africa.

In Asia, 60 per cent of humankind, the great shift will be between China and India. Some time in the early 2020s, India will pass China in population for the first time since the early 1700s. From the time of the Roman Empire, right through to the dawn of the eighteenth century, India had more people than China.[10] In 1700 it is estimated that India had 165 million people, China 135 million. Then China pulled ahead, so that by 1900 China had 400 million, India 285 million. In 1982, three years after China brought in its one-child policy, its population passed the one billion mark. India at that time had 700 million people. Even adding the 93 million people in Bangladesh and the 91 million in Pakistan, the Indian subcontinent still had fewer people than China. China has dropped its one-child policy, and indeed its two-child policy, but despite this the dynamic between the two giants that has lasted for three centuries, with China having a larger population than India, is about to be reversed.

We can be pretty sure that India will increase its lead in the years to come. It is harder to be so certain about the ways in which population dynamics will feed back into the national psyche, but we can have a feeling for the differences between an ageing society and a youthful one. At the moment, China still displays the vigour of its transformation from a command to a market economy – from subsistence to consumerism. But like Japan before it, that vigour will wane as the country ages. By contrast, India's youth will ensure that it remains boisterous, energetic and self-confident for many years to come.

India's relative youth is also its challenge – and this also applies, of course, to Pakistan and Bangladesh. How do you ensure that young people are adequately prepared for a world that requires people to be better educated and better trained – not just for the roles that exist now, but for those that have yet to be created? Booming numbers of young people hitting the job market need booming numbers of jobs. In many parts of the world there is a struggle to combat youth unemployment, but in India that challenge is staggering. Some ten to twelve million pour into the workforce every year, and around one in five people between the ages of fifteen and twenty-eight in urban areas are unemployed.[11] Creating those jobs is arguably the Indian subcontinent's most daunting task.

THE SOARING POPULATION OF AFRICA

Projected population growth in Africa is extraordinary, almost unbelievably so. We'll come to the questions about it in a moment. Start with what the UN expects to happen. The 2019 UN projections[12] suggest that the population of sub-Saharan Africa will double between 2019 and 2050: from 1.05 billion to 2.1 billion. Add in North Africa and the total goes from 1.3 billion to 2.5 billion, one-quarter of the world's people. Every country increases its population, but some of the highest proportionate increases will be in some of the countries already under economic stress. As a rule of thumb, the lower the present level of economic development, the greater the projected increase in population. Thus the relatively advanced South Africa is projected to increase from 59 million to 76 million, while the similarly sized but lower-income Tanzania will rise from 58 million to 129 million. Among Africa's poorest states, Niger will triple from 21 million to 66 million.

Or at least it will if these UN numbers prove broadly right. They are based on projected changes in fertility, and are shown in the graph opposite.

But UN calculations have changed over time, largely because fertility has not fallen as fast as expected ten or twelve years ago, and there is little consensus among scholars as to what will happen now.[13] The great question is: how quickly will fertility fall? We know, given the number of girls in sub-Saharan Africa

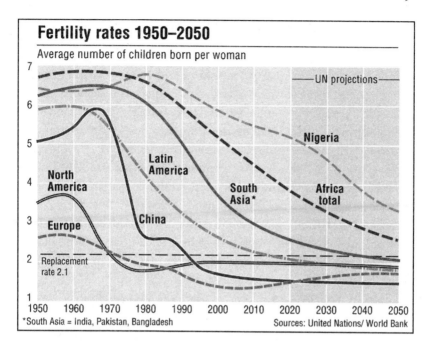

Fertility rates 1950–2050

Average number of children born per woman

North America

Europe

Latin America

China

North America

South Asia*

Nigeria

Africa total

UN projections

Replacement rate 2.1

*South Asia = India, Pakistan, Bangladesh

Sources: United Nations/ World Bank

who will be of child-bearing age over the next thirty years, that the population of Africa will rise sharply. So that projection of it doubling will be broadly right. But what we don't know is whether by then the growth will have tailed off, as women's education rises, or whether it will race onwards to 2100 and beyond. For the record, the UN projection of Africa in 2100 has a population of 4.3 billion, 40 per cent of the total of 10.9 billion. By then the population of the rest of the world will be falling, but that of Africa will still be growing. It will be young; most of the rest of the world will be old.

It is hard for us now to envisage such a situation, but I think we have to accept that it is the most likely outcome. Even with a faster than projected decline in fertility Africa becomes more important to the future of the world. African people become more important, the African environment becomes more important and African ideas of how societies should be organised will become more important.

WHY DEMOGRAPHY MATTERS SO MUCH

These three themes – the ageing developed world, the shift of the balance of population between China and India and the growing weight of Africa – raise some fundamental questions about the world's ability to manage the huge challenges of long-term demographic shifts. There is the popular phrase 'demography is destiny', originally applied to the implications of demographic change to politics in the United States, but often used in a wider context.[14] It has a natural resonance; perhaps that is why it is so often quoted. But I suggest the more helpful, if less neat, phrase is 'coping with demography is destiny'. Societies can cope either well or badly. The lives of all of us, wherever we live, will be shaped by demographic changes, and the challenge therefore will be to respond to them in a positive way.

There is a serious problem for the world as a whole – how to protect the planet on which we live, so that ten billion people or more can have decent lives without putting too great a burden on its resources. That will be dealt with in the next chapter, which looks at the environment. There is also a question as to whether an increasing population is a strength or a weakness – or, rather, how to turn what might appear a weakness into a strength.

But given the sketch of demographic trends in the first part of this chapter, there are a number of specific challenges facing different countries and different regions, so what follows is some guesses as to how they will tackle them. Here are the six biggest challenges:

1. How Europe should adjust its policies to meet the needs of its ageing population.
2. Whether the United States can continue to grow, in the words of Emma Lazarus's famous 1883 poem, welcoming the world's 'huddled masses yearning to breathe free', yet maintaining a harmonious society.
3. How regions with plunging populations, notably Eastern Europe and Russia, deal with this decline.

4. To what extent China manages to adapt to an ageing society.
5. How India and the subcontinent use their youthfulness in the most positive way.
6. To what extent Africa and the Middle East, the two youngest regions, can cope with their booming population so as to give their young people satisfying lives.

Europe has no choice but to adapt. It is unrealistic to think that birth rates will rise sharply enough to reach replacement rate. It may happen in some smaller countries, perhaps in Ireland and Scandinavia, but it will not happen for the continent as a whole. There are two broad paths forward. Europe can encourage immigration, attracting people from the rest of the world to do the jobs it needs doing. And it can reorganise its own work and social patterns so that the existing (though in many countries, shrinking) population gets the work done. That work will, of course, include looking after increasing numbers of elderly people.

It will do both, but the emphasis will vary across Europe. The pressure for greater immigration will be huge, particularly from Africa and the Middle East. We have a glimpse of that now. But European nations will increasingly want to choose which immigrants they accept, based on the skills they bring. However, the key point, brought out in a European Commission study in 2019[15] is that increasing labour participation rates will have a bigger impact on the size of the European labour force than immigration. Higher immigration naturally increases the size of the labour force, but if immigrants bring their families it does not do much to change the ratio of workers to non-workers. Increasing that ratio is crucial to improving living standards. So, too, is lifting the quality of the labour force. Education and training, always important, become even more so with a shrinking number of people at work.

These points also apply to the United States. But it faces a little less pressure. It has a somewhat more productive workforce than most European nations. It will have a rapidly growing population, instead of a stable or declining one. And it has a much longer tradition of receiving large numbers of immigrants. The challenge is less 'how do you get the work done?' and more 'how do you maintain social harmony?'.

History can give a guide to how America will react. It has had many bouts of high immigration, followed by periods when it has restricted the inflow and devoted energy to assimilating the new arrivals. The first two decades of the twenty-first century have seen very high immigration, both documented and undocumented. That has led to a reaction, one aspect of which was the plan by then president Donald Trump to build a wall on the border with Mexico to keep undocumented migrants out. Many Americans, by contrast, have sought to show their openness to immigrants in a variety of ways, including the idea of 'sanctuary cities' in Canada as well as the United States, where the rights of immigrants have special protection.[16]

This tension will continue. From the perspective of potential immigrants, the economic allure of the United States is likely to remain so strong that they will find ways of entering the US job market whatever measures are taken to stop them. But pressure against undocumented immigration will not go away. A plausible outcome would be a decade or more of restrictions followed by a decade or more of more relaxed controls. Though the detail is hard to envisage, the overall outcome is pretty clear: the US population will become more diverse: more mixed in race, culture and social norms. And it will become much bigger.

Coping with population growth is easier than coping with population decline, the challenge that faces a number of developed countries, as we have seen particularly in parts of Southern and Eastern Europe. For governments to do nothing will be politically impossible, but coming up with effective policies to counter the impact of population decline is extraordinarily difficult. It is easy to say that the key is to improve job opportunities for young people – to retain and encourage local talent. But it is much harder to point to success stories, where a developed country has turned round a declining population by that means.

Harder but not impossible. The best example of just such a turnaround is the Republic of Ireland, which was once beset with the emigration of its young. Its population slid from 3.2 million at the time of partition with Northern Ireland in 1921 to 2.8 million in the 1960s. (It had been 6.5 million in the 1840s before the famines.) A set of business-friendly reforms from the 1950s onwards gradually brushed up its economic performance, and reduced emigration coupled with relatively high fertility rates led to a rising population, in 2019 approaching 4.9 million.[17]

Could Ireland's revival be a model for Bulgaria, or Italy? Ireland has many built-in advantages, including the English language and legal system. But it has also invested heavily in education and crafted a tax and regulatory regime that has coaxed other countries to set up businesses there, particularly the United States. There are elements of its policies that carry lessons for other developed nations. Being friendly to international investors is a start.

There is some experience of declining populations in the developed world but hardly any among emerging nations. So China, whose population is projected to start falling by 2027,[18] maybe earlier, will become a pioneer. It is true that China will by then not really be an emerging economy; it will be a middle-income one. But actually, hardly any middle-income economies have experienced a falling population. The question for China is whether it can continue to grow reasonably rapidly and push on, so that by 2050 it reaches what you might call low-end developed country living standards. It will be a fully developed country, but not as rich as countries in Europe, or the US. Will that be enough to satisfy the ambition of its people? Will it continue to want to look outwards to the world?

The issues for the other giant, India, are quite different. The most populous country on earth will have millions of young people hitting the job market each year, brimming with energy and ambition. They will be well-educated, increasingly so, and demanding. They will need job opportunities, of course, but they will also need satisfying lifestyles. Some of their needs will be met by greater investment: in homes, transport, public services and so on. But to provide comfortable living standards for more than 1.6 billion people in the limited land area of India will need a mix of thoughtful public planning and innovative market solutions.

Government and the private sector must work in a more cooperative way than they have achieved to date. The potential is enormous, but so, too, are the risks.

The challenges for Africa are even greater. It is hard to overstate the importance of demography not only to its future, but also to the future of the rest of the world. It is the youngest and poorest continent, with the fastest-growing population. If you take conventional measures of wealth and wellbeing – GDP per head, access to medical care and so on – it is and will remain below the standards not just of the developed world, but viewed in aggregate below those of almost everywhere else. Its young people will look at the opportunities available to their peers elsewhere and wonder why they are not available to them. The more connected the world, the greater their sense of dissatisfaction.

Yet Africa, as noted earlier, is growing fast. That growth is supported by inward investment, notably from China, and by emigrants' remittances, both of which are likely to surge in the years ahead. Further, conventional measures of wealth are not necessarily the best indicators of economic opportunity. It is impossible to generalise sensibly about the economic prospects for an entire continent. But it is worth making the point that for many young people in Africa, it may turn out that they will have better life chances within the continent than if they were to leave.

Many of the issues facing sub-Saharan Africa also face North Africa and the Middle East. In terms of demography they are quite similar. The median age in Nigeria is eighteen; in the Palestinian territories it is nineteen; in Iraq twenty.[19] However, while all these countries need to provide good jobs for the young, the political and economic backdrops against which these jobs will be created are very different. Investment in education brings great long-term rewards, but in the short term countries may be educating people for jobs that are not there. The sad but inevitable result for the young graduates is huge frustration and a scramble to find another country where their skills are better rewarded.

There are no easy solutions to these challenges. We know, or at least can reasonably expect, that some parts of the world will have declines in their population, while others will experience increases, sometimes rapid ones. We know this will create social and economic tensions. We know, too, that there is both a need and an opportunity for population growth, and the prosperity that will result from that. But that growth will place a greater burden on the planet's resources. If there are to be more people in the world, which there will be, and if those people are to have higher living standards, which most people would hope for, then the world faces some very tough questions.

The tensions will be all the sharper because of the rebalancing of the world's population towards the old, both within countries and between them. We have no experience of this, no roadmap to help us navigate between these tensions, no lessons from history.

Those issues will be tackled in subsequent chapters on the environment, on technological advance, and on trade and economic activity, and on government. But we must accept that the world's population will continue to grow for another generation at least, and that its average age will continue to climb. There are many uncertainties in the future. But the continued growth and the continuing ageing of the world's population are as near inevitable as could be.

3

Resources and the Environment – Decarbonising the World Economy

FROM MANY CONCERNS TO ONE HUGE ONE

The mood has shifted. Whereas concern about the environment in the 1990s focused on a string of different issues, the great overriding anxiety now is that of climate change. A generation ago, environmental experts were worried about whether the world could feed more than seven billion people by 2020, when oil supplies might start to run out, the threats to biodiversity and to habitat, the hole in the ozone layer and so on. Of course, they were also concerned about the ways in which human activity was increasing the levels of carbon dioxide and the consequences for global warming. But at that stage climate change seemed a more nebulous, distant worry.

Perceptions now are vastly different. Climate change is at the very centre of current concerns. It is a huge, hulking, holistic, interconnected and existential problem. There are a number of reasons why. Thirty years ago, there was already a mounting pile of evidence supporting the view that the world was warming and that this was almost certainly associated with rising levels of carbon dioxide in the atmosphere. But while this was generally accepted by most of the scientific community, the general public was only just beginning to become aware of it.

Then, over a fifteen-year period from 2005 to 2020, everything changed. Four things happened. Governments the world over realised that the economic arguments for tackling climate change had gathered pace. Consumers' and investors' attitudes evolved, with people demanding products that had the least impact on the environment and better corporate environmental practice. Advances in technology made it possible for business not only to meet the new demands from governments and customers, but to profit massively from the shift. And the Covid-19 crisis speeded up trends that had already begun.

The trigger that shifted government attitudes was a report by a British economics professor, Nicholas Stern, who had worked in several public roles including chief economist for the World Bank. In 2003 he was recruited by Gordon Brown, then Chancellor of the Exchequer, to join the UK Treasury as chief economic adviser. In 2005 he led a team that produced a report on the economic impact of a warming planet: *The Economics of Climate Change: The Stern Review*.[1]

His key point was that there was a strong financial case for seeking to slow down changes to the climate, beyond moral or conservation reasons. This changed the argument. Countries needed to act because it was cheaper to start transforming their economies now than to face the costs of climate change later. To appeal to economic self-interest is usually more effective than appealing to altruism, and while some of the estimates and calculations of the report have been criticised, its conclusions were generally accepted.

The report paved the way to the Paris Agreement in 2015,[2] where 197 countries agreed to curb their greenhouse gas emissions. Inevitably both that agreement and the decision in 2017 of the United States to withdraw from it were controversial. In 2021, President Biden rejoined. But despite American ambivalence, from the point of view of global governance Paris moved the whole debate about climate change onto a different plane. It also helped budge the needle on how ordinary consumers chose to spend and invest their money.

The story then swung from a British academic and civil servant to a Swedish teenager. If Lord Stern, as he became, was the driving force behind the transformation of government attitudes towards climate change, the single most important person to push consumers to rethink their environmental footprint was Greta Thunberg. The extraordinary story of a sixteen-year-old young woman sailing across the Atlantic to address the United Nations in 2019 is so well known that there is no need to repeat it here. What is worth shouting from the rooftops is that she achieved something that no one else had done: she encouraged young people across the world to push their elders into taking climate change seriously. This shifted the political dial, marginalising politicians who spoke out against her, but also had a profound impact on the corporate world. Companies that failed to follow good practice found consumers and investors punishing them. Thunberg gave a new impetus to the E of ESG investing – Environmental, Social and Corporate Governance. Investors started to divest from firms that were perceived to have low environmental standards.

The origins of ESG investing go back to 2004, when the then secretary-general of the UN, Kofi Annan, wrote to the heads of large financial institutions calling for them to support the idea of responsible investment. But the ideas had only gradually filtered through markets.[3] Greta Thunberg's actions led to a tipping point. Before her UN speech, most quoted companies in the developed world would publicly support environmentally friendly policies. After it, they began to deliver them.

For the winners, the companies that were on the right side of the shift in investor sentiment, the rewards have been huge. The people who invested in environmentally responsible companies have done well, too. The companies have thrived thanks to advances in technology. These advances have meant they could create the sophisticated products and services that people want without imposing a heavy burden on the environment.

Most of those winning companies are American, the high-tech juggernauts of the West Coast: Apple, Microsoft, Amazon, Alphabet, Facebook, Netflix and so on. You could argue that good

ESG practice was a relatively small contributor to their success, but, nevertheless, they were astute enough to ensure they ticked the ESG boxes. More generally, these companies benefited from the shift of consumption towards electronic communication. To print a newspaper means chopping down trees and transporting heavy newsprint; to deliver news online does not. Of those many high-tech winners, one stands out: Tesla.

Elon Musk stands alongside Nicholas Stern and Greta Thunberg as someone who shifted the entire debate about climate change. His contribution has been to end the reign of the internal combustion engine. Thanks to his genius in seeing that laptop batteries could be scaled up to power a car, and then creating a seductive example of that, the Tesla Model S, he transformed the entire global motor industry.[4] By 2050, hardly any new petrol- and diesel-powered vehicles will be manufactured and those still on the roads will be fast disappearing. The technologies that made this possible – the falling costs of batteries to store electricity and of wind and solar power to generate it – have leapt forward. This has created a commercial case not only for decarbonising road transport, but also for decarbonising the world economy in other spheres.

All this was happening at the beginning of 2020, when Covid-19 struck. Writing in early 2021, the long-term consequences are still hazy. But it is easy to see several ways in which the disruption from the public health crisis will change environmental behaviour. For example, supply chains will become simpler, air travel will be more restricted and commuting patterns will untangle and shorten. Most of this was happening already, but the crisis meant that structural changes that might have taken a decade happened in a few months.

Pull all this together and the outcome is that the rumbling concerns about climate change have moved to the very centre of our lives. We come back to what might actually happen to the world's climate later. But it's worth remembering that climate change will also profoundly impact every other issue related to the environment and natural resources. We look at them now, starting with whether there will be enough food and water for ten billion people. Then, will there be enough energy to sustain middle-class lifestyles? Next, can the world's megacities function without environmental breakdown? Will shrinking habitats lead to loss of many species of wildlife? Finally – and most chilling – are there other potential environmental disasters that we have hardly begun to think about?

FOOD AND WATER WILL BE TIGHT

If we have the water, we can probably grow the food – or at least we can if we are able to persuade people to eat rather less meat. Without fresh water we can't. Water is the pinch point. A quarter of the world's population does not have enough water for their daily needs.[5] Some large cities have come close to switching off the taps altogether: Cape Town and Chennai, for example. Agriculture in the Murray-Darling River Basin in Australia has been devastated by water mismanagement. Infamously, the Aral Sea – which lies between Kazakhstan and Uzbekistan – has shrunk to a fraction of its former size[6] as a result of too much water being drawn off for irrigation of cotton and wheat crops. There are lots of things that can be done both to use water more efficiently and to increase supply. The costs of desalination have fallen steadily, and for locations near the sea that is part of the solution. In 2018, Cape Town in South Africa came within a few days of having to shut off its municipal water supply and make people draw a ration from standpipes. That emergency forced people to be much more economical with their use of water.

Development of drought-resistant crops will help, too. Most wealthy countries will find ways of providing enough water to meet their needs. It is the poorer ones that will suffer.

For India, China and parts of sub-Saharan Africa, it will be a continuing struggle. Technology will help. Better food distribution will certainly help. Maybe wiser policies will help, too, for misguided political decisions have been responsible for a string of environmental catastrophes. Diverting the rivers that flow into the Aral Sea to irrigate cotton crops was arguably the worst. Yet the struggle to feed people must be seen in the context of the stunning decline in the number and extent of famines that has occurred over the past century. If countries make sensible decisions about water use, most of them should be able to scramble through.[7]

Professor Amartya Sen, who won a Nobel Prize for his work on the problems of the world's poorest people, argues in his essay on poverty and famine that issues such as land tenure and distribution of food matter more than actual supply. If people own or have a long lease on the land they farm, they will make sure it is not degraded. Cutting food waste is obviously a win-win, for everyone.[8] We know what we need to do. The challenge is to do it.

So the world should be able to feed its increasing population. But there will probably need to be more of an effort to slow the increase of meat consumption, simply because feeding plants to an animal is an inefficient way of using the calories in the foodstuff. A good example of the way consumer pressure has started to move people in the developed world away from meat has been innovations such as Burger King's vegetarian burgers. This may be the start of something big.

There is a further twist, essentially a failure of policy. That is the growing of crops, not for food, but as fuel for vehicles. As noted later in this chapter, more than half the palm oil imported into Europe is turned into biodiesel,[9] putting pressure on countries such as Indonesia to turn diverse tropical forest into palm plantations. Similar objections apply to the addition of ethanol to petrol, where sugar beet or maize is turned into fuel, and to using woodchip pellets to fire thermal power stations. Such policies enable countries to claim they are reducing their carbon footprint, which, if calculated narrowly, is correct. But this is achieved at the cost of increasing carbon emissions elsewhere.

A common-sense conclusion would be that the world as a whole will be able to feed ten billion people, and will be able to manage its water supplies so that in aggregate there will be enough water to fulfil everyone's needs. But there will be continuing local and regional crunches, when, for example, some cities regularly run out of water, and this will lead to political and maybe military conflict. Obvious flashpoints will be where rivers cross national boundaries: notably the Nile and the Mekong. Just because things should be manageable does not mean they *will* be managed.

THE SEISMIC SHIFT IN GLOBAL ENERGY SUPPLY

A generation ago the fashionable phrase was 'peak oil'. The idea was that at some stage oil production would decline because supplies were being used up faster than new fields were being discovered. The crunch time was rolled forward as new fields came on stream, but since the amount of mineral oil is finite, sooner or later we would run out.

People still talk of peak oil, but now the phrase is used to envisage the moment when oil *demand*, not oil supply, peaks. The rapid development of solar and wind power to generate electricity, coupled with the falling cost of batteries, seems to be leading to a faster switch away from fossil fuels than was predicted even five years ago. Nevertheless, demand for energy will continue to climb. That demand will be driven partly by a larger global population, and partly by the increase in living standards, particularly in the emerging nations. The economies of the developed world will probably not increase their overall energy needs very much, maybe not at all. Take the UK. Total energy used was lower in 2019 than in 1970.[10] This was partly because of greater efficiencies – better home insulation, more economical cars, etc. – and that is fine. But it was also because of structural changes in the economy, in particular the switch to services. The UK imports half its food,[11] and has a large deficit on traded goods more generally. If you import a tomato, or a car, you are in effect importing the energy used to grow that tomato or build that car. The UK has a surplus on its exports of services, but they are not so energy-intensive. Seen like this, the UK's ability to grow its economy while using less energy is rather less impressive.

If you take the world as a whole, there are two prime questions. How quickly will overall energy demand grow? And how quickly can the world switch from fossil fuels to renewable sources?

The answers to these questions have changed. It is becoming increasingly clear both that energy growth is slowing down faster than expected, and that renewable technologies are advancing faster.

BP, the oil giant, has a long track record of analysing global energy. In 2019 it sketched four main scenarios of what might happen to both demand and supply through to 2040.[12] All acknowledged that economic and population growth would mean the world used more energy. In the first, if we carry on pretty much as usual, the energy used would be about half as much again, and the level of carbon dioxide emissions would carry on rising. In the second, if the present movement to decarbonise the world economy continued, boosting renewable sources, cutting the use of coal, etc., then carbon emissions would stabilise at present levels even though more energy was being used overall. Third, very relevant after the Covid-19 pandemic, if globalisation and economic growth faltered that, too, would stabilise emissions. Only the fourth scenario – a faster transition in energy use, in particular a massive fall in the burning of coal – would result in a sharp decline in carbon emissions.

That last scenario is our best hope. A richer emerging world will use more energy, notwithstanding the efforts of the present developed world to curb energy use. The switch to renewable sources will help, and the faster the switch the more so. BP's best scenario still had the three big fossil fuels, which currently supply 85 per cent of primary energy, providing half of it in 2050. But with the falling cost of solar and wind power, and better and cheaper batteries, that tipping point may well come sooner. We should all hope that it does.

Timing is crucial. Eventually the combination of conservation and renewables is the only way forward. But electricity generated by natural gas produces half the carbon emissions of coal.[13] So, as a stopgap, the fastest way to cut carbon emissions could be to switch out of coal and towards natural gas. But it is important to acknowledge that gas is only a stopgap.

If advocating gas as a stopgap sounds unambitious, history tells us that we should be cautious about the pace at which new technologies are adopted. Nuclear power is the greatest disappointment of the energy field. It is more than sixty years since the first nuclear plant, Calder Hall in England, was connected to a national grid in 1956. British schoolchildren were taught that the UK was the leader in peaceful uses for nuclear power and that when they grew up the world would have clean, cheap electricity. Yet now only 11 per cent of the world's electricity is produced by nuclear power and the number of power stations in the world has barely risen since 1990.[14] A combination of cost, safety fears and local objections has rendered it a niche technology.

By contrast, both wind and solar power have leapt forward, with costs plunging. Together they generated much more power than nuclear by 2020, and their role will continue grow rapidly, as the graph here shows.

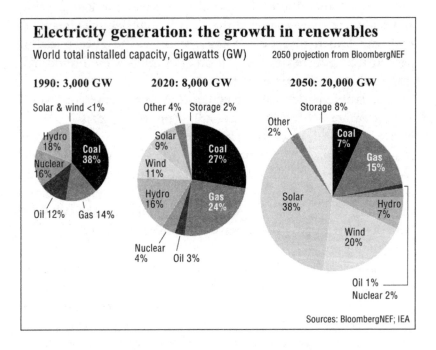

Electricity generation: the growth in renewables

World total installed capacity, Gigawatts (GW)   2050 projection from BloombergNEF

1990: 3,000 GW   **2020: 8,000 GW**   **2050: 20,000 GW**

1990: Solar & wind <1%; Hydro 18%; Coal 38%; Nuclear 16%; Oil 12%; Gas 14%

2020: Other 4%; Storage 2%; Solar 9%; Coal 27%; Wind 11%; Hydro 16%; Gas 24%; Nuclear 4%; Oil 3%

2050: Storage 8%; Other 2%; Coal 7%; Gas 15%; Solar 38%; Hydro 7%; Wind 20%; Oil 1%; Nuclear 2%

Sources: BloombergNEF; IEA

There are environmental costs of both wind and solar, for both need to be stored to give a continuous supply, and the present technology of batteries requires the mining of rare earths. Further, there are some areas, notably shipping and air travel, where oil will be the main source of energy for another generation at least. Nevertheless, it is possible to envisage a world economy that by 2050 is rapidly moving away from its residual reliance on fossil fuels. If that proves right, it should be possible to combine rising living standards with falling carbon emissions. There is currently great political pressure to do so, and solar and wind power look like they will succeed where nuclear power failed. But the push towards the better use of all resources, not just energy but also food, water and minerals, will be relentless. There will be no quick fix. The old developed world will become less profligate, if not as swiftly as it could and should. But the new middle class of the emerging world, some two-thirds of the world's population by 2050, will rightly want to enjoy higher living standards. The energy to drive this transformation will be available. The question is its cost. There is an unavoidable trade-off. The more expensive energy is, the harder it will be to increase those living standards. But though there is no simple way of reconciling the aspirations of the still-poor with those of the now-rich, human ingenuity must find ways of curbing the otherwise growing burden on the planet.

URBANISATION, BIODIVERSITY, PRESSURE ON OTHER NATURAL RESOURCES

There is a temptation to focus on food, water and energy as prime challenges and neglect some of the others. Three central ones stand out.

The first will be to manage the continuing flow of people from the land into the cities. The scale of that movement was touched on in Chapter 2, with almost all the growth being in the emerging world. This is, from an environmental perspective, really welcome, for the density of cities means that goods and services can be created and distributed more efficiently than they can in the countryside. People have voted with their feet to live there. But for cities to give a decent quality of life as well as higher living standards, they need planning, investment and administration. The market cannot provide these. It creates the demand in the form of jobs, services and homes – though municipal authorities frequently step into housing provision. But the market cannot create an overview of how cities should develop. So there has to be a partnership between national and local government on the one hand and the private sector on the other, and that relationship has proved fraught.

There is a spectrum. At one end, urban expansion has been directed by powerful national and municipal authorities, a top-down movement most evident in Beijing and Shanghai. At the other end, great cities have grown with relatively light central planning, such as Jakarta and Lagos. There is a temptation to assume that planning brings better results, and for many functions such as water treatment it certainly does.

But there are many examples where outcomes have been perverse, notably when heavy-handed planners have destroyed long-established neighbourhoods. There was the so-called slum clearance in London, Glasgow and other British cities, particularly after the Second World War. More recently in Beijing the hutongs, narrow alleys with courtyard homes, have been bulldozed and replaced by tower blocks and eight-lane highways. Similarly, there are examples where shoddy planning has rendered parts of cities prone to flooding and other environmental disasters. Jakarta is sinking by six inches a year, with the outcome that in 2019 the decision was taken to move the capital to Kalimantan.[15]

There are certain things giant cities must do: provide decent sanitation and have reasonably effective public transport among them. But the way they do it depends on many things, including location, social attitudes and level of wealth. It would be nice to be able to declare that there is one model megacity from which others can learn. But there isn't.

There is, however, one common challenge facing many of the world's largest urban agglomerations. It is whether there might be an overriding environmental issue that could become a threat to their very existence. You cannot move a city – pick it up and pop it down somewhere else. You can run a city down, reducing its importance, and its people will leave. A political decision to move a capital can have that effect, but more usually it is a shift in industrial structure that has led cities into a decline. In the United States, Detroit is the most obvious example. But the greatest single challenge to large cities is the environmental one: water. Some cities in low-lying areas near the coast may become increasingly difficult to protect from flooding. Other cities in inland areas (and, indeed, on the sea, such as Cape Town and Chennai) may run out of water. The people of the world are moving to giant cities. But some of those cities may be unsustainable even at their present size, let alone with millions more citizens.

If it is hard to be optimistic about the future of some of the world's great cities, it is even harder to be so about the threats to biodiversity. It is quite correct that several of what were thirty years ago the world's most endangered species are no longer so threatened, as Hans Rosling points out. But other less glamorous species are in worse trouble. Successful conservation efforts for specific animals, such as the Siberian tiger and the white rhinoceros, grab the headlines. Massive declines in creatures further down the food chain don't. For example, the decline in fish stocks is widely reported,[16] but only of the fish we humans catch to eat. We don't know much about the loss of insects, except when declines in pollinating species hit agricultural production.

It gets worse. We know nothing at all about the millions of species that we have yet to identify. We have recorded some 1.2 million species, but there are an estimated 8.7 million animals, plants and fungi still to be discovered.[17] The growing number of humans on the planet will inevitably do some damage to the future of those species. But we have no idea of what, when or how.

So we don't know enough about what is happening to species that are not of direct commercial importance to us to make sensible judgements about what is happening, or to frame policies to counter the damage we are doing. Even when we do identify a problem, we sometimes do more harm than good.

This applies particularly in our demand for natural resources, where a well-meant action to protect the environment may have the reverse effect. There are several examples of this. Here is one specific instance and one general one.

The specific example has been the EU's promotion of biofuels in an effort to reduce carbon dioxide emissions.[18] This seemed a great idea at the time. Not only would mineral oil be replaced by renewable produce, but pollution would be lower, too. In 2009 the EU introduced a binding target: a 10 per cent share of renewable energy in European transport by 2020, with biofuels making a 'substantial contribution to this aim'. The only problem was that Europe could not produce enough oil-generating plants to meet the targets, so it had to import the palm oil instead.[19] That in turn meant countries such as Indonesia and Malaysia cut down even more of their forests to convert the land to grow palms. By 2018, half of Europe's palm oil imports were being used for transport. When the damage became evident, the politicians did an about-face. The result was a complete reversal of policy, with palm oil being phased out as fuel by 2030. Sadly, huge swathes of Borneo's virgin tropical forests, notably the home of threatened orangutans, have already been cleared,[20] never to return to their original state.

The general example is the global switch from the internal combustion engine to electricity to power cars, trucks and buses. This will race on apace through to 2050 for many reasons. Electric vehicles eliminate tailpipe emissions, which improves urban air quality. If the electricity is generated from non-carbon sources, it cuts carbon dioxide emissions. And since electric motors are inherently a simpler and more elegant technology than petrol or diesel engines, they will eventually be cheaper to manufacture and service, and more reliable, too.

There are costs, however. A good example is the environmental impact of the mining of cobalt, an essential mineral for lithium-ion batteries.[21] Two-thirds of the world's supplies come from the Democratic Republic of the Congo, where Amnesty International claims children as young as seven are working in the mines.[22] There are suggestions that, as demand grows, the world will have to resort to mining under the seas,[23] where apparently much of the world's cobalt resources lie. Now, it may turn out that an alternative technology is developed that enables batteries to be made without cobalt, or at least using less of it. Greater focus on the mining practices will surely improve conditions. It may be possible to dredge cobalt from the oceans' depths without too much damage being done. But we have to be honest about the costs and the environmental implications of the switch to electric vehicles, and we must acknowledge that the efforts of the developed world to be 'green' sometimes have perverse environmental outcomes on the other side of the planet.

It is easy to mock well-meaning politicians for their stupidity, but the scientific community that advises them is culpable, too, and politicians have to respond to the popular demands of the time. If the challenge is obvious and immediate, and the technical fix well tried, then their decisions should be reasonably straightforward. So, for example, if the citizens of a city in the emerging world (or, indeed, the developed world) demand action against poor air quality, the politicians know what they have to do. The decisions they must make are about how quickly to take the action needed, and how to fund the upfront costs of doing so. At least they and their constituents will start to see the results within their period of office.

If, on the other hand, the challenges are nebulous and distant, and the appropriate technical responses unclear, it is much tougher. How do you assemble an orderly and rational set of policies when you have no idea of the gravity of the problem, the timescale for action, and the appropriate technology to deal with it? When you also need international cooperation to achieve anything significant, your chance of framing effective policies is frighteningly small. You have to do something because voters are clamouring for action. But the history of environmental intervention suggests that what you do may turn out to be ineffective, or, worse, completely wrong.

There lies the greatest environmental challenge of our time: climate change.

CLIMATE CHANGE – WHAT WILL HAPPEN, AND WHAT CAN WE DO ABOUT IT?

Start with the science. There is going to be massive change, whatever we do. We have to accept the broad body of scientific

---

opinion that climate change is happening and that it is caused by human activity, in particular the build-up of greenhouse gases in the atmosphere. The projections from the Intergovernmental Panel on Climate Change of the extent to which global temperature could rise are shown here:

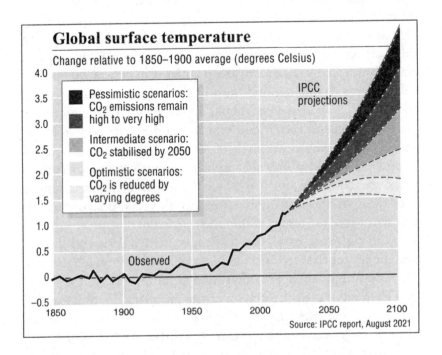

Global surface temperature

Change relative to 1850–1900 average (degrees Celsius)

Pessimistic scenarios: CO$_2$ emissions remain high to very high

Intermediate scenario: CO$_2$ stabilised by 2050

Optimistic scenarios: CO$_2$ is reduced by varying degrees

IPCC projections

Observed

Source: IPCC report, August 2021

Worryingly, the pace at which the world is warming seems to be speeding up, and the more pessimistic ranges are scary indeed.

Some people will be sceptical of these predictions, and that is natural. Anyone brought up in the 1950s will recall that the great fear then was of global *cooling* – that the world was heading into a new Ice Age.[24] That proved wrong. But because the scientists were wrong then does not mean they will be wrong now. Even if you accept the minority view, and it is a small minority, that such evidence as there is of global warming is caused by factors other than human activity, it must be right to try to limit carbon dioxide emissions. As the world's population rises and the standard of living of most of its people climbs, too, common sense says that we should try as far as possible to limit the burden we put on the planet.

If then you see action on climate change as an insurance policy – that it makes sense to tackle this issue even if the scientists *turn out to be wrong* – then everything becomes clearer. There is less need to argue about the detail of the science. Instead the focus can be on the most cost-effective way to deal with the problem.

What will happen? Here is a proposition. Now, in 2021, the world is rather more than 1° Celsius warmer than the average of 1850–1900, before the effect of emissions from rising populations and the Industrial Revolution took hold. The aim of the Paris Agreement was to keep the increase in temperature by 2100 'well below' 2° above pre-industrial levels – in other words, well below another 1° from present levels – with a target of keeping the overall increase below 1.5°.

So, the proposition is that current efforts to reduce carbon emissions will be partially successful – but only partially so. By the middle 2020s we will have a good idea of how well, or how badly, they have worked. We will know a lot more about what is happening, but also a lot more about the likely consequences of global warming. Then one of two things will happen.

If the aim to hold down the rise in temperature to 1.5° looks like being met, then the pattern through to 2050 will be one of incremental advance. A combination of government action, consumer pressure and technical advance will continue to push the world to a steady-state economy, where growth can continue without much increase in carbon emissions. Indeed, by 2050 these will have started to decline. While the world will continue to get hotter, thanks to the legacy effect of previous action, a topping out will be projected by 2100.

If, on the other hand, it becomes clear by the middle 2020s that the likely rise in temperature will be 2° or more, then a massive shift in policy will take place. We will realise we are not doing enough. The world will throw everything it has at the problem to reverse it.

Think of the way it has thrown everything at the Covid-19 crisis. The world's universities and pharmaceutical companies, funded partly by governments, raced to create a vaccine. Governments ploughed trillions into economic support. Businesses and people adapted with astounding resilience. There was a mix of cooperation and competition that helped haul the world economy through. Inevitably, given the origin of the virus and the response of the Chinese authorities to it, there was also suspicion and anger about the causes, and rivalry in the drive to create vaccines. But the outcome was an extraordinary global effort on behalf of humankind.

Expect something similar to happen in the response to a climate crisis. The politics are straightforward. The world's three largest economies, China, the United States and India, are all particularly severely affected by climate change. China suffers seriously from water shortages as well as heat and pollution. The United States has huge investment in real estate in low-lying areas such as Florida, which are gravely threatened by rising sea levels. And India is already acutely affected by rising temperatures as well as precarious water supplies.

This is not to dismiss the importance of the rest of the world. Far from it. In terms of human beings most affected by climate change, there are hundreds of millions in sub-Saharan Africa. In terms of land area Russia is the largest nation by far, so what it does matters enormously. The Amazon basin has more than half the world's remaining rainforests, so local policies to protect them have a significance far beyond South America. But the three most populous countries have the most to lose, and getting agreement among three is vastly easier than agreement among twenty or more.

What is the balance of probability between the 'incremental improvement' and the 'throw everything at it' scenarios? I don't think we can know, just as we cannot really assess the appropriate balance between the efforts to adapt to a warmer world and attempt to prevent it happening. What worries me most is that we could be heading past 1.5° by 2030. If that happens the world will be in a really bad place. The politics are shifting, but maybe not quickly enough. This makes the next ten years critical.

We know that there is a massive difference between a world that warms by 1.5° and one that warms by 2°. The first is difficult but manageable; the second grave indeed.[25] We also know that the sooner we take action, the more effective that action will be. It is possible that a series of catastrophic events will trigger a massive and coordinated response sometime in the 2020s or 2030s. But the reality is that whatever we do, and despite the huge uncertainties, climate change will be a profound concern not just in the years to 2050, but far beyond. It dwarfs all other environmental issues.

THE PATH FORWARD

It is easy to be despondent about our increasingly heavy footprint on the planet. The environmental costs of what we call our increased standard of living are obvious to all. To give middle-class lifestyles to a majority of the world's population – by 2050, a large majority – will require technologies that have yet to be developed. There need to be advances in crop yields, new forms of energy generation and storage, better construction of homes, more efficient transport – the list is almost endless.

We are also ambivalent about such progress. We talk about the elimination of poverty as a goal, and rightly so for a noble one it is. But eliminating poverty means people using more energy, having larger homes, consuming more calories, being able to travel, living longer and enjoying all the other benefits of economic development.

Ultimately, to be despondent is to ignore the ingenuity and adaptability of humankind. We have made many mistakes, sometimes unwittingly, sometimes wilfully, and often with profound stupidity. Through war we destroy the environment and waste resources, as well as killing each other. But our intelligence has pushed forward the frontiers of good practice in many developed countries, so that we are now living longer and healthier lives than our parents, grandparents and great-grandparents, and generating relatively less pollution as we do so. The demands on our intelligence and ingenuity will go on rising, but looking backwards at our response to the demands we have faced in the past, is it not reasonable to think that we can meet this next crop, too? I suggest that the rational answer must be yes.

4

Trade and Finance – Globalisation
Changes Direction

THE SCARS OF THE FINANCIAL CRASH OF 2008/9

The great questions for trade are whether globalisation has stalled and whether the next thirty years will see a slide into trade barriers and other restrictions. The great questions for finance are how much damage has been done by the crash of 2008 and the ultra-loose monetary policies of the central banks over the past decade. Does the entire financial system need a radical overhaul to survive – and, if so, what form will that take?

International trade has been, with technology, one of the two main drivers of prosperity for the world since the Second World War. It has been especially important from the 1980s onwards, when first China, and then – with the fall of the Berlin Wall - Eastern Europe abandoned communist economic policies and became functioning market economies. They were joined by India, starting in the 1990s and gathering speed since 2014 with the reforms of Narendra Modi. By 2019 India had become the fastest-growing large economy in the world.[1]

If greater freedom of international trade was a key driver of this spread of prosperity, the financial system was the oil that lubricated and accelerated the process. It ran the payments system – trade finance, foreign exchange markets and so on – that made possible the surge in trade, but it also provided much of the capital to fund the investment that lifted two or three billion people out of poverty and into a middle-class lifestyle.

You might imagine, given the evident success of the global market economy, that both the greater freedom of trade and the contribution of the financial system would be cheered to the rafters. Not so. Both are under attack. Greater freedom of trade means fiercer international competition. When foreign competitors undercut local ones in price – or supply goods of better quality – local companies close, or maybe move their production offshore.

So free trade is regarded within much of the developed world as a destroyer of jobs. In the sense that it is one factor speeding up the switch of labour from manufacturing to services, that has indeed been the case. But that shift is taking place throughout the developed world for two other reasons as well. Because it is easier to increase productivity in manufacturing than in service industries, the number of people employed in making things has inevitably fallen relative to those providing services. What is more, as people become richer they tend to spend more of their income on services than on goods. Once you have one or perhaps two cars you don't buy another. Instead, you spend the money on eating out, or maybe going on more expensive holidays.

But there is a profound political problem. The benefits of international trade in the form of cheaper goods are spread widely and thinly across the entire population. That is not a news story. But if a factory closes because of foreign competition it is very much a story, for people lose their jobs and an entire community is damaged. Globalisation gets the blame. This may not be fair. The British car industry was ravaged in the 1960s and 1970s by poor products and poor labour relations as much as by foreign competition, and it was foreign companies, notably Nissan, that paved the way for a rebirth by investing in the UK. In US states like Ohio, Honda has been responsible for providing jobs and reviving the car industry. But fair or not, the impact of globalisation on the job market has given it a bad name.

As for finance, the industry can be blamed for bringing much of the opprobrium heaped on to it by its behaviour in the run-up to the 2008 financial crisis, and indeed since. Bankers have long been unpopular in fiction, with villains from Shylock to Gordon Gekko. In the real world, people accepted that they were overpaid, but at least they appeared to be competent at their jobs. Then suddenly that aura of competence was stripped away. Banks and other financial institutions around the world had to be rescued by governments. Taxpayers had to bail out the banks for fear that if they failed to do so something much worse would hit the global economy. To add insult to injury, even though the banks were saved, the world was plunged into the deepest recession since the 1930s, and the recovery has only been sustained by very low interest rates which have cheated savers out of their money.

How could ordinary, hardworking voters have any trust in the financial services industry after that? All the achievements of the industry, from making the international payments that enable the food to be in the supermarkets, to funding the development of the apps everyone has on their iPhones, to organising the mortgages that enable people to buy their homes – all this somehow falls by the wayside. The reputation of finance is currently determined by its few catastrophic failures rather than its vastly more numerous successes.

There is a balanced response to all this. It starts by looking at what financial services do. It is an industry that has over the centuries displayed many weaknesses, which regulation has sought to counter. The inherent nature of finance involves two risks. One is credit risk: if you take people's savings and lend them to others there is always the possibility that the borrower can't or won't pay back. The other is liquidity risk: if you lend money out for a long period, what happens if the savers suddenly want their money back? The borrowers may be sound but cannot repay the debt immediately. The result is a run on the bank. Elementary? Well, yes, and that is exactly what happened at the UK home lender Northern Rock in 2007, followed by a string of other banks around the world. The most serious of these was the failure of Lehman Brothers, which declared itself bankrupt on 15 September 2008.[2]

But then ask why things went so wrong. It is very hard to defend the banks and they were indeed appallingly badly led. But the regulators, the central banks and some of the politicians must also take some of the blame. The regulators allowed banks to run with much smaller liquidity buffers than they had a generation earlier. The central banks were tardy in increasing interest rates despite the evidence that the boom was getting out of hand. And politicians on both sides of the Atlantic urged lenders to loosen their lending criteria and make more funds available to less creditworthy borrowers.

However, while this was a story of multiple failures, the banks shouldered most of the blame. They had to live with that legacy. For the next decade they were forced to pay huge fines for their misdeeds. Their employees and shareholders suffered. Staff lost their jobs and investors lost their money. But the most lasting legacy of the financial crisis, more lasting even than the recession that followed, stemmed from the principal measure used to tackle it: ultra-easy monetary policy. Central banks pumped money into the system, and clamped interest rates to the floor.

The classic response to a financial crisis is for the central bank or banks to flood the markets with liquidity. In other words, they make sure that all financial institutions have enough funds to meet their immediate obligations. If depositors ask for their money back, they get it without question. That deals with the liquidity issue. Again and again, since the middle of the nineteenth century when central banking in its present form was developed, this has proved the cheapest and least disruptive way of coping with a banking crisis.[3]

The solvency issue is more complex. If, once the dust settles, some banks may find the people or companies they have lent to are unable to repay, then the government of the country concerned has the tricky task of deciding whether to use taxpayers' money to save the bank itself. The general principle is that if a collapse is systemic – if it will lead to further collapses even of basically solvent institutions – then the bank should be saved. If it is too small or too specialised to matter, then it can be left to go under.

How do the authorities make that judgement? The answer is they sometimes get it wrong. There is a strong case to be made that Lehman Brothers should have been rescued in 2008. Not only would fewer other banks around the world have needed to be rescued but the scale of the subsequent recession across almost the entire developed world would have been much less savage.

So in 2008 the world's governments and central banks found they had to rescue the banking system. Put simply, they did three things. They flooded the world with cheap money. They saved the major banks. And they brought in new regulations on banking to try to make sure that a similar collapse never happened again.

All those measures were necessary, but they have had lingering side effects. The decade-long period of very low interest rates has been associated with a surge in asset prices, which has increased social tensions. If asset prices go up, those with the most assets, the rich, gain at the expense of those without as much wealth. And low rates made it harder for less sophisticated savers to get a decent return on their funds. Saving the banks with taxpayers' money has left resentment towards banking in general, and encouraged a defensive, cautious approach among bankers in response. And the regulations designed to make banks safer meant that they were discouraged from lending to potentially risky customers, notably small businesses. The economies of the developed world were still living with the legacy of the 2008/9 financial crash more than a decade later when the next global crisis – the blow from the pandemic – struck. So how might global trade and finance develop over the next thirty years? Trade first.

THE CHANGING NATURE OF INTERNATIONAL TRADE – FROM TRADE IN GOODS TO TRADE IN IDEAS AND CAPITAL

The next thirty years will see a radical change in the nature of global trade. Of course, there will still be the need to move goods around. Countries that are rich in raw materials will continue to export those, while countries with specialist expertise in manufacturing will continue to sell their products around the world. But the idea that trade in goods should become ever freer will fade into the background. The reason is not so much political forces in favour of protectionism, though they will play their part. Rather, it will be that there will no longer be so much *need* to ship, or fly, goods around the world. Instead, the emphasis will shift to local production.

By the middle 2010s, well before Donald Trump launched his attack on NAFTA, the North American Free Trade Agreement between the US, Canada and Mexico, and his trade war with China, the growth of world trade had already started to ease off. Instead of trade rising faster than the growth of global GDP, it had started to climb more slowly. Why?

There seem to be four broad reasons. One has been that the difference in wages between much of the emerging world, particularly in China, and the developed world had started to narrow. Wages rose sharply in many emerging countries while they stagnated in most of the developed world. Add in transport costs and it no longer made as much sense to move production offshore. The ugly expressions 'onshoring' and 'reshoring' began to sprout, as companies started to bring production – and jobs – back home.[4]

The second is that manufacturing is changing. Far fewer people are working on factory floors, and far more on design and automation. So the costs involved in making something are less about the actual production and more about the expertise of the design and making team. You make things where convenient, typically close to your market, rather than where is cheapest. And you locate the design team where people with those skills are available. That means the many technology hubs of both developed and developing countries. The expertise flows around the world; the goods are made locally.

The third reason is consumer choice. It is hard to pin this down and there seem to be several drivers that together will limit the growth of international trade. One is the environmental impact of transport, a particularly important concern among the young. Phrases such as 'food miles' crop up. Celebrity chefs urge people to buy seasonal food grown locally, rather than imported produce. This leads into the drive to encourage people to repair existing products rather than throw them away and buy new ones. The attack on 'fast fashion' is part of this. There are even some particular products, including the most expensive consumer durable of all, the car, where demand is falling in the developed world. The shift to electric cars, which are simpler and accordingly last longer than petrol or diesel ones, will further cut demand. If fewer cars are bought, fewer cars will be shipped around the world.

Finally – and perhaps most important – there is a seemingly relentless shift in people's purchasing patterns from buying goods to buying services. Services differ from goods in that they generally have to be created at the same place that they are consumed. Your car can be made anywhere in the world before being shipped to the dealership where you buy it. But if you buy a restaurant meal, it usually has to be served to you in the restaurant where you are, or delivered to your home before it gets cold. It follows that if people spend more on services and less on goods they will, other things being equal, spend more of their income locally. Trade in goods as a proportion of GDP will tend to fall.

This leads to a further twist. What about trade in services?

Services account for a much larger part of the economy than everything else – about two-thirds of global output, and some 80 per cent in some developed countries including the US and UK. They are also more labour-intensive, accounting for three-quarters of the jobs in the world. There is, however, much less cross-border trade in services than there is in goods, accounting for only about 24 per cent of total international trade in 2019.[5] Services trade, however, is rising steadily, both in absolute terms and relative to trade in goods, for it was only 17 per cent of global trade in the early 1980s.

It is smaller than trade in goods for a number of reasons. One is that services like your restaurant meal must be created at the point of delivery. There is no international trade in haircuts. Another is that whereas a product is the same in every country, services are different. Thus a Toyota sold in Japan is similar to one sold in the US, but the pension plan of a Japanese worker is different from that of an American worker. A third reason is that there are more restrictions on trade in services than in goods: American doctors are not allowed to practise in Europe, and vice versa, without requalifying.

However, trade in services seems likely to carry on growing relative to goods, because the forces driving the growth in international service trade seem likely to continue. Take the communications revolution. That has both cut the cost of international transfer of information and allowed the creation of global social networks such as Google and Facebook. The market for entertainment has also become more global, a trend that has particularly benefited English-language enterprises. Sports have gone global, too. A large proportion of financial and business services now operate internationally rather than nationally. And once it recovers from a pandemic dip, the biggest single industry in the world – travel and tourism – seems set to continue to grow faster than global output, as the new middle classes of Asia decide to spend more of their income on foreign holidays.

So it could be that while the world may be approaching peak globalisation in goods trade, peak globalisation in services trade is a long way off. It is quite plausible that by 2050 half or more of international trade will be in services rather than goods. This means that globalisation will take a new direction over the next thirty years from the direction it has taken since the Second World War. The drivers of competitive advantage will change. We are used to a world where the key skills are how to make excellent goods that the rest of the world wants to buy. That is what pushed Germany to becoming the world's largest exporter of manufactured goods and fuelled the more recent growth of China. But now the added value is more in designing products rather than manufacturing them. Apple became the most valuable company in the world in 2020, but subcontracted much of its production to China and South East Asia. In the future, the most important skills will be how to create services the rest of the world wants to buy.

It is already pretty clear what some of these services will be. Education and healthcare come top of the list for there seems to be almost unlimited demand for both. That will continue. As people become richer, they choose to spend more on education, and as populations become older they have to spend more on their health. The entertainment industries have gone global, too, though international trade in entertainment is limited by differences of language and culture. Language barriers may well decrease, but it is quite possible that cultural gaps will widen.

But demand for other services is less clear. One of the extraordinary features of the communications revolution is that no one knows what services we want to buy until someone creates one. We did not know we needed a Facebook until we were offered one. The same applies to the entire social media industry. Most of the information services that will dominate the years to 2050 probably do not yet exist. The question then is: which countries will create them?

This will be one of the great battlegrounds between the US and China, with the other English-speaking countries drawn into the sphere of America. No one should doubt the ability of China to develop its information technology industries. That has already happened. Whether China will be able to generate a true export-oriented business in services is less clear. We can see the fields of conflict, but have to guess where the tussle ends up.

There is, however, an overwhelming probability that trade, viewed overall, will remain reasonably open. The benefits so outweigh the costs that some way will be found to keep those benefits. Even if the world does divide to some extent into regional trading blocs, members of those blocs will still have to do business with each other. Total free movement of goods and services will not happen. Total free movement of people will not happen either; indeed, freedom of movement may move into retreat. The task will be to find a way of garnering the main benefits of globalisation while minimising the costs – and that will be a thirty-year slog.

FINANCE AND INVESTMENT – NEW CHALLENGES, NEW FORMS OF MONEY

Finance was battered by the crash of 2008, but has staged a partial recovery. It now faces three great questions. Will financial flows remain free, or will barriers be put up over the next thirty years? Will the present structure of the industry, with banks, stock markets, foreign exchanges and so on, be retained in a world where China is the world's largest economy and India number three? And will national currencies, issued by central banks and guaranteed by governments, remain dominant, or will new forms of money, including digital currencies, replace them?

For anyone in the developed world, the idea that people and companies might not be able to move currency across national boundaries seems strange. But much of the emerging world retains foreign exchange controls of some kind, as did the UK from the beginning of the Second World War in 1939 to 1979, when Margaret Thatcher's incoming government abolished them.[6]

As of 2020 both China and India have retained exchange controls. True, these have gradually been relaxed and they may be relaxed further. But if they are not, by the middle 2030s global trade and financial flows could become seriously restricted. After all, by then the world's largest and third largest economies will be China and India.

In any case, when it comes to funds for financing investment rather than funds for financing trade, nearly all countries impose restrictions of some sort or other. Some of these are for national security, for example all countries have restrictions on foreign investment in defence contractors. Others are to protect local populations from the distorting impact of inward investment, a situation in which wealthy foreigners snap up relatively cheap local assets, pushing up prices. Thus many countries try to control foreign purchases of residential property, and some actually ban it.

On the other hand, inward direct investment – setting up plants by foreign companies – is not only almost universally accepted, it is positively welcomed, sometimes by giving special tax breaks that are not available to domestic businesses. Show up in an area of high employment saying you want to build a factory and the local mayor will roll out the red carpet.

The world has got along with this hotchpotch of incentives and controls, with capital and currency movements gradually becoming easier since the Second World War. But now there are two reasons to suspect that progress may be halted or even pushed into retreat. One is rising nationalism, hard to quantify but evident across much of the world. The other is the rebalancing of the world economy, and in particular the impact of excess savings in much of East Asia, including China.

Of the first there is not much to add here, except to note that this is a movement the world will have to cope with for the foreseeable future. The second, however, has a mathematical impact on global investment. Two-thirds of the world's savings are generated in Asia. While there are many domestic opportunities for investing those savings, simple prudence means that savers should seek to diversify their assets. That means investing abroad.

That happens at a personal level, for as we are seeing, wealthy Chinese, Indians and other people in Asia want to get some of their money out. A flat in London or Vancouver is an obvious step. Nearly 20 per cent of the condominium apartments built in Vancouver in 2016–17 had at least one non-resident purchaser.[7]

It also happens at a corporate level. This is particularly evident in the motor industry, with the Chinese Geely buying the Swedish manufacturer Volvo, and the Indian conglomerate Tata buying the UK's Jaguar Land Rover. Those two purchases have been both welcome and successful. Less welcome was the attempt by the Chinese oil group CNOOC to buy the American company Unocal back in 2005, for the US saw that as an effort to take strategic control of a key energy company.

Since then, Chinese efforts to invest in the US have been more circumspect, taking care to invest only where such investment is welcomed. But the simple numbers – the size of the Chinese and Indian economies relative to the rest of the world – mean that they will have the firepower to dominate finance. This will be difficult, to put it mildly, for the US and European nations to accept. That leads to question two: will the present structure of the financial services industry, which is a European and North American model, survive in an environment where they no longer dominate?

There are a number of practical reasons to believe that in some form it will. The basic structure of modern finance – collecting savings and allocating them via banks and securities markets – has been around a long time. It precedes the Industrial Revolution, with banks going back to the Middle Ages, equities as a way of financing companies and trading in government stocks to the seventeenth century. It has survived the creation and end of the Gold Standard, two world wars, the rise and demise of communism, the great inflation of the 1970s, and most recently the financial meltdown of 2008. So it is pretty robust.

It also does the job. For all their imperfections, banks continue to take deposits and grant loans. Governments fund their deficit by issuing bonds. Companies raise money by issuing shares on stock exchanges. Pensioners receive income from investing in stocks and bonds.

Most recently, it is a system that has been at the forefront of financing America's high-tech boom. It created the first ever trillion-dollar company, Apple.[8] And by the start of 2020 it had launched more than 400 'unicorns', companies floating on a public market with an initial valuation of more than $1 billion.

China has very much shared in the high-tech financial boom, with giants such as Tencent and Alibaba going public in the US, and roughly half of those 400 unicorns were Chinese. China has not merely fitted in with the American version of the financial system. It has positively embraced it.

There was a further vote of confidence in the Western financial system from Saudi Arabia. It floated a small portion of the shares of its state-owned oil giant Saudi Aramco at the end of 2019, making it the world's most valuable company. It listed locally rather than in the US, and most of the shares on offer were bought by Saudi and other Middle Eastern investors. But the mechanism, a shareholder-owned company with a public quotation, was entirely Western.

Yet all this comes at a time when there are clear weaknesses in the capitalist system. An economic recovery has been sustained since 2009 by super-low interest rates. In 2020, more than a decade on, official interest rates in much of the developed world remained at or near zero. In the eurozone they were negative. With inflation running at around 2 per cent in most countries, real interest rates were negative across almost the whole of the developed world for most of the decade. A long economic expansion was sustained, and in that sense the policy was seen as a success. But the costs of the policy were becoming evident, too. These costs will hang over finance for the next thirty years.

One obvious cost has been the social impact of the growth in asset values. Cheap money has not fed through to any great extent in goods and services inflation but has led to a surge in asset inflation. Homes, most other property, equities and most bonds rose in value, typically by two or three times. The US Dow Jones index ended 2009 at 10,428 and ended 2021 at 36,338. That might seem welcome in that some people have become richer, but the cost has been a sharp increase in wealth inequality. People who were well off already became even better off, and the more sophisticated they were – the more access they had to professional advisers – the more likely they were to benefit. Poorer savers were held back by low returns when they put their money on deposit in banks.

There have been other less obvious negative effects. One has been to weaken commercial banks, particularly in Europe where they have to place deposits with the European Central Bank at a negative rate. Another has been to encourage savers to seek riskier investments to try to maintain their returns. Looked at from the other side, riskier borrowers have been able to raise funds more easily and cheaply than they otherwise would, increasing the probability of defaults in the future.

These increasing risks suggest that at some stage in the 2020s there will be another financial crisis. There is no obvious precedent here as to how this might develop, for interest rates have never been so low for so long in recorded history. There is a hot debate as to whether this is a temporary phenomenon in some way associated with the relatively slow growth of most developed economies – relative, that is, to their past performance. But there are other possible explanations. Maybe it was a policy failure by the central banks, which mistakenly pushed interest rates down too far.

Maybe it is a response to the excessive savings of Asia. Maybe it is a function of the West's ageing population. Or maybe it is simply part of a 700-year trend for real interest rates to decline. That was the theme of a paper published by the Bank of England in 2020, which charted European interest rates back to the early 1300s.[9]

The honest answer is that we don't know. What we do know is that the capitalist system is under strain and this is a sign of that. You cannot run a market system on negative real interest rates for very long, because people will find other ways to safeguard the real value of their money. So some sort of denouement will occur, probably before 2030.

What happens then? It may be that the leading world economies will get together and agree ways in which the financial system can be reformed. Or it may be that financial tensions will push the world more swiftly into regional trading blocs, with China, the US and Europe taking leading roles in this process. In other words, financial disruption reinforces the trend towards trade disruption. Or it may be that something else will replace money.

What happens to money is the biggest question of all. Money might appear to have been around a long time, and in some form it has. But all currencies are issued by nation states and have been devalued to a greater or lesser extent over the years. There is one dominant currency, the US dollar, reflecting the US economy's importance in the world. But as the US will be in some relative decline, there will be pressure to use other currencies alongside it. Which ones? The euro is untested and may well not survive through to 2050. In any case, Europe will account for a shrinking proportion of economic activity. The Chinese renminbi is the obvious candidate, but may not be acceptable in much of the present developed world.

In the twentieth century the world managed to engineer a shift of importance from the pound sterling to the dollar, but the transition was far from smooth. The Bretton Woods fixed exchange rate system, created after the Second World War, broke down after twenty-five years in the early 1970s, and the floating rate system that replaced it led to the greatest surge in inflation that has ever occurred in peacetime. In theory, it should be possible to shift to a multi-currency world, without a dominant currency. But the experience of the past century suggests that in practice it will be difficult to do so.

So what gives? It is possible that people will abandon national currencies for international trade. If this were to happen, within a country people would still use dollars, euros, pounds, renminbi and so on. But for cross-border contracts they would find some other way of making the exchange.

It was this desire to sidestep national currencies that has led to the creation of private crypto-currencies, of which the best known is bitcoin. Bitcoin and the other crypto-currencies are seductive for a number of reasons. For a start they operate under the radar of central banks and governments, and are, for the time being at least, untraceable by the authorities. Thus they avoid both tax and scrutiny. The soaring price has enabled early adopters to show huge capital gains, though later purchasers may well be sitting on large losses. They also have a fashionable element: they are young, high-tech creations a million miles from the fuddy-duddy world of the central banks. There is a further twist. Crypto-currencies were created during the period of ultra-low interest rates. So the financial penalty for holding them vis-à-vis money was zero.

But crypto-currencies are not really currencies, for they don't fulfil the functions of conventional money very well. The classical analysis of money is that it does three things. It is a unit of account; a medium of exchange; and a store of value.

On the first function, you cannot really use them as a basis for pricing anything because the value of the crypto-currencies varies too much. On the second, they account for a small body of transactions, mostly for purchases of software, but their use is minuscule compared with the volume of regular transactions. As for the third, they may have proved a store of value for people who bought early, but are no store for people who paid too much.

There are other objections, including the environmental cost of the energy used to so-called 'mine' them, but the biggest one is the mirror of their attraction that no country or central bank authorises their use. It is that if people wish to cash in their holdings there is no country behind them. Ultimately, currencies have value because of the power of the authority that issues them. A dollar is worth a dollar because the US Federal Government is backed by the US economy. So if you take a dollar and want to use it to buy some goods or services, someone else in the US will exchange it for what you want: a car, a haircut, a diamond ring, or anything else.

It is better to see crypto-currencies as an asset class, such as equities, bonds, property, artworks, classic cars, or notably gold. Like the last three of those, it produces no income so there is no value to be calculated by looking at the future income stream. The value therefore is simply what another purchaser is prepared to pay for it. There is always a possibility that people will not want to hold such assets. That even applies to gold – except that humans have valued gold since the late Bronze Age, more than 3,000 years ago, which gives comfort to the idea that they will continue to do so for a while yet. Bitcoin is little more than a decade old.

All this suggests that crypto-currencies are a blind alley, assets that will at some stage become worthless. National currencies will beat off the attack from technology, though the role of the dollar will gradually recede.

Technology will, however, transform finance in other ways than creating new pseudo-currencies. For a start, online transactions will gradually replace cash. There are huge advantages to getting rid of physical notes and coins both to users and to the governments that issue the cash. For private users, a ledger transaction – be it on a card, a phone, an iris scan or some other means – is swifter, cheaper and more secure than physically using notes and coins. For businesses it is cheaper, too, while for governments it cuts fraud and tax evasion. It also enables governments and the owners or administrators of the transaction medium to track the financial activities of everyone who uses it. Cash is anonymous. Any transaction that goes through a bank account is not.

The shift to online transactions is already gathering pace. In much of Scandinavia, cash is a rarity for most day-to-day use. Governments around the world have become concerned about the social impact of the disappearance of physical money. Obviously, people who do not have access to bank accounts find it hard to carry out their daily lives. Immigrants, elderly people and casual workers suffer. Charities that rely on street donations find their income falls. But the trend seems set to continue, and it may well be that, by the 2030s, cash transactions will have more or less disappeared in much of North America and Western Europe. If this happens, it will be because consumers make that choice, and governments will be hard-pressed to defend it. If, however, significant numbers of people *do* want to keep using cash, then they will probably be able to do so. But the tide will be running against them. The use of physical cash will ebb away.

Cash, be it in notes or coins, is still the embodiment of a national currency. Thus there is a temptation to think that if cash disappears, national currencies will not themselves survive. That view is surely wrong, for the notes and coins are really only symbols of the economy of the country that issues them. A currency is a claim, whatever its form. At the moment, the most powerful claim is based on the productive power of the American economy. So the key issue about the future of money is how the world will move from a currency system that relies overwhelmingly on the dollar, as power shifts towards the emerging nations. As of 2021, some two-thirds of the world's foreign exchange reserves were held in dollars,[10] as were more than 40 per cent of cross-border transactions. The next most important global currency was the euro, but its use had been declining. Will the renminbi take up the slack?

Reason says it will. To do so it needs to have been made fully convertible for some years. There must be confidence in Chinese monetary management. And there has to be confidence more generally in Chinese governance. Other currencies, notably the Indian rupee, are also likely to play a greater role in international finance, though again they will have to be fully convertible.

So the most likely pattern of finance will be that, by 2050, national currencies will remain, and trade will be denominated in a mix of these currencies. In other words, the world's present currency system, with national currencies that are convertible

into each other on the foreign exchange markets, will continue
for another generation, but with the balance of those currencies
shifting towards the emerging world.

That is the most likely outcome – an updated and rebalanced
version of the arrangements that have enabled the great burst of
international trade and finance to take place since the 1970s. For
anyone who believes that the world economy works better with
open markets and reasonably free international transactions that is
a comfort. The system works. Why change it?

But this benign outcome is by no means certain. A number
of things can go wrong. One would be a loss of faith in what is,
and will still be in 2050, the anchor to the entire system: the US
dollar. If the US retains its position as the most sophisticated and
dominant economy, even though it has become somewhat smaller
than that of China, then the dollar is likely to remain king. But
even if this happens, there could be some set of circumstances, for
example were there to be a surge in inflation in the US but not in
the rest of the developed world, where foreign holders did not wish
to hold dollars or to use them for contracts.

Or the challenge may not come from concern about the dollar,
but concern about national currencies in general. The parallel
would be the bloated inflation of the 1970s and 1980s, but back
then there was no viable alternative to national currencies. In the
future, some form of digital currency might become more credible,
particularly if it were backed by commodities or raw materials.

The euro is probably the weakest link in the web of national
currencies. It is the only major currency not guaranteed by a single
government, but, rather, by a collection of separate jurisdictions.
There is no mechanism for a country to revert to its own national
currency, and the euro will remain vulnerable unless and until there
is something close to political union among the states that use it.
Were the eurozone to break up, which is quite possible, that event
would almost certainly put pressure on other currencies, too.

A further danger would be widespread defaults in the bond
markets. The governments of emerging market economies do
frequently default on their debts. Argentina has defaulted eight

times since the country achieved independence in 1816.[11] But developed countries only rarely have an explicit default, instead relying on interest rates held below inflation rates to reduce the real value of their debt. Greece was a rare exception in 2015. If a major country were to declare a default – and Italy looks the most vulnerable large economy – that would deal a grave blow to the entire financial system.

What then? Well, if pressure on national currencies were to mount, it might be that the world's governments and central banks would themselves agree to create a common digital currency that commanded confidence. This would have to be done with the support of national governments – the politics would have to be right – but there could be a set of circumstances where a majority of governments saw that as in their self-interest.

The main point here is that the world has a globalised economy without a global currency. The nearest thing it has to that is the dollar. But the dollar is and will continue to be managed in the interests of the US – or at least what the US sees as its interests. This is not a stable situation. We must hope that it is good enough for a few years yet, and if some sort of revolution takes place in the financial system, the world economy as a whole is not unduly damaged.

TRADE AND FINANCE IN 2050

There is inevitably a danger that there will be some great disruption to international trade and finance, akin to that which took place in the 1930s. It is easy to see some of the tensions that could lead to this. These include the rivalry between the US and China, pervasive economic nationalism and populist pressure against financial institutions. Globalisation, both in trade and in finance, has many enemies. Concern about its perceived adverse impact on communities will not go away, and it may turn out that the late 2010s represent the high-water mark of globalisation if you take as a proxy the amount of international trade as a proportion of global GDP.

The 2020s are likely to be particularly difficult. Quite apart from the massive disruption caused by the pandemic, the world economy was already likely to face some sort of reversal. The ability of the governments and central banks of the major economies to counter a slowdown will be limited by the surge in inflation. In addition, efforts to bump up the economy have increased inequality within countries and thereby inflamed populist resistance to globalisation. Increasing controls over cross-border trade and investment seem inevitable.

The key question is whether this rumbling discontent evident in much of the developed world bursts out into something more serious. If the political response is simply putting up some limited restrictions on international trade and investment, then there may be little lasting damage. Common sense says both should remain reasonably free, and the negative short-term impact of barriers in terms of higher prices and limited consumer choice should make politicians wary of erecting them.

The balance of probability is that, after a choppy decade, a reasonably open global trading system will be sustained. Trade will change its nature, with more goods being produced locally. But finance will keep flowing across borders, and investment funds will therefore continue to seek out attractive opportunities. Innovative ideas will also continue to fly around the globe, and the world economy as a whole will benefit.

A middle-class world – for, as the graph overleaf illustrates, by 2050 some two-thirds of the world's population will enjoy middle-class or higher living standards – will want access to the world's best products and services.[12] That should give new impetus to globalisation from 2030 on to 2050 and beyond.

It may turn out that the greater threat is not trade but financial barriers. These could be triggered by the growing awareness in the developed world that its financial hegemony was disappearing. In 2020 two-thirds of the world's savings were being generated in Asia. Much of that money is being invested locally, but there is a surplus to be invested abroad. Asian investors can, so to speak, buy up the world. As we noted earlier, they are increasingly doing so.

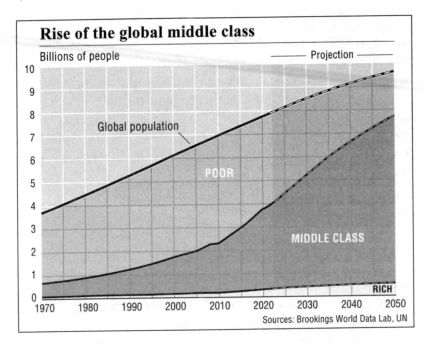

Rise of the global middle class

Billions of people   ——— Projection ———

Global population

POOR

MIDDLE CLASS

RICH

1970   1980   1990   2000   2010   2020   2030   2040   2050

Sources: Brookings World Data Lab, UN

As financial power shifts, the West must contemplate a situation that would have been hard to imagine thirty years ago: wealth will increasingly be generated in the emerging world, not the developed world.

This leads to a further point. How will competitive advantage evolve in the years to 2050? Trade and financial patterns will be shaped by that. We are used to a state of affairs where the West has the technology, and exports that in return for cheaper manufactured goods, some types of food and raw materials. To oversimplify, the US exports aircraft and financial and social media services; Germany exports cars and capital goods. The US imports cheap manufactured goods and some luxury items; Germany imports oil, gas and raw materials.

But by 2050 many countries of the emerging world will be able either to match the West in technology, maybe exceed it, or at least be close behind. There will be, and this is troubling, some regions, countries and people who will remain poor. But the advantage in economic competence that the West still enjoys over the emerging nations will certainly have narrowed, and in some cases may well have disappeared. Present trading and financial patterns will inevitably be transformed by this shift in power.

The tough question for every advanced economy is this. What can it do that others cannot do more cheaply or better? If the answer is not much, the living standards of what are now comfortable, prosperous countries will gradually slip backwards, at least in relative terms. Argentina's experience of going from an extremely wealthy to a middle-income country will become more widespread.

That is, for anyone in rich Europe or North America, a troubling thought. But the evidence of the first two decades of this century is that the West can still innovate, can still supply intellectual leadership and can still develop the goods and services that the rest of the world wants to buy. The market will continue to signal where these advantages lie. But this does mean open borders for trade in both goods and services, and it means keeping financial flows free, too. If governments are pushed into restricting trade or finance – and the pressures to do so won't go away – then much of the developed world could see flat or falling living standards.

Looking from the perspective of the developed world, there are the two main headwinds discussed in the two previous chapters: demography and the environment. They must both be tackled if the world economy is to make progress pushing against them. To curb trade or finance would be to add another headwind.

As far as trade is concerned, the world has to get through the problems and pressures of the 2020s. Next, it has to find some way of acknowledging the shift of power to the developed world. We cannot yet see whether this shift will take place under the umbrella of the existing multilateral institutions, the IMF, the World Bank and the WTO, or whether it will be with a series of regional bilateral agreements. It probably does not matter too much either way. What matters is that trade remains open and that freedom of trade in goods gradually extends to freedom of trade in services.

For trade, the difficult period comes in the 2020s; for finance the difficult period comes later, in the 2030s and beyond. That is because, while a system based on the US dollar will be good enough to carry the world through the next few years, it will become progressively harder to sustain once the US is no longer the world's largest economy. There is nothing obvious to replace the dollar.

The greatest concern must be that there will be some widespread collapse of faith in national currencies. That nearly happened in the 1970s and 1980s, when inflation was destroying their real value. The world pulled back from that as the central banks, led by the US Federal Reserve, regained control. We can all take comfort from the history of the twentieth and twenty-first centuries, when the financial system managed to survive two world wars, the depression of the 1930s, the great inflation and the Covid-19 pandemic.[13] But it would be naïve not to expect some similar shock, perhaps in the 2040s, that would threaten again to bring the world economy to its knees. We cannot hope to see the detail, but it is uncomfortably easy to see the dangers ahead.

5

Technology Races Onwards

THE BIG QUESTIONS FOR THE NEXT THIRTY YEARS

History helps. We know with a high level of confidence that technology will push forward over the next three decades, because we can see what has happened in the past three centuries, from the Industrial Revolution of the mid-1700s onwards. We can see both how incremental advances have improved the quality and lowered the cost of many familiar technologies like air travel, and how they have also enabled utterly new products and services to be developed. We know that the technology has advanced for the past thirty years, though there is disagreement as to whether the pace of such advance has speeded up, remained constant, or perhaps even declined.

From this experience we can see that such innovation can be divided into two broad categories: incremental and revolutionary.

Most advances are incremental, but, despite their slower pace, over time they can have profound consequences. The falling cost of air travel and transport has not only opened up mass travel for the global middle class, it has also made possible complex supply chains, where parts for goods are flown around the world from different locations before final assembly.

Revolutionary advance comes either when there is some sudden scientific breakthrough, or when several existing technologies are grouped together and refined to create a product or service that sweeps across the world. The development of antibiotics is a good example of the first; the iPhone of the second. One transformed medical treatments, with a massive impact on human health; the other transformed the way people use global communications, with a massive impact on human behaviour.

Revolutionary advance creates a problem for anyone trying to predict the direction and application of technology. We can make reasoned judgements about how incremental advance will affect us, and, while these may turn out to be right or wrong, at least those judgements will be based on what we can already observe as possible or seems likely to happen. We are dealing, so to speak, with 'known unknowns'. With revolutionary advance it is a case of 'unknown unknowns' – things that are extraordinarily hard to envisage.

The classic example of that has been the impact of the iPhone. Steve Jobs, presenting it in 2007, famously said: 'Every once in a while, a revolutionary product comes along that changes everything.'[1]

He was right, of course. It did. But even he could not have imagined the scale of the revolution. How could he? He presented it as an iPod on which you could make telephone calls and connect to the internet. He didn't present it as an entry point to location-based services such as Uber, because Uber did not exist. Nor could Uber have existed until the collection of technologies including online maps became available. And he certainly did not envisage things like selfies, for the early iPhones did not have a front-facing camera.

So the difficulty in predicting revolutionary change is that while once they occur they may seem obvious – why did no one think of that before? – until they come about they are hard to envisage. Why would anyone want to take a selfie?

Fortunately, there are two anchors. One is that we know that the laws of physics don't change. What does change is our ability to create products and services within the scope of those laws. We do things cheaper, better and faster, and it is the consequent improved quality of goods and services that lifts our living standards. But there are limits, and, as we approach these, innovation slows down. It takes the same time now to fly across the Atlantic from London to New York as it did in 1960. At some stage, the speed of microprocessors – the silicon chips that are in just about everything – will reach a plateau. But there will be new and unpredictable advances in other areas where we have not yet explored the limits of physics. One obvious broad area to look for them will be that of biotechnology; another will be artificial intelligence. But we cannot predict quite what we will find.

The other anchor is that while the aspirations and desires of human beings may shift gradually over time, our core hopes and fears are pretty constant. The big things we want from technology do not change that much. They include peace, community, families, health, entertainment and so on. So technologies that help us towards those goals will drive onwards. A good current example of a technology that helps us towards those universal goals is social media. Families and friends are important; a WhatsApp group helps keep families and friends together by allowing them to dip in and out of conversation with each other. The usefulness of any technology is not just about its impact on economic efficiency. It is about something much deeper: it is whether it helps us fulfil ourselves as human beings.

Combine physics and human desires and that gives us a framework for thinking about how technology will advance over the next generation. There are two tests. First, can something be done, and done at a price society can afford? And, second, do people need and want it to be done? The answer must be yes to both for technological advances to change the way we live.

There is a further twist. What we want technology to do changes over time. For much of our species' history we have needed it first and foremost to feed us. So we gradually developed better methods of farming, crops that produced higher yields, and clever ways of storing and conserving food products. We have needed it to heat our homes more efficiently and safely. More recently, since the Industrial Revolution, we have used technology to make huge increases in living standards, lifting an increasing proportion of the world's population out of subsistence towards middle-class lifestyles.

Those earlier objectives still hold true, for there are still too many people in the world who go to bed hungry. But, looking forward, the focus is shifting again. We now need technological advance to do something else. We need it to reduce the footprint humankind has placed on the planet. That will be one of the great themes for the next few decades.

INCREMENTAL ADVANCE MATTERS MASSIVELY

It is unglamorous but it transforms our lives. Day-to-day products gradually become better and, in relative terms at least, cheaper. They become more efficient, more reliable, easier to use and so on. This we can see: those of us who are old enough will know how rarely we pass cars that have broken down by the roadside today, compared with the way things were, for example, in the 1970s. Harder to see are the advances in production methods that have brought about these advances. Unless you do a tour of a car assembly plant, you are not aware of the way human workers have been replaced by robots, or how electronics have transformed quality control. Harder still to grasp are the ways in which incremental progress has resulted in higher crop yields and the greater variety of foods available in the supermarkets of the developed economies. Maybe Northern Europeans should not expect to be able to buy strawberries at Christmas, given the cost and environmental impact of flying them from warmer and sunnier climes. But without the falling air-freight costs that have come from incremental advances in transport, it would not have been practical to give them the choice to do so.

Seen from the perspective of the developed world, incremental advance gives middle-income people the choice of goods and services that were, a generation earlier, only affordable for the rich. Seen from the perspective of the emerging world, it gives many people the chance to experience a middle-class lifestyle for the first time. The spread of the technologies generated mainly in the developed world has been transformational in the emerging world, and this transformation of people's everyday lives will continue for the foreseeable future.

We can rely on technology to continue to advance. Nevertheless, there are several challenges. One is that in some areas we are reaching the limits of the possible. For example, in aircraft engines each sequential increase in efficiency has become harder, and when engineers have tried to gain an extra edge, they find reliability suffers.

Another and greater challenge is that, while most manufactured products continue to forge ahead, it has been harder to secure similar improvements in either efficiency or performance in many service industries. An example here is higher education. The costs of providing a university education have risen faster than other service industries, and if there have been incremental improvements in the way students are taught, these are hard to identify.[2]

Similar concerns apply to other service industries. Healthcare, viewed globally, may be making progress, and the experience of battling the Covid-19 pandemic will bring medical advances that we cannot yet foresee. But it is not clear that healthcare is becoming generally more efficient. Some countries may be achieving this, but in much of the developed world there seems to be a pattern of rising costs without always producing better overall health outcomes. Medical technology has made extraordinary advances and will continue to do so. Nothing should take away from that. But the healthcare industry struggles to contain costs.

Education and healthcare will inevitably account for a rising share of GDP over the next thirty years, as the world's population ages. So if living standards are to continue to rise (and, yes, whether that word 'continue' is correct is debatable) these two industries have to find ways to behave more like manufacturing. There will be technical breakthroughs that will transform both of them, and we can glimpse where these might spring up. Some areas will be sketched later in this chapter. Meanwhile, both education and healthcare will have to get better at making small but useful advances.

There are many other aspects of the world economy where improvements in technology can help solve apparently insurmountable problems. One obvious one will be helping the booming cities of the emerging world offer better lives to their inhabitants. How do you channel their growth so that they are habitable and efficient, instead of sprawling nightmares?

Here it is possible to be optimistic. There is a string of advances that will help. Take water. Gradually cities are learning how to provide decent living conditions while using much lower levels of water consumption per head than is typical in developed countries. Jordan has the lowest availability of water per head of population of any country in the world. It is, and will remain, under great pressure, as a small, arid country that serves as a haven for many refugees,[3] yet it manages to provide a reasonable middle-income lifestyle for its ten million inhabitants, partly by straightforward conservation measures but also by becoming a testbed for new technologies. One example is a more efficient system to water its orchards, developed with the Massachusetts Institute of Technology.[4] Ideas that work in Jordan can be applied around the world, notably in the new megacities.

By 2050 two-thirds of the world's population will live in cities, with perhaps a quarter in cities of more than ten million. If they can use good practice in key areas such as transport, public services and housing, most of the world's people will be able to live decent lives. The key to that good practice is incremental technical advance. So public transport must be non-polluting. The falling costs of electric vehicles will fix that. The efficiency of health and education services can be steadily lifted by information technology, although this will be trickier. As for housing, again a series of advances, each one small and unflashy in itself, will continue to lower both building and maintenance costs.

There is a further point. The importance of incremental advances lies not just in the obvious – that over time they bring widespread changes that benefit the human condition. Less obvious are the combined benefits of better dissemination of improved technologies. When lots of people make small changes, the bigger picture is transformed. For example, the most efficient new air-conditioners use up to 70 per cent less energy than the current average ones. Any one home or office that upgrades its system to the latest model will save energy. But from the perspective of the overall energy efficiency of a country, what matters most is that lots of people install generally efficient systems, rather than a few install highly efficient ones.

Governments can help. In Europe, requiring vacuum-cleaner manufacturers to produce lower-powered models (and banning high-wattage ones) has forced them to find ways of getting better cleaning performance from less power. Making all electrical appliance producers show the efficiency of their products has made buyers aware of the savings they can make by buying higher-ranked items.

But perhaps what helps most of all is the way knowledge is disseminated much more rapidly, as a result of the communications revolution. That is driving consumer choice, and consumers generally want to buy the best performing products. If you want to buy a product that is more efficient, more reliable, or simply more stylish, anyone with online access can read reviews and choose the product that fits the bill. That is a spur. So both the pace of incremental advance and the spread of better products and services are driven by better information, which in turn is driven by electronics. The less glamorous, but arguably more important, incremental aspect of technological progress works in conjunction with its 'gee-whiz' cousins of the communications revolution, to which we now turn.

HOW FAR WILL THE COMMUNICATIONS REVOLUTION RUN?

The communications revolution was in early middle age before the pandemic struck. Then suddenly it shot forward by a decade. Transformations that might have taken ten years to work their way into daily lives happened in a few short weeks.

Take the use of cash. In Scandinavia, physical cash had already been replaced by online transactions, and its use was slipping elsewhere. But in Germany and much of the rest of Europe, cash remained king. Then suddenly its use slumped as people switched to cards or mobiles. When the pandemic hit, the shift in the retail distribution system from shops and supermarkets to home delivery was already spreading around the world, with the highest proportion in the major economy being in the UK, where one-fifth of retail sales were online at the end of 2019. But with shoppers quarantined at home, that proportion surged to more than one-third in a few weeks.⁵ The same sort of thing happened to home working. It, too, had already been gradually rising as it became more practical to work remotely, but the shuttering of offices across the developed world had a profound impact on everyone's lives. The Zoom conference became one of our many new daily experiences.

The first point here is that all the technical advances that transformed our daily routines existed before the pandemic. Phone payments were growing; online shopping was climbing; online conferencing was creeping up – Zoom was founded way back in 2011. What the pandemic did was to speed up the social revolution in the use of technology, rather than triggering a revolution in the technology itself. Even the work on vaccines was well advanced before the scientists and drug companies switched their energies to developing several new effective vaccines against Covid-19 in record time.

However, there is also a second point. The companies that developed these winning technologies will now have the resources and self-confidence to press ahead and seek other ways in which people's lives can benefit.

This gives some clues to what will happen next. Technology will be deployed to do what people and their governments want it to do. That will differ in different parts of the world, because different societies have different priorities. Take two extremes. China prioritises social control, while the US prizes the ease of personal mobility. So China has bolted together a number of technologies, including facial recognition, to create the most advanced system of surveillance in the world, although there may be pushback from its citizens. At the other extreme, self-driving cars have driven millions of miles in the US, mostly in California and Arizona, though quite how close they are to widespread adoption is not clear.

It is easy to see that there will be a gradual spread of these changes running through the 2020s, 2030s and beyond. In some areas the plateau – when explosive growth shifts to incremental growth – will come quite soon. The most dramatic advances of social media seem already to have started to slow. There are social and practical limits to the amount of time even teenagers want to spend communicating with each other. But there are other areas where the revolution has yet to begin, and we have to guess at where these might be.

The easiest way to get our minds round this is to think of areas of the economy and how they might be affected. Here are five: healthcare, education, distribution and transport, the changing uses of the home, and what technology does to the job market. Some thoughts about each.

Healthcare will be vastly better and probably cheaper by 2050. Not only will we know much more about what can go wrong, but we will be able to monitor people's health in real time. Diagnostics will be automated, and medical intervention tuned to the optimal response for whatever is going wrong. There will always be difficult ethical decisions, but many of the routine tasks of healthcare – helping people lead broadly healthy lives – will have become just that: routine.

Not everyone will take part in real-time monitoring, some from choice, some because of cost and limited availability. But the two-thirds of the world's population that have middle-class incomes will be able to access the level of care currently available to the wealthy professionals of the present developed world. However, instead of having the regular six-monthly or annual check-ups requiring a visit to a clinic, they will not have to do anything. Technology will pick it up.

We cannot know the detail of the technologies that will do the job, but we can envisage how they might work. Anyone looking at their mobile phone is being watched by the camera. So any change in their health that might be spotted, for example, by a retina scan, will be known by the phone. The technology to send that information back to a care centre already exists. Add this information to all the other things that are stored on a phone, including how much exercise they take, the speed at which they are walking and so on, and it is possible to build up a complete picture of behaviour, and how it changes. If someone has a health problem, their phone will be able to diagnose it, and much of the time decide what should be done.

This will, of course, be intrusive. So social attitudes, including those towards privacy, will help determine the extent to which monitoring becomes universal. Potentially it is a powerful tool against many of the challenges public health in the developed world now faces – obesity, junk food, legal and illegal drug use, alcoholism, and many more – but it may be a hard sell.

It is hard to predict the interchange between technology and social attitudes. Both change over time, but whereas one almost always advances, the other shifts in sometimes puzzling ways. Health is a fascinating frontier between public and private responsibility. Governments set the rules that determine the broad environmental conditions in which we live, an extraordinarily wide range of regulations from food standards to air quality to land use. These have a massive impact on general health. We are vaccinated against common diseases because governments mandate it. But we as individuals sometimes push back against this. Sometimes we refuse to take full responsibility for our health, or we distrust the advice of government and medical experts.

So the challenge in using technology to improve the health of a country or community will be one of persuasion. Medical technology at an acute level will continue to advance. We will be able to treat more conditions more cheaply and more effectively, and we will be able to pick up problems more swiftly. But the greater contribution will come from the way in which technology helps change lifestyles. We cannot know the game-changing app that will push people across the world to lead healthier lives. Maybe smartphones are the wrong place to look for things that will transform healthcare. Maybe advances will come not from the existing set of communications technologies, but from somewhere quite different. But we can be reasonably sure of two things: healthcare will improve massively over the next thirty years, and technology will have a crucial role in driving that improvement.

Next, education. Technology has transformed education by distributing almost infinite information, which is wonderful, and by undermining intelligent discussion about that information, which is not.

It was easy to see thirty years ago that by now an individual with an internet connection would have as much access to information as the research department of a multinational corporation had then. Search engines have changed education because they have made knowledge available to all. But they have not changed people's ability to assess that information. Worse, infinite access has created a market for rubbish. Too many people are highly skilled at promoting ideas, while too many are dreadful at assessing their worth. Disinformation is just as easy to distribute as the real stuff.

One consequence of this has been to strengthen the position of the education industry worldwide. The long-established structure of education – books, schools, universities, on-the-job training – has been less changed by the information revolution than might have been expected. Children still have satchels on their backs and are still 'creeping like snail, unwillingly to school' as they were in Shakespeare's Seven Ages of Man more than 400 years ago.[6] A top-branded university of, say, the 1960s, is still a top-branded university now. A doctorate is still a doctorate, and now an even more essential qualification for a career in higher education. Expertise is still prized, even if it is sometimes disregarded. The louder the background noise, the harder it is to distinguish the signals. So trusted education and research institutions matter more than ever.

The other consequence has been the growth of a parallel knowledge industry. Technological advance has often come from plucky outsiders: it was the Wright brothers who pioneered flight, rather than the great industrial corporations of the early twentieth century. But what has happened in the IT revolution is that the thousands of entrepreneurial start-ups are now backed by big money. The quest to create the next 'unicorn', a start-up with a value of more than $1 billion when it comes to the market, has poured huge resources into new technologies. Good ideas (and inevitably many bad ones) get backed on a scale as never before.

This links with the established education institutions. Universities and their alumni have a role one way or another in creating many, perhaps most, of the start-ups. The challenge for the universities is to garner some of the rewards of their students' enterprise. But they also have to appreciate that, often, they just provide the spark. The fire bursts out somewhere else.

The frontier between the education industry and the businesses that the industry inspires will become more blurred over the next thirty years. Universities will become more like businesses and businesses more like universities. This is already happening. The change will move much faster. We may even see the growth of for-profit universities that explicitly seek to develop commercially successful outcomes from their research. That will probably happen first in Asia rather than Europe or North America, but if it does happen and is successful, expect the West to copy.

The other broad change that technology will bring to education will be to cut costs and speed up the time it takes. Higher education is too expensive for most students in the developed world and takes too long. It makes no sense for young people to start their working careers saddled with a deadweight of debt, or for them to spend much of their twenties still not earning their living. In the emerging world, the booming middle class will want the best education for their families, but will not have the resources to replicate Western-style institutions.

The only realistic way forward is to use information technology to deliver greater efficiency. As far as costs are concerned the process should be straightforward. You use teaching time more judiciously. But the aim will also be to improve outcomes: to find ways of teaching and learning better. Obviously, what you do in a primary school in rural India will be different from what you do at Harvard University. But the principles are the same. In fact, they are the same as in any manufacturing facility. Some things have to be done by human beings; indeed, are better done by people. But many functions are better automated, and the challenge is to know which ones are which.

We all know this. But it has been tough to push through educational reforms for all sorts of reasons. What is changing is the awareness that education is becoming a global industry rather than segregated national ones. But technology is universal. When one country, region or establishment shows it can do something better, expect the rest of the world to follow. The prize is huge. Get technology right and you not only have a more successful industry, you have people better able to make a success of their lives.

As for distribution and transport, distribution has already begun its technology-driven revolution with the move to online. The shift from shopping that requires a visit by the customer to a retailer, to ordering online and having the product delivered to the buyer's door, has been running since the early 2000s.

Many of the consequences of that shift were evident before Covid-19 accelerated it: the loss of retail jobs and the rise of warehouse and delivery gigs, the pressure on high streets and out-of-town shopping centres, the creation of databases of personal buying choices and so on. This will run for another twenty years at least, and the question is when the shift to online reaches a plateau. Our experience of previous socio-economic transformations suggests that it will be when somewhere around half of all retail sales, maybe a bit more, take place online and are delivered to the buyer. As is so often the pattern, the luxury providers will prosper and the bargain-basement ones will find a ready flow of customers. But the middle will shrink.

This change in distribution will be the largest single force to transform the world's urban environment. Retail space will be turned into living and entertainment space, continuing the present trend for commercial space – warehouses, multi-storey car parks and lofts – to be turned into homes.

The result will be more habitable cities. The challenge will be to make the new distribution chains as efficient as the old ones. It is more complicated to get products to lots of different private homes than to a few large shops. On the other hand, city-centre shops are more expensive to run than out-of-town distribution warehouses. Much will depend on advances in transport technology. The shift from the internal combustion engine to electricity for road transport will race forward, but much of the hype about the impact of this on our lives will look quaint by 2050 – as quaint as predictions in the 1960s that by 2000 we would be flying around in our own helicopters.[7] The physics doesn't change.

What will change will be patterns of behaviour. Cars will still be the main form of personal transport, but we will use them less. The developed world may have reached 'peak car' in terms of vehicle miles travelled in 2019. The different emerging economies will reach that point later, but almost all will have done so by 2050. Cities in the developed world will have become calmer, less polluted, more liveable places. And to generalise, cities in the emerging world will have gone through a period of chaotic, headlong growth, but by 2050 most of them will also be firmly on the same trajectory towards greater liveability.

The key point here is that most of the debate about technology and transport is in terms of it becoming cleaner and more efficient. That will happen and is welcome. But the bigger impact will be on the way changes to transport and distribution systems affect the urban environment. Cities must become better places to live. Only technology can help them become so.

We are all aware of the changing use of the home. The IT revolution is, for many people, already changing our homes from a place of consumption to a place of production – from somewhere we spend money on creating a nice place to live, to somewhere we earn money that we spend elsewhere. True, that does not apply to everyone. You cannot drive a bus or teach someone to swim from your home office. But one of the effects of the Covid-19 crisis has been to show how much work can be done from home. That will have a lasting impact akin to that on retailing: it speeds up something that was happening already. It will also reinforce the trend towards home entertainment, as people choose to stay in to watch a movie rather than go to the cinema.

All this we know. So the questions are: how far will these trends run before they plateau and maybe fall back – and how will homes themselves be changed.

We will probably reach the limits of home working well before 2050. One of the legacies of the Covid-19 pandemic is that we will learn quite quickly when it is more efficient to do some task online and when it is essential to do the task in person. The technology, extraordinarily competent already, will become even more so, thus the limits will not be technical but social. When do human beings need to chat with each other in person, and when do they work best on their own?

We should get an idea of this very soon, though it will take a long time to adapt our physical environment to fit social needs. One clear consequence is that homes will need to be bigger. There will need to be dedicated workspace, just as there is dedicated space for food preparation, entertainment, sleeping and so on. As people become richer, one of the early signs of increased wealth is demand for larger homes. Now there is an economic justification behind that consumer aspiration. Some regions will find this easier to meet than others. It is easier to expand a suburban villa than a high-rise flat. So North America, Australia and New Zealand will be at an advantage vis-à-vis Europe, and particularly vis-à-vis urban Asia. But housing will adapt. Homes will always be homes, but increasingly they will also become factories.

Finally, technology and the job market. If communications technology makes it possible for people to do much of their work at home, it inevitably rebalances the relationship between an employer and an individual. People working remotely are measured by their output, and manage their time by themselves. Home working is not the only force pushing people towards self-employment rather than taking a job – others include the shift from manufacturing to services, the need to cope with flexible demand, and the ageing of the workforce – but it is a powerful one.

That is evident. But there are huge uncertainties. One is how far the trend to self-employment goes. In the UK it had reached 15 per cent of the workforce by 2020, the highest since the 1860s when records began, and nearly double the 8 per cent in 1979.[8] The proportion of self-employed will almost certainly carry on rising, though it will by 2050 have levelled out at perhaps 25 per cent of the workforce. For many people the freedom to work for oneself is a great liberation, but it does require an attitude of mind that many don't have. Corporate structures will remain the norm.

Another uncertainty is what new communications technologies will do to the quality of jobs. Will they continue to displace routine, repetitive tasks and therefore lift overall pay and job satisfaction, or will they hollow out the jobs market, destroying the middle and driving growth only at the top and the bottom?

They will almost certainly do both. Many mid-skilled repetitive roles have already been eliminated. Hardly anyone in business has a letter or a memorandum professionally typed, so the job of the stenographer has gone the way of the blacksmith. Travel is largely booked online, destroying employment in travel agencies. One of the side effects of the Covid-19 pandemic has been to speed up the switch from physical to online meetings, cutting the travel time needed to get to the meeting – and the jobs of the people working in transport.

Yet technology has created more jobs than it has killed. Total employment has risen across the developed world, and, insofar as it can be measured, overall job satisfaction seems to be stable or rising. If you take labour unrest as a measure of whether people are happy at work, the decade from 2010 to 2020 has been reasonably calm by historical standards. Job satisfaction surveys in the US suggest that people became more content in their work once the impact of the 2009 recession faded.[9] Despite reasonable concerns about insecurity, forced self-employment, temporary work and the so-called 'gig economy', there does not seem to be a general, overall decline in the quality of work. What has happened is that the share of labour in GDP – the amount people get paid relative to the size of the economy as a whole – has been falling since the 1960s, and that has continued through this century.[10] There are some signs that labour will do rather better from the 2020s onwards, but it is too early to be confident about that. This is the thesis in an important book by Charles Goodhart and Manoj Pradhan.[11]

But there are many forces at work there, including the rise of China to become the world's second largest economy, so it does not seem right to blame the new technologies for a trend which was well established before they took off.[12]

What will almost certainly happen will be that two trends evident now will become more intensely so. One is that the demand for highly skilled labour will increase. The second is that all working people will need to become more resilient. There will be plenty of work, but people will have to be both well educated and appropriately educated to do it. And everyone will have to be flexible not only in building their skills, but also more generally in managing their time. Home life and work life will blur together, as we have seen during the pandemic.

The most important single reason for this is that the next burst of technological advance, similar in its impact to the communications revolution, will be artificial intelligence, or AI.

WHY AI MATTERS SO MUCH

The idea of AI – getting computers to think like humans – goes back to the 1950s,[13] but it has really only been since about 2015 that it has begun to have much practical use. And the reason for that is the tidal wave of data generated by the world economy. AI is wonderful at analysing data, far better than we are. But it is useless at much else: it cannot unload a dishwasher. So until we had the deluge of data, it was essentially a toy. It could beat us at chess, but it could not help us find a cure for cancer.

We are in the very early stages of learning what AI can do, but we already have several areas where its ability to pick its way through a forest of information is transforming things. There are thousands of examples already. Moorfields Eye Hospital in London[14] found that if AI was used to scan patients' retinas, it could identify eye diseases earlier than even the most experienced doctors. AI is being used in facial recognition, in hiring, in marketing, in supply chain management and so on. During the Covid-19 pandemic it was used in a number of ways, including predicting outbreaks by tracking carriers through their mobile phones, forecasting risks for people and scanning databases for molecules that might be helpful in the quest for a vaccine.

There are inevitably a host of challenges, which are already cropping up. One is privacy. To what extent do we want not just our personal data to be analysed, but all the data we create as we move through life? Another is bias, for it has become clear that AI can develop biases just as human intelligence can. Still another is how to use AI's hard skills of analysis and reason alongside human beings' soft skills of empathy, creativity and imagination.

Where might AI take us in another generation? There are two ways of thinking about this. One is to start from what it can clearly do very well, the other to ask what we as a society want from it.

As far as the first is concerned, we know AI is wonderful at examining databases and drawing conclusions from these. This ability will lead to many practical uses in medicine, environmental studies, human behaviour, business practice, social policy, etc. The more data that is thrown at AI, the more surprising facts it will unearth. Example: in the Covid-19 crisis, it discovered that people were much more likely to be infected by someone they knew than to catch the virus from a stranger.

This quest – what can AI do? – will lead to unexpected places, places that we can barely imagine. It will make possible some services that we cannot yet think we want or need, rather in the way that the communications revolution made possible social networks such as Facebook and Twitter. But we don't yet know what they will be.

This is rather unhelpful. If, however, you start from the other end and ask what we might want from AI, things become clearer. For example, ageing societies will need better healthcare, and, in particular, more advance warning of health problems among the elderly. We don't know quite *how* AI will help, but it's a safe bet that it will do so. We know too that education is changing, from being something that young people get at school and university to a life-long process. AI will help us see what works and what doesn't. The world will need to manage its human resources more effectively and AI will help us do so.

We will also need to reduce the environmental burden we place on the planet, so again there will be huge scope for AI. As the quality and quantity of data increases, we will use AI to help us work out which changes to our lifestyles will be positive for the environment and which will be counterproductive. We will certainly learn much more about climate change, as we need to, but also learn more about the most effective ways of slowing and perhaps reversing it.

All this is welcome. The main difficulties will come in applying AI to human behaviour. Can we use it to cut crime? The answer is almost certainly yes. We will soon be able to predict where crimes are likely to happen, what they will be and who is likely to commit them. The ethical question will be what should be done with that information. Do you lock someone up because the computer says there is an 80 per cent chance they will commit a murder?

To take the same point further: should AI become a normal tool of daily life, guiding people as to whom they should choose as friends or lovers, or how they should plan careers and manage their family finances? Should it be used by insurance companies to decide the rates to charge on car insurance, or life assurance? And, finally, where does the state step in, monitoring people's behaviour and seeking to change it?

We will come to the changing ideas about the nature of government in the next chapter. The point here is that the confluence of big data and AI is huge. This will probably lead to the biggest changes we make in our daily lives over the next thirty years. It will make things possible that we now only dream about, and while we manage it sensibly it will have great capacity for making our lives better. But there is also a less benign outcome ahead.

THE SURVEILLANCE WORLD

There will always be a trade-off. There is already a trade-off between using data for benign purposes such as trying to target appropriate advertisements for social media users, and less benign ones such as using data to silence critics of an oppressive political regime. There is an inevitable conflict between privacy and security, and all societies are wrestling with that. But if, as seems inevitable, we are still in the early stages of the AI revolution, the present obvious conflicts are minuscule matters compared with what is to come.[15]

Imagine a society where every moment of someone's life is known, stored and can be analysed. Where they are educated, what grades they got, who they have worked for, who they had dinner with on a particular evening and what they ate, every word they have written in an email, when they have gone to the doctor and why, where they went on holiday, who they have had relationships with, who their genetic parents were – every tiny detail about a person's life from infancy onwards can be instantly available.

There will, of course, be exceptions. There will be some people even in advanced economies who try for whatever reason to conceal what they are doing, and there will be people in emerging economies who are simply below the radar. But a global database will exist that has just about everyone on it, and the challenge will be to use that to benefit both humankind and the planet on which we live.

There is no precedent. We have never had a world where just about everything is known about just about everyone – and where a red flag pops up if there are gaps in the data. So there will be two or three decades of experiment, where different societies stumble about as they try to decide where the boundaries should be between privacy and disclosure, and how to protect the former and deploy the latter.

At the moment it seems likely that Western democracies will incline towards protecting personal privacy, while China and perhaps India will incline towards promoting collective values. That may change. It is quite possible that liberal democracies will become less liberal, accepting that privacy is a false goal. The Scandinavian model, where most information about people is already made public, may become more widespread. (In Norway, everyone's tax returns are published online in summary form.) It is equally possible that the growing middle classes of China and India will seek different lifestyle choices for their families and friends than the current objectives of the state, and aspire to greater individual privacy.

Ultimately the balance may be determined more by the benefits that detailed personal monitoring can provide. The obvious one is better health. The present proposition from social media services of 'let us have your data and we will show you more interesting adverts' is not particularly attractive. But 'let us monitor your health and we can help you live a longer and healthier life' is rather more compelling. And what about this one? 'Let us monitor your lifestyle and you will pay lower taxes.' People who make healthy lifestyle choices put less of a burden on the rest of society than those who make less healthy choices. So it might suit countries to find ways to incentivise their citizens to make 'better' choices, and cutting their taxes would surely be an effective way of doing so.

This does assume, however, that governments will be reasonably benign in how they use technology for the common good, not just in surveillance but in other regards, too. In the main they will, but we have to accept that some won't. War has over the centuries been a powerful driver of technological advance. One of the underlying assumptions of this book is that there will be no conflicts on a scale of either of the two world wars during the first half of the twentieth century. If there are, then all predictions are pointless and the future does not bear thinking about. But there will be conflicts – or at least a level of global competition that nudges towards conflict – and technology will have a role in that. This is one of the outliers that we must acknowledge may transform the next thirty years.

WHERE MIGHT TECHNOLOGY'S WILD CARDS LURK?

There will be surprises – sudden leaps forward with profound implications for our societies. We cannot know what they will be: they would hardly be surprises if we could. But we can have some ideas about the places where they may come from and so where we should start to look. Here are five.

The first is energy. One of the disappointing features of the past half-century is that the world has failed to move away from carbon fuels. As we saw in Chapter 3 the three main sources of primary energy remain oil, gas and coal. Advances have taken place in efficiency, and progressively through the twenty-first century fossil fuels have been supplemented by wind and solar power. But wind is one of the oldest sources of energy, with windmills developed in Persia around AD 600, and the Romans used solar power to heat water for their bathhouses. The great breakthrough might have been nuclear power, but it has been deeply disappointing. It can be made to work, but it is expensive and creates serious environmental concerns.

There will be huge pressure on both energy suppliers and energy users to wean the world off carbon fuels more swiftly. It is, of course, conceivable that there will be some leap forward on primary production. The obvious area here is nuclear fusion, the technology behind the hydrogen bomb, and in the 1950s the British ZETA reactor was expected to be the next great development in nuclear power. It failed. Since then,[16] the quest for a commercial application of fusion has been a long story of disappointment. Reason says it will continue to be so.

More likely, the breakthroughs will come in energy storage and energy efficiency. The cheapest ways to generate energy are sun and wind. If it becomes possible to store solar and wind-powered electricity cheaply and safely, then it won't matter so much that the wind doesn't always blow and the sun doesn't always shine. Present battery technology will improve incrementally but batteries are inelegant. They are heavy and use huge amounts of rare earths. What is needed is a step change, and that can only come from a completely different technology. This is likely to happen. The winner or winners probably exist now, but we don't know what they will be.

There may also be a new technology that brings a sudden leap in energy efficiency. The example of the past twenty years has been the light-emitting diode replacing the incandescent light bulb. Suddenly a technology that had been around for more than 120 years was swept aside by something that was between five and ten times more efficient. Maybe there is a similar leap out there, perhaps in the efficiency of computers and other internet-connected devices.

A second area where technology may leap forward will be in healthcare. Writing in early 2021 amid the devastation brought by Covid-19, it is easy to predict that the massive global effort to create a vaccine will bring other advances. Can human ingenuity beat viral infections in the way that it has, for the moment, seemed to control bacterial ones?

Or maybe the outcome will be much more negative and humankind will be in an endless fight against both bacteria and viruses that keep evolving faster than we can contain them. We may lose. In that case, medicine could go back to the situation it was in during the 1930s before penicillin was invented. We would have to rely on good practice in hygiene, exercise, eating habits and lifestyles more generally, to keep people healthy. Average life expectancy would at best plateau, and might start to fall.

That leads to a third area where there will almost certainly be surprises and quite probably shocks: biotechnology.

Questions abound. Will the rich of the developed world try to create perfect babies, whatever that might mean? Or maybe there will be a more general desire in many countries for people to seek to manipulate the genes of their offspring so as to boost their chances of being balanced, happy people? These questions are uncomfortable, but as gene technology advances they will become impossible to avoid.

What about agriculture? There will certainly be great pressure to transform food production. At the moment, the agricultural science industry is mostly trying to produce higher crop yields and varieties better suited to harsh conditions. Thanks to this, land use has been contained and the planet has managed to give a better diet to its less-advantaged people. The next stage, already rumbling, will be to replace meat and fish in our diets, or at least reduce the inefficiency in the food chain brought about by feeding vegetable protein to animals and getting them to convert it into animal protein. Much of the developed world has already begun to adjust its diet – milk consumption in the US has been falling since the 1970s – and that trend will eventually spread to the emerging nations, too.

If the possibilities in agriculture are reasonably clear, they are less so in industry. The question here is whether some present industrial processes, including the many uses of plastics, might be transformed by biology. Could the plastic revolution, with all its benefits but also all its environmental disasters, be coming to a close? It feels as though it is, but the *coup de grâce* could be delivered by advances in biotech. We would not need to tell people not to use plastic bags; there would be no plastic bags because a better and cheaper biological alternative would have taken over.

There is a broader issue here. Maybe manufacturing will shift from making things out of metal and plastic to making them out of bio-engineered natural materials. This would only happen if the latter became cheaper and better, but that may come about. Construction may shift, too, moving away from steel and concrete to wood composites. Fashion changes as well as technology, but often technology is the driver of a change in fashion. A new process to mass-produce steel beams, and the invention of the electric elevator, helped pave the way for the skyscrapers of the early twentieth century.

There are two further possibilities, both far beyond the outer limits of our present knowledge. One concerns the way our brains sometimes operate in ways that cannot currently be explained.

Many of us seem to have some sort of connection with other people at a preternatural level. It could simply be that we think of someone on the other side of the world and discover they were thinking of us at exactly that same moment for no apparent reason. Some people have premonitions about something that is going to happen, usually something bad. Or sometimes coincidences occur, where the odds against them happening are so enormous that it is hard to believe that they are quite random. It's easy to dismiss such events, and many people do. But many serious scientists are open-minded about this. Alan Turing[17] believed in telepathy, and according to Pew Research[18] 18 per cent of Americans believe they have seen a ghost. We certainly have a huge appetite for there being some sort of a world beyond our understanding. Look at the triumph of Harry Potter.

Now suppose we come to understand how our brains can communicate at a different level – how telepathy works. We may not be able to become time travellers or be able to communicate with the dead, but maybe there will be some radical advance in our knowledge that explains some aspects of the paranormal. How would we then think about our species? Where might such a discovery take us? How would it change our attitudes to religion? Maybe many puzzles of the past would fall into place, an 'aha' moment. Maybe we would simply become more confused as to what it is to be human, and search for some higher force governing us and our planet. In all probability, such a discovery will not happen – but we should not exclude the possibility that it will. Everything, starting with our understanding of physics, would change.

The other transformative discovery would be for us to learn that we are not alone in the universe. Given the sheer size of the universe, it would be amazing if we were. So the issue is more whether there are other life forms that are close enough to us for us to be able to engage with them. What we know about physics suggests that this is most unlikely. But suppose there is another parallel physics, deployed by other intelligent life that is far more sophisticated than our own. This is not the place to go through the evidence of sightings of UFOs, or to speculate on what other life forms might exist. My point is simply that, should we find we are not alone, that too would mean that everything we think we know would change utterly.

But we have long known this, haven't we? As Shakespeare had Hamlet observe: 'There are more things in heaven and earth, Horatio, than are dreamt of in your philosophy.'

6

How Governments – and Governance – Will Shift

THE MANY CHALLENGES TO DEMOCRACY

These are tough times for believers in democratic governance, but governance is bigger than government. We think in terms of countries and the governments that run them, and most policy is framed by them. National governments cooperate at international and regional levels in many ways but they remain, and will remain in the future, the main decision-making entities. So what happens to the relationship between the US and China, or China and India, will be at the centre of the world in the years to come. The issue here, which we will come to in a moment, is whether representative democracy will retain its prime position as the gold standard to which most of the world, China apart, aspires – or at least professes to aspire.

But there are other forces that will help determine how our planet and our lives are organised. There are hundreds of multinational bodies of one sort or another. These include the clutch of international institutions founded after the Second World War: the United Nations, the International Monetary Fund, the World Bank and so on. There are international financial institutions, including the Bank for International Settlements, a tribute to the staying power of such entities, for it was founded in

1930 to help with German reparations after the First World War. These include regional development banks, such as the European Investment Bank and the Asia Development Bank. There are regional economic associations, of which the European Union has been the most successful, and there are government-supported industrial cartels, of which the best known is the Organization of the Petroleum Exporting Countries.

Next, there are the governance systems that give order to the worlds of commerce and finance: how companies are organised, who owns them, how they are financed, the ethical and environmental issues they encounter and the financial system behind it all. A global standard for private corporate ownership has emerged, for both state and cooperative ownership have been in decline. Under this standard, larger companies tend to be quoted on stock exchanges, while smaller ones are family-owned or backed by private equity. Trade and finance are supported by a network of national and international banks, some state-owned but mostly at least partly in the private sector, even in communist China.

This whole edifice of market capitalism operates under a mixture of legal, accounting and regulatory standards that have shifted over time, and will continue to shift. But whereas for much of the post-war period public support tended to increase, that support has waned since the financial crisis of 2008/9. While its future looks at present reasonably solid – what do you replace it with? – its governance is under increasing scrutiny.

That will be a huge issue, but it leads to an even greater one: how will social attitudes and behaviour shift over the next thirty years? Will East and West converge or diverge? What changes will take place in the way societies govern human behaviour, including the relationship between men and women? This is not really a political matter or even a legal one, because both politics and the law tend to lag behind public opinion. But one has only to think about the way the #MeToo movement has transformed some aspects of US life, to acknowledge that there may be radical shifts in attitudes ahead that politicians will have to cope with. But first, let's think about the political system itself.

WHY HAS SUPPORT FOR REPRESENTATIVE
DEMOCRACY WANED?

The easy assumption of the 1990s after the fall of the Soviet Union, that some form of liberal democracy would become the dominant form of global government, has been shattered. Communist China has achieved a fair degree of economic liberalism while tightening the control of the party leadership. The rough democracy of post-Soviet Russia has become very rough indeed. Even where democracy has given clear signals of the sort of government that a majority of the electorate wants, such as in India and Russia, the West's liberal elite has been shocked. To that elite, electorates in several European countries and in the US have also given the 'wrong' answers.[1]

Some of these concerns were entirely predictable. It was possible in the early 1990s to predict that in the US there would be some sort of populist rebellion against the liberal elite – I did so in *The World in 2020*. It was also possible to predict that the UK would probably leave the European Union, as that book did. What was harder to foresee was how China would develop, and it seemed unlikely that the country could be sufficiently successful in economic terms under a centralised regime to satisfy the aspirations of a growing middle class. But, so far, it has done so. That has been a very considerable achievement, but one that carries the message that you don't need to live in a democracy to have a good chance of becoming reasonably prosperous. Some democracies have been more successful in economic terms than others, but just about everyone accepted that communism as practised in the Soviet Union, its Eastern European satellites and Maoist China kept the vast majority of the population poor. The rise of China changed all that.

The outcome is that representative democracy is under attack from many quarters: from the left and the right, from at home and abroad, from supporters and from enemies, from advocates of direct democracy and from believers in 'strong man' leadership … the list goes on. The difficulty is to get these challenges into some sort of perspective, separating them from the ideological stance of the challenger. The two challenges sketched here are an attempt to do that.

First there is the perceived lack of success of most of the developed world since the financial crash and recession of 2008/9. According to the official figures, GDP growth was relatively slow even in reasonably successful economies, productivity growth was poor, median incomes stagnated, income and wealth inequality rose, and, in much of Europe at least, unemployment remained high and opportunities for the young remained dismal.[2]

Supporters of democracy have two broad answers to all this. One is to argue that the decade has, despite this perception of failure, actually been a considerable success. The other is that the problems that have arisen have little to do with the system of government but stem, rather, from other factors such as the ageing populations of most advanced economies, which inevitably depress living standards.

The main argument behind the first is that we have been under-measuring economic growth and the associated rise in living standards that the growth has generated.[3] The iPhone boom with the plethora of apps, selfies, free communication across the world – all shows up as a net loss of GDP because the old technologies displaced by this boom, such as newspapers, required more input and employed more people. Paradoxically, the young, the most avid users of these technologies, feel most disadvantaged. The capitalist system that flourished under democracy created the products and services people love to use but they don't credit the system for this. The statistics say living standards have not risen, or at least not by much. But allow for these new services and they have carried on rising, particularly for the young.

The problem with this answer, however rational it might be, is that if people feel their living standards are not rising then telling them that they are wrong will not win much support. Besides, for many people in middle-skilled jobs economic transformation has left them with skills that are no longer needed, or at least less valued in the workplace.

Enthusiasts for the democratic market system also have to acknowledge that all advanced economies face demographic headwinds. As pointed out earlier, if a stable or shrinking workforce has to support a growing number of non-working pensioners, that will inevitably require higher taxes and hence depress the real wages of those at work. Gradually but inexorably through this century that headwind has strengthened. It will go on doing so. Politicians may be able to make a case that if people want better public services they will have to pay more tax, but it is very hard to explain that people will have to pay more tax simply to maintain the present level of service. This difficulty is compounded by a harsh fact: younger people pay more of the tax, but older people have most of the votes.

The second challenge is less about the mathematics of the economies and of public finances and more about the response of politicians to these pressures. We are, in 2021, too close to the populist revolution to be able to set it in historical context. But it will eventually peter out, perhaps in the 2030s, and what will people say about it then?

I suggest it will be seen as an inevitable reaction to the arrogance of too many mainstream politicians. The early signs of a rebellion against elites were evident in the early 1990s, but it took until the 2010s before this burst through. Examples include obviously the election of Donald Trump, the political outsider who beat the establishment candidate for the US presidency, and the UK's decision to leave the EU. They also include the election of Narendra Modi as prime minister of India and of Viktor Orbán as prime minister of Hungary, both of whom presented themselves as against the old establishment. Other examples include the rise of what were once fringe political parties just about everywhere.

It would be wrong to see this as a coherent global force running through all or at least most democracies. What has been happening is much messier than that. Insofar as there is a common theme, it is that successful politicians have to present themselves as outsiders, even if they are not. It is almost as though mainstream politicians have become disconnected from the hopes and values of ordinary people, sometimes almost looking down on the electorate – a range of things such as not understanding patriotism, or sneering at people with values other than their own. Hillary Clinton's labelling in the presidential campaign of 2016 of half of Donald Trump's supporters as a 'basket of deplorables' captures this disconnection.[4]

These divisions are not new. In the past political leaders have frequently become disconnected from the mass of people. Nor is it confined to politics. Across much of the developed world other focal points of power and influence, including the law, parts of the media and much of academia, have similarly found themselves out of step with a large part of the populace, sometimes a majority of it. The difference appears to be that the gravitational pull of the centre seems to be weaker relative to the centrifugal forces pulling societies apart. Democracies struggle to cope. The legitimacy of the leadership derives from the voters. But the leaders don't do what the voters want, and despise them for their primitive views.

If the gap is wide at a national level, it is even wider at a supranational one. The new global order established after the Second World War created a series of institutions to help national governments cooperate at many levels: the United Nations, the International Monetary Fund, the World Bank and so on, with Europe creating the Common Market in 1956. This was a top-down 'vision' project, for obvious reasons. The failure of national elites had led to two world wars, the Holocaust and the division of Europe. The second half of the twentieth century created institutions that would prevent a rerun of the first half. The inadequacies of these institutions were ignored or tolerated for at least their existence gave some hope that the catastrophes of the past would not be repeated.

The forces that drove populist criticism were partly the growing awareness of these inadequacies. When the world faced a truly grave challenge such as climate change, the chosen forum to agree action was indeed the UN: the Paris Agreement of 2015 was under the United Nations Framework Convention on Climate Change. But when Donald Trump became president he gave notice to withdraw from it. That decision was reversed within hours of Joe Biden taking office on 20 January 2021, but the damage to the UN's authority remains.

Big countries have always ignored the UN when it suits them, so maybe more corrosive is the growing sense that such organisations were no longer needed. A good example of this was the argument advanced in the UK referendum campaign against leaving the EU that the EU was created to prevent war in Europe and the UK leaving might weaken it. For many this was absurd – the Germans were not going to invade 'plucky little Belgium' ever again. But the EU did win the Nobel Peace Prize in 2012 for 'the advancement of peace and reconciliation, democracy and human rights in Europe'. It was instrumental, the citation said, in 'transforming most of Europe from a continent of war to a continent of peace'.[5]

To many people, even before Russia invaded Ukraine, this does not ring true. It was US leadership that created NATO in 1949, not the EU. Thanks to the NATO shield, the Berlin Airlift the previous winter and other US and UK initiatives, Western Europe was already a continent of peace in 1956 when the Treaty of Rome was signed. It was the defeat of the Soviet Union in the Cold War that led to most of Eastern Europe joining that continent of peace from the late 1980s onward. It was an American president, Ronald Reagan, who declared in West Berlin in 1987: 'Mr. Gorbachev, tear down this wall!'[6]

None of this is to argue that these international organisations should be abandoned. Nor is it to devalue the positive contribution such organisations have made, and will probably continue to make, as a key element of the global economic and political system. Rather, it is to explain the scale of the challenges they face and the reasons for the ramping-up of populist attacks on them. Like government at all levels – national, state and local – they have to lift their game. Can we reasonably expect them to do so?

CAN DEMOCRACIES LIFT THEIR GAME ?

Most democracies are not very well managed. Or to put this disagreeable point another way, the levels of competence across the countries of the developed world vary widely both in the skill with which they formulate policies and the efficiency with which they carry them out. There are a few examples of excellence but a long tail of mediocrity.

Policies are created without a lot of evidence, sometimes none. Instead, politicians see opportunities of generating support from special interest groups: old-age pensioners, students, public sector workers, charities, gun owners and so on. We regard it as normal for politicians to have 'beliefs' as to what they should do, things they 'stand for', 'platforms' of policies. It is normal but it is odd. Most other parts of our societies are not run in this way. True, some academics have strong views about their subjects, and religious leaders naturally do have things they believe in strongly. But most other people, whatever they are doing, try to do whatever seems to work best. That could be designing aircraft engines, marketing new brands of toothpaste or treating coronary patients in hospitals.

Countries that choose policies on the basis of their success elsewhere also tend to be good at putting them into practice. But many national bureaucracies struggle not only to deliver services but also to regulate effectively.

There are a handful of market economies where the government has adopted a technical approach both in forming policy, delivering it and regulating the private sector. Singapore is perhaps the most cited example, but there are others where there is a record of rational policy-making over a long period. They include New Zealand, Taiwan, South Korea and Switzerland. Estonia has the most advanced system of putting services online. Others are pretty poor.

Covid-19 has been another test of government competence, and while the knee-jerk reaction of many in the West has been that democracies have performed badly, that doesn't really stand up. China *may* have contained the virus more effectively than most European nations, and the US. But several democracies including South Korea and Japan seem to have avoided the worst outcomes, and the true costs to China will only emerge over several years. Besides, the combination of governments, universities and the pharmaceutical giants has delivered effective vaccines, which have been distributed reasonably swiftly.

What the crisis did reveal once again was the trust deficit. Governments are less trusted than many of the services they provide. This pre-dates the crisis. The OECD found in 2015 that on average only 43 per cent of citizens trusted their government, compared with 75 per cent trusting their local police and more than 70 per cent trusting their healthcare services.

This is obviously corrosive, and populism has been one result. But it is also a puzzle. If people in general trust the services governments provide but not the governments themselves, what then?

There will be a range of outcomes. The best would be for governments across the developed world to be honest about why they are distrusted, by improving the efficiency of the services within their own control, and explaining more about the limits of what they can achieve. The historical parallel to the first would be the string of public sector reforms, such as competitive entry to the civil service, from the 1840s onwards, pioneered in the UK then spreading across the world. The historical parallel to the second – well, there aren't really any because it seems very difficult for governments to acknowledge their own limitations. Some will manage to do this, but not many.[7]

The worst outcome will be that politicians continue to over-promise and under-deliver. They are trapped by the Juncker dilemma: 'We all know what to do, we just don't know how to get re-elected after we've done it.'

That was how Jean-Claude Juncker, prime minister of Luxembourg and later president of the European Commission, put the problem in 2007. He was talking about the need for structural change in Europe, but it applies universally.[8]

It would be naïve to expect this dilemma to disappear. Governments will do some things to improve their delivery, notably applying technology wisely, and they can try to explain how pressures will contain what they can achieve. But to be realistic, given the demographic headwinds nearly all of them face, they will continue to disappoint their voters.

The troubling answer to that question posed above – can the democratic system lift its performance enough to satisfy electorates? – is probably no, it can't. What then?

MUDDLE THROUGH, LESS DEMOCRACY OR MORE DEMOCRACY?

The democratic model is so powerful, so entrenched and so resilient that it will survive in some form in most countries that are at present some form of democracy. But if it continues to disappoint, it will be battered. There are really only three possible outcomes. It muddles through; there is less of it; or there is more of it.

Muddling through will be the most likely outcome in most democracies. This is what has happened so far to the populist revolution. The US has muddled through its populist experiment with Donald Trump as president, although it replaced him after four years. France chose a charismatic but untried leader in Emmanuel Macron. Hungary's Viktor Orbán has been contained within the country's political system. We should therefore expect a messy couple of decades, with some countries flirting with radical leaders of left and right, but then returning to the mainstream. That, at least for most of the developed world, seems likely to be the norm. Voters will be disgruntled, but not sufficiently so to wreck their particular models of representative democracy. The constitutions will hold.

But it is possible that some countries will choose less democracy. In other words, they will back a single leader or an elite corps of rulers. Russia has moved some way towards that, though Vladimir Putin has had broad popular support. Italy could choose a single strong leader who rejected the constitutional model. India could move to a more presidential system. It is impossible to generalise. The wider point is that if representative democracy leads to chaotic government, people may reject it and hunt around for an alternative. Order, albeit not very democratic order, will be preferred to chaos.

The other path is much more direct democracy. If people can vote for winners in reality show games, why should they not vote for policies of governance? Switzerland is the pioneer of such government, with referendums on such matters as increases in VAT and bans on minarets. But using referendums to determine policy is really a twentieth-century rather than a twenty-first-century model in the sense that, perhaps surprisingly, it has not been given an obvious boost by technology. You could very easily ask people to vote on everything on their mobile phones. But that has not happened. So Swiss practice has not become widespread even in Europe, except when countries are considering huge constitutional issues such as their relationship with the European Union, or independence for a region or country – examples being Quebec, Scotland or Catalonia. Elites do not like it, and frequently try not to accept the results. The UK experience with ending its membership of the EU was certainly an uncomfortable one for many established politicians, and will probably be held up as an example of the perils of allowing that particular version of direct democracy to take place.

But the idea that ordinary people should determine policy will not go away. Technology has advanced massively, and people have become accustomed to voting online for a vast array of things. A world where you vote for unimportant matters but not for important ones is absurd. The problem is that a small number of people who feel very strongly about some issue, and have the time and money to mobilise support for it, can hijack the agenda and impose policies on the mass of the electorate that a majority of them don't really want. Equally, if people are used to voting for things that don't matter, maybe they won't take the responsibility seriously when they do. Notwithstanding all these reservations, direct democracy will not go away. If representative democracy disappoints there is always the alternative: ask the people what they really want. It will be the default option when representative democracy is perceived to have lost its legitimacy, but the outcomes it produces will be unpredicted and unpredictable.

If national politics will have a very difficult thirty years ahead, what about international politics? Will the carefully constructed web of multinational institutions crumble? Or, faced with grave global challenges, will they have a resurgence and become part of the solution?

WHAT HAPPENS TO GLOBAL INSTITUTIONS?

It is easy to be cynical. Whenever governments spot the potential for an institution to fulfil some fashionable function they create one. These are mostly staffed by skilled bureaucrats, who are good at creating the services that the politicians want. When the original tasks become less important they figure out other useful things to do. As an example of the latter, once German reparations after the First World War became irrelevant, the Bank for International Settlements reinvented itself as an economic research group and a clearing house for central banks to settle balances between each other. The IMF, created to help manage the post-war fixed exchange rate system, took on a new role after that had collapsed, monitoring fiscal practice and encouraging countries, mostly smaller ones, to run prudent budgetary policies.

As a good example of the way an institution is created because it is fashionable, the BRICS Development Bank was created in 2014 by Brazil, Russia, India, China and South Africa, following Goldman Sachs's idea. When the concept of the BRICS became less fashionable it was renamed the New Development Bank.

On one level there is nothing wrong with this. The New Development Bank may not be necessary, but it won't do any real harm. Some such bodies, particularly the ad hoc ones, have been enormously important at key moments. The Group of Seven, originally with five members, helped coordinate the developed countries' response to the oil shocks in the 1970s. They were then the seven largest economies in the world. Now, as the balance of economic might has shifted to the emerging nations, the G7 has been supplemented by a broader group, the G20. Having twenty members makes it more cumbersome, but to be able to get the leaders of about 85 per cent of world GDP in one room at one time is really useful. The G20 came into its own in the 2008 financial crisis, coordinating plans to help engineer the recovery.

But there is a problem. Multinational bodies with specific tasks, such as the various development banks, the International Energy Agency (IEA) and the World Health Organization (WHO), will continue to carry out those tasks. But they will matter less. A world where there was a shortage of capital needs development banks, but that situation is long past. There is now a global glut of savings. The IEA was founded in response to the oil shortages of the 1970s. Now there is a glut of that, too. As for the WHO, it has done much useful work, but when the world faced the Covid-19 pandemic, it did not distinguish itself. National governments were the only bodies that could take charge of policy and the WHO was much criticised for its tardy and timid response.[9] The vaccine programme of the European Union was hardly an initial success either.

So we have a world where governments act through multinational bodies when they feel it suits them, but ignore them when they feel it doesn't. That situation may simply continue, particularly if a new cold war between the US and China takes the place of the Cold War between the US and Russia. It is not a comfortable way of tackling global problems, but it may be good enough. There is, however, one particular multinational organisation, the European Union, where the tension between national governments and a supra-national organisation is likely to burst out. The world can bumble on ignoring the UN when it suits, but EU members cannot do that within Europe. This is a particular issue for Europe and the likely outcome will be described later. The general point here is that all these bodies only have the authority that national governments have agreed they should have, and if they exceed that authority then they find themselves cut back.

WHAT HAPPENS TO MARKET CAPITALISM?

The dominance of Western models of democracy has been mirrored by the growing spread of its commercial and financial models across the emerging economies. The reason is that for all its imperfections it has delivered the goods. It is the system that drove previous waves of innovation, from the railways to the motor car. It continues to do so. In the twenty-first century it has brought us the iPhone, the apps, 5G communications, Tesla cars and so on. The modern world would be inconceivable without the goods and services market capitalism has delivered. But since the financial crash of 2008/9 it has been under increasingly vocal attack.

The attacks are likely to become more intense for four reasons. First, governments (i.e. taxpayers) have had to step in twice to prop up the system. They had to bail out the banks and some commercial companies after the financial crash of 2008, then again in 2020 after Covid-19 hit the entire world economy. It is a slightly unfair prospect because most large companies have a wide range of shareholders rather than a single family in control, but seeing billionaires begging for bailouts does not play well with ordinary working people.

Second, the rising inequalities of wealth (and to some extent income) in most of the developed world will lead to discontent. Leave aside the fact that ultra-loose monetary policies after the financial crash of 2008 are partly responsible for the rise in asset prices – in other words, it was national governments' policies that caused at least some of the rising wealth differentials. It happened, and the winners will be blamed by those who feel they are losers.

Third, the bargaining power of employees vis-à-vis that of employers is likely to rise.[10] There are several reasons why power shifted away from employees, including the decline of the power of trade unions, and decline in demand for middle-level skills. But the biggest one was the rebalancing of the world economy towards the emerging world. Workers in the West found they had to compete against people who were just as well educated, just as highly skilled, but worked for far less money. But that competition will ease. Wage differentials have narrowed. High-cost economies have learned to use expensive labour more efficiently. And the more general move against further globalisation will support local production. Taken together the effect will be to increase the power of working people in the advanced economies, which in turn will lead them to take a more confrontational attitude to the corporate world.

Fourth, rising environmental concerns will encourage more attacks on big business. These attacks are often unfair. For all their faults, commercial companies only survive if they offer products and services people want. If people want to buy, for example, prime steak, then it is unfair to blame farmers, meatpackers and supermarkets for bringing steak to people's dinner tables. Many of the world's environmental problems – the air pollution in Europe and the UK caused by diesel cars, for example – have been the result of government policies, not commercial greed. But unfair or not, the attacks will continue.

So what will happen?

For a start, business will adapt. You can already see this in the ways in which it is moving. It will improve its environmental, social and governance practices – its ESG ratings.[11] It will find ways of giving incentives to all layers of workers, not only the most senior ones. It will change its strategy towards globalisation. Instead of shipping jobs abroad it will try to source them locally, responding to the pressures outlined in the trade and finance chapter.

It would, however, be unrealistic to expect the global business community to satisfy the attackers. So the tensions will continue and will burst out in unpredictable ways. Government regulation will become more onerous as politicians respond to the more questioning mood of voters. Tension between the business and political worlds is not new, of course, and actually it is in the main healthy. Governments need the private sector to get things done, but the private sector needs the framework set by government to flourish. But the tensions will break out into open conflict and in some countries at least the business community will find itself an embattled island, where the climate becomes too hostile for some to survive.

Viewed globally, the market capitalist system may look secure for the foreseeable future. But in some countries, maybe many, it will no longer be the all-conquering winning way of organising production. There will be experiments where finance for projects is gathered in other ways, such as crowdfunding. There will be more regulation on quoted companies, which will encourage people to keep firms privately owned. The distinction between state-owned and companies quoted on stock exchanges will blur, as governments come to own large parts of commercial enterprises. This will be driven by two completely different forces: the growth of sovereign wealth funds and the need to rescue important businesses (including banks) when they get into trouble.

There may also be a revival in other forms of ownership, akin to the reform movement that started in the eighteenth century and gathered pace in the explosion of wealth of the Victorian middle classes in the nineteenth century. The eighteenth and nineteenth centuries saw the creation in the UK of the mutual life assurance companies, the building societies, the trustee savings banks and the cooperative wholesale groups – all owned by the people who used their services. Some of these remain but most have been converted into joint stock companies. Sadly, not many new cooperative enterprises are being created, at least in the developed world.

This may change. There is plenty of both political and social pressure to do so: incentives for employee ownership, tax breaks for not-for-profit enterprises, fair-trade initiatives to encourage primary product producers, and massively important, the whole charity sector. The question is whether economic drivers will reinforce social pressure. If the global middle class feels it is being ill served by the existing corporate structures, it will create new ones. Ultimately all economic activity is governed by what people want. If the mass of the population want the products and services that market capitalism creates, that model will continue to dominate. But the edges will be chipped away. How fast that happens will depend on the ways in which our societies are transformed over the next generation.

GOVERNANCE AND SOCIETAL CHANGE

Most people are prepared to go along with the social attitudes of the present moment. We have to do so if we want to enjoy happy and successful relations with everyone about us. So we accept that over time attitudes and values change and will continue to do so.

But while most of us do try to fit in with the accepted norms, looking back it is extraordinary how these shift over one or two generations. You might expect Victorian morality to be different from current morality. That was a long time ago. But most people would think of the 1960s being much the same as today – perhaps a little more libertarian then than now, in contrast to the stitched-up 1950s. Yet homosexuality was illegal in the UK until 1967, and the idea that the sexes should be treated equally in the workplace had barely begun to take hold.

Along with the shift of ideas since then, there has been a shift in political attitudes. In the 1960s it was, to generalise, the left that had supported individual liberties while the right believed in social control. This has now flipped. It is the right that is libertarian and the left is authoritarian. This is particularly evident over freedom of speech, and in some universities – to judge by the attitudes of many students towards right-wing speakers – even freedom of thought.[12]

The point here is not to make any judgements but simply to note that we must accept that by 2050 current ideas about the organisation of society may seem as quaint, as strange and even shocking as the ideas of the 1950s did in the 1980s.

So where should we look for the ideas that will shape societies a generation hence?

Economic success is something of a guide. The United States shot to global leadership after the Second World War, while Europe struggled to recover. The lifestyles of the huge American middle class were the envy of the world, especially in contrast to the relative poverty in Europe. So many characteristics of American society, including consumerism, individualism and eventually a form of feminism, spread across the rest of the world – or at least to those parts of the world that could afford them. But it wasn't just fashion, popular music and day-to-day lifestyles that all became more American. The informal rules that govern the workplace, shopping, schools and so on were massively influenced by US norms, too. McDonald's taught diners everywhere how to eat American-style. That's obvious. Less obvious was the way it taught restaurant owners, through its franchise model, how to run an American-style business.

That dominance remains. At a cultural level, it is US-style social media that governs the lives of young people the world over. At a financial level, the dollar is still king. The professional classes of the rest of the world may sniff at the excesses of US society but they still want their children to go to MIT or Stanford for their post-graduate studies.

As we have seen earlier the US share of global GDP will almost certainly decline, and as it does so it would be reasonable to expect other countries' ideas to move forward. But where might they come from?

That is the problem. There is no obvious alternative. The governance systems of China may be attractive to some emerging countries, but it is hard to see widespread adoption across the developed world. There may be aspects of Chinese systems that will spread to the rest of the world, rather in the way the 'just in time' manufacturing system of Japan revolutionised Western car companies from the 1980s onwards. Companies seeking to sell or invest in China will naturally continue to follow national standards. But it will not be a general model.

Europe has ambitions to be a global leader in regulation and has certainly become a regional one. But the numbers do not work. The EU economies will by 2050 account for about 12 per cent of global output. That is not a strong enough base from which to try to impose standards on the rest of the world. It also assumes that the EU will still exist in 2050, which, as discussed later, while probable is by no means certain. There are many aspects of European society that are enviable, including the comprehensive welfare systems in most of its northern member states. So there are elements of the European system that will probably be adopted elsewhere. In this regard, Europe may come to influence US policy more than it has in the past. As the balance of the Chinese population ages, China will pay attention to the ways in which Europe tries to care for its senior citizens. But Europe's influence will be limited by its relative economic decline.

India will inevitably make some contributions to global governance. It will be the world's most populous nation, its third largest economy, and probably the fasting-growing of all large countries. This combination will give it great influence. Other countries, particularly in Africa, will seek to emulate aspects of Indian practice. But as with China, this is likely to be a pick-and-mix process. Thus, some aspects of the way India orders its commercial companies will be adopted elsewhere, though it is hard at this stage to see what these might be. But it is less likely that Indian practices and social trends will become a global model adopted in the advanced world. Hollywood will continue to influence Bollywood, not the other way round.

What seems likely to emerge from all this is a set of codes of governance that will still be led by US practice but will have other elements grafted onto it. There will continue to be regional and national variations, both at an official legal level and at an unofficial social level. There will be common international codes only where there need to be, as indeed exist now. There have to be common rules for airline safety but not for food safety, unless the food is to be exported.

There may even be greater divergence over international standards than there is now. For example, the concept of universal human rights may shift to a more fluid set of ideas. Why should India be pushed into adopting a similar code of human rights to Sweden? Given the disparity in population, maybe the relationship should be the other way round. The whole idea that the West should set the appropriate rules of governance for the rest of the world will seem increasingly anachronistic. Besides, the West's ideas will change.

Remember, this will be a middle-class world. Two-thirds of the population will be middle class or rich.[13] The majority of these people will be in the emerging world. They will be well educated and articulate. Their ideas will matter. Perhaps the most interesting possibility will be that many people in the West will find some of the moral attitudes of parts of the emerging world more attractive than their own.

So how might the current ideas of how societies should organise themselves shift? It is guesswork, of course, but maybe this thought is helpful. Mark Twain is credited with the quote 'History doesn't repeat itself, but it often rhymes' though it is not clear that he ever said or wrote the second part of this aphorism. So maybe we should be looking for rhymes: possible swings in social and governmental attitudes that chime with swings that have taken place in the relatively recent past. They won't be the same. This will not be a simple swing of a pendulum. But there are some clues in history.

IDEAS ABOUT GOVERNMENT AND GOVERNANCE IN 2050

As far as the ideas of the West are concerned there are two particularly interesting periods that may help us here. One was the early Victorian period, the other the first decade of the twentieth century in the run-up to the First World War.

The essence of the first period was the growing weight of middle-class attitudes as the Industrial Revolution transformed economic power. This showed itself in many ways, including ending civil service jobs being granted on candidates' influence rather than their merit, stopping military commissions being bought, an orderly taxation system and so on. The essence of the second period was less happy – the burst of globalisation that ended with the catastrophe of war and the social and economic disruption of the first half of the twentieth century.

So there could be a positive rhyme, and a negative one.

The positive rhyme would be that the rest of the twenty-first century would see the middle classes of the emerging world having a similar influence in their countries as did the middle classes of Britain, Europe and the US in the nineteenth century. If this is right, we should expect there to be a progressive improvement in governance standards at every level across the emerging world: in taxation and government spending, in corporate practice, in the law, in public services and so on. This does not necessarily mean that it will be current Western practices that are adopted. There are enough obvious flaws in these for the new middle class to cast around for something better. Indeed, it would be arrogant of people in the present developed world to think that the emerging world won't do better. It would be wonderful for humankind if it does. But the general hope – that people may look back in another 100 years and regard this century as one of overall progress – surely stands as a plausible projection.

The negative rhyme would be that the world makes as much of a mess of the next half-century as our ancestors did of the first half of the last one. There are uncomfortable parallels. National rivalries can be motors of growth and scientific achievement, as they were around 1900. Think of the race to create and then mass-produce the motor car; or the competition to build a heavier-than-air flying machine. But leaders became overconfident and the wealth of the world economy seemed so secure that a short war seemed something that Europe could afford with only minimal disruption.

The present period has uncomfortable echoes. You can catch examples of hubris and aggression among politicians in the US, China, India, Russia and Europe. Even when there is no aggression there is frequently unpleasantness. Most troubling of all is the quite widespread assumption that the world economy will continue to make progress, whatever politicians do. This is not to attack any particular current leader or policy. Rather, it is to point out that there are fragilities now in the way the global economy is run that resonate with the fragilities that existed in 1900.

How the world is governed over the next thirty years will depend to a large extent on how the balance between these two forces plays out. That is the framework – what I hope is a helpful way of thinking about global attitudes towards governance. But there are many forces that will pull against each other within that framework. Here are some thoughts about these, starting with religion.

Religion is and will remain an enormously powerful force shaping social attitudes. It is not helpful for economists to try to predict trends in global religions. What is perhaps useful is to observe that, far from there being a clash of cultures driven by religion, it is possible that the various religions could become a unifying force. They could help create paths for people of different religions but often common moral codes to live together in harmony. After all, there is no religion that encourages cheating or stealing. The vision of Samuel Huntington in his 1993 essay *The Clash of Civilizations*[14] of competing civilisations is a helpful, if troubling, way of thinking about this. There are certainly many clashes on the frontiers between one dominant religion and another, and those will doubtless continue. But these present tensions may prove a passing phase. Just because they have increased over the past thirty years does not mean they will continue to do so. They may. But it is equally possible that religion, far from dividing people, will become, if not a unifying force, at least a buffer between different ideas of how they should live their lives.

We must hope that it does. By 2050, while Christianity will still be the most prominent religion, Islam will have closed the gap, as you can see from the graph here.

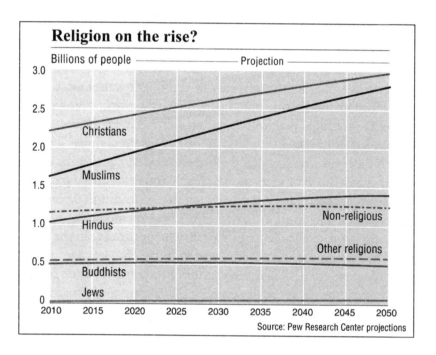

Pew Research[15] calculated that Christians will account for 31.4 per cent of the world's population, the same as 2015, while Muslims will have risen from 23.2 to 29.7 per cent. Four out of every ten Christians will live in Africa. India, a Hindu-majority nation, will nevertheless be home to the largest national group of Muslims. The scope for tension, and indeed conflict, is obvious. Reason says that people of different religions should be able to live together in harmony. We have to hope that reason prevails.

If reason can be the glue that binds together people of different faiths, or of no faith, then maybe reason will bind together different political ideologies. The idea behind Francis Fukuyama's *The End of History and the Last Man,* that there was no viable systemic alternative to Western liberalism, was over-influenced by the collapse of the Soviet version of communism. Actually, there are many other forms of political organisation that can be made to work, including and perhaps especially the Chinese mix of single-party state control and the market economy. There does not need to be a single political system, or a single version of the mixed market economy, or indeed a set of common ethical values. We all just need to get along with each other.

That hope gives us a vision of how the world might manage to negotiate the next thirty years in reasonable harmony. I think this prospect holds true, notwithstanding the war in Ukraine and the other conflicts that will sadly but inevitably break out. There are a number of issues that have to be tackled on a global scale, of which the most important is the preservation of a planet on which humankind can continue to live, feed, clothe – and enjoy itself. The pursuit of happiness is not an ignoble goal. But there are also many issues that can be tackled effectively by the major nations agreeing on a particular policy on an ad hoc basis. If the post-war institutions such as the UN and IMF become less relevant, so be it. A reasonable level of cooperation between the major powers should be enough. How those major powers are likely themselves to develop in the years to 2050 is the subject of the next section.

How the World Will Look
in 2050

7

The Americas

THE UNITED STATES – STILL THE GREAT GLOBAL LEADER

The United States will remain the dominant global power in 2050. Its economy will be slightly smaller in aggregate size than that of China, but it will lead the world in other ways. It will be the wealthiest large economy, and quite possibly the fastest-growing one. It will remain the global intellectual leader and the dollar will remain the most important national currency. Perhaps most significantly, after two or three decades of internal and external tensions it will have become more comfortable with itself. Nothing is set in stone, and there are huge challenges that the world will face – and which will require American leadership to tackle. But the long-term outlook is more positive than it appears to many Americans in the fraught early 2020s.

How is it possible to be so confident? Of course, there could be some unforeseeable catastrophe that would wreck this positive outlook, but there are three solid reasons for optimism. First, the US is likely to remain a magnet for global talent. Clever, energetic, entrepreneurial people from all over the world are still choosing to make their lives in the US, and, while immigration has led to tensions within the country, it is hard to see this attraction waning. Where else do you go? Second, the social, political and economic problems of the US are fixable. It is reasonable to think that between now and 2050 resources will have been devoted to promoting greater equality of opportunity, building a more effective social safety net, improving the nation's health, preserving the environment – and all the other challenges the country faces. Third, the principal challenger for global leadership, China, will lose much of its dynamism as its population ages and declines. What happens to China will be tackled later in this section. We look now at how being that magnet for talent will change the US over the next three decades.

We can be confident that the population of the US will carry on rising. There will be about 400 million people living in the US by 2050, maybe a bit less, maybe more if immigration and birth rates pick up a little. The latest UN estimates[1] put it at about 380 million, though back in 2008 the Pew Research Center[2] estimated that it would be 438 million. Either way the country will become racially more diverse. Pew estimated that just under half the population will be non-Hispanic white and just under one-third Hispanic Americans. Black Americans will remain around 13 per cent while Asian Americans will have risen to nearly 10 per cent. So at some stage, probably in the 2040s, the white majority will have become the minority. The US has always been a nation of immigrants, but at that moment, when the majority becomes the minority, it will have become a truly multiracial one.

Long before that, however, the growing ranks of Hispanic and Asian Americans with Black Americans, will account for more than half the workforce. That is where much of the drive will come from that will sustain another generation of American exceptionalism.

How can we be so confident of this? Well, of course, we can't be. This is simply a reasonably likely outcome. For it to happen, several things need to go right, of which the most important are that the US remains open to immigrants and that it continues to offer them a clear path to economic and social advance. There are several issues embedded here that will have to be tackled. There is the politically sensitive matter as to the legal status of the undocumented arrivals. There is a strategic question as to whether the US, insofar as it is able to make that choice, should seek to attract lower skilled workers as well as the elite ones. But what are skills? After all, energetic, clever people without much formal education can create wonderful businesses if they have that entrepreneurial streak in their make-up. There are many cultural questions: for example, to what extent should immigrants be required to sign up to US cultural values? That is tricky, not least because those values keep on changing.

Anyone making the case for immigration must acknowledge the reasons why it is resisted. Every country in the world controls who can and cannot come there to live as citizens. The US has had alternating periods of high immigration followed by periods when it has clamped down on arrivals. As a result, the proportion of foreign-born citizens has swung from 9.7 per cent in 1850 to close to 15 per cent from the 1870s through to 1910, then to fall to only 4.7 per cent in 1970, before climbing back up to 13.6 per cent in 2017. Pew projects that it could rise to 19 per cent by 2060. That is certainly plausible but, given current concerns and the traditional swings in immigration, maybe not that likely. More probably it will continue at somewhat more moderate levels, maintaining the proportion of foreign-born citizens at around 15 per cent.

The most important point here is that the US will remain the magnet that it currently is. It surely will. More than this, the US has the pick of the crop of would-be migrants. The balance of inward migration is likely to shift from Mexico, currently the largest source, to China and India. The other options for ambitious Chinese and Indians are in theory widespread – they can go anywhere in the world that feels it needs their skills. But in practice, for reasons of culture and language they are likely to prefer countries where English is the principal language, or at least is widely spoken. Some will continue to come to the UK. Already many Indian and Chinese families are either established in the UK or have bought property in preparation for migrating. Others will choose Canada and Australia, as they do now. But the combined population of these three countries, plus Ireland and New Zealand, is some 140 million in 2020, against the US's 331 million. Unless the US were to clamp down severely on migration, it will end up taking the lion's share.

That leads to a further thought: that the US role as de facto leader of the Anglophone world will become more explicit. The UK is turning away from Europe. Canada is already closely integrated with the US. Australia and New Zealand face difficulties in their relations with the great power of their time zone, China. Links of language and culture will grow in importance vis-à-vis physical proximity. Quite how this Anglophone community might organise itself is sketched in the final chapter. The point here is that it is and will remain a magnet for ambitious immigrants.

And so to the obvious challenge. Large-scale immigration is disruptive. The US needs skilled immigrants to retain its position as global leader. How will it preserve and hopefully improve social harmony? And can it?

Right now this looks a momentous task. There is zero common ground between 'build a wall' and 'open the gates'. There is no agreement on how to cope with the 'dreamers', the undocumented children and young adults brought into the US by their parents. To be realistic, these tensions will probably get worse before they get better. The 2020s are likely to be a period of social and economic conflict more generally, as will be discussed shortly, and the debate over the levels and form of migration will be an element of this conflict. But this will not continue for ever, and by the 2030s and 2040s an accord on how to manage migration will have been reached. Being a magnet for talent creates problems, but if you create a society that repels talent your problems are vastly worse.

The tensions between populism and elite liberalism that broke out into the open with the election of Donald Trump in 2016 will continue through the 2020s. There is a temptation to see one side emerging as a winner, but it is much more likely that some sort of consensus will be established by the 2030s. The best historical parallel is the way the student protests of the 1960s and early 1970s waned as other concerns, particularly about unemployment and inflation, moved to the forefront. Surmounting what now looks an unbridgeable chasm between different ideas as to how the US should be governed may become more manageable if other issues, such as a new cold war with China, pull left and right together in common endeavour.

If this is right, then the US will move through the 2030s and 2040s into adopting its own version of the Western European welfare model. Government at both a federal and a state level will probably account for a slightly larger percentage of GDP than it does in 2020. There will be slightly more progressive taxation, though nothing like European levels of taxes on the rich, to pay for improved care for the elderly. By the 2040s Americans will feel more comfortable with the way their country deals with social and economic hardships, and the ideological battles of the early 2020s will seem almost irrelevant, rather in the way that so many battles of the past seem odd today.

We can't be confident, of course, but remember that the population balance of the US in the 2040s will be very different from the population in 2020. The values of the Hispanic and Asian minorities will be more pervasive – and, for the politicians, more persuasive. It is a numbers game. Politicians will only succeed in getting elected if they accept the changing shifts in the size and make-up of the electorate. It will be more multi-ethnic, but it will also be older. In shorthand, any tilt to the left from the rising numbers of Hispanics (many of whom lean right on some issues) will be offset by a tilt to the right from the ageing of the entire population. So it is at least plausible that US society will be calmer and less divided by the 2040s than it has been at the beginning of the 2020s.

What might make such an outlook more likely would be if the US manages to achieve a reasonable increase in overall living standards, and in particular for its huge middle class. There are several reasons to be hopeful here. One, as argued in Chapter 5, is that the benefits of the online revolution are being under-measured and will in any case flow through as we get more accomplished at using the technologies that have become available. Another is that the healthcare sector, now absorbing 18 per cent of US GDP for what are by world standards not particularly good outcomes, will become radically more efficient.[3] Still another is that the US will continue to pioneer further technological leaps, as it did with the development of the iPhone and social media. Above all, if one of the core arguments of this book is correct – that the US will remain the world's most vibrant, innovative society – then the benefits will flow through in higher living standards for most of its people.

So it won't be a question of one or other tribe winning the current battle of ideas as to how the US should organise itself; rather, there will be a broad consensus on economic policy issues, just as there was in the 1950s and 1960s. The populist revolution will have done its job in reconnecting the elite with the middle class. Instead, there will inevitably be many other issues that will trouble the country.

These will include the impact of climate change. The effects of this, as outlined in Chapter 3, will have started to become quite evident across the nation. Put bluntly, parts of the south will be at an increasing disadvantage vis-à-vis much of the north. There are too many uncertainties for it to be possible to calibrate the impact, but, put at its most optimistic, a lot of resources will have to be devoted to coping with environmental degradation. The most pessimistic possible outcomes, such as the loss of parts of some low-lying coastal cities to rising sea levels, don't really bear thinking about. It is small comfort that some other countries are likely to suffer more.

What can be said with confidence is this. If, or maybe better when, it becomes clear that the US faces an environmental emergency, it will mobilise the resources needed to tackle it. Some actions will come from the federal government, others from the individual states, still others from national and local businesses, and some from private philanthropy. We cannot see what will be done or how it will be done. We have to accept that huge mistakes will be made, and that action will probably be taken too late – perhaps is already being taken too late. But as in tackling so many troubling issues, the best should not become the enemy of the just about good enough. At some stage, perhaps in the 2030s, there will be an investment drive to tackle environmental degradation akin to the Marshall Plan that helped rebuild Europe after the Second World War. It is reasonable to expect that it will be adequately successful at keeping the country a place where its citizens can live, bring up their children and be optimistic about the future for their grandchildren and generations to come.

A second set of challenges will come from the nation's inequalities. These are frequently discussed in racial terms. Why, for example, do African Americans have worse health or lower incomes than white Americans? The wide differences in health and economic attainment for different ethnic groups in America are one dreadful manifestation of the country's inequalities. However, when looking forward to what the US might look like in 2050 it is probably more helpful to think about the country's social problems more generally.

The issue is not inequality as such. Big countries are inevitably less equal than small ones. The gaps between the poorest and richest regions in Europe are comparable to those of the US, though within the countries of Europe they are much smaller. China and India have much larger wealth gaps than the US. Immigration generally increases inequality in the host country because new arrivals usually earn less, at least initially, than the host population, and the US is and will continue to be attractive to immigrants.

Rather, the issue is the social costs of inequality, which must be carried by the whole community, not only those who are most disadvantaged. These costs include crime, a less healthy workforce and seniors who need more expensive care, as well as all the intangible costs. No decent person, however wealthy, wants to step past homeless people sleeping on the street. Will the US tackle these social costs effectively over the next thirty years, and, if so, how?

Actually, considerable progress has been made over the past generation or so. All big cities have social problems, but New York in 2020 is a shining, successful enterprise compared with the tatty, rundown city that it still was in the 1980s. The much-criticised New York healthcare system responded reasonably well[4] to the Covid-19 pandemic. Where ground has been lost, for example in tacking obesity, the US faces problems that are common to the rest of the developed world. But there are also several measures that suggest that the US is an outlier, notably the number of people in prison.

There are two broad political responses. One, espoused by many Democrats, is to call for the state to do more to promote equality by taxing and spending, moving towards the model of Western European countries. The other, favoured by many Republicans, is to emphasise personal self-discipline: to caricature, if people work hard and lead orderly lives then everyone will become richer and inequality will decline.

The tensions between these two very different approaches will continue through the 2020s and probably the 2030s. The most likely outcome will be some combination of both themes. There will, as noted above, be more government intervention. The electorate will vote to improve the US welfare safety net. There will also be legislative action to curb what is seen as abuse of monopoly power – a rerun of the trust-busting movement of the 1890s and early 1900s. These actions will be carried out alongside an acceptance of unequal outcomes, provided a majority of the country is confident that the system is not rigged in favour of the 'haves'.

This will be difficult. One of the core problems of any meritocracy[5] is that people who are doing well feel deep down that they have earned a right to do well, thanks to their education, intelligence and energy. It is hard to accept that, in addition to their personal application and hard work, they owe their success to a series of chances: to happen to have parents who could afford to fund them through a top college, to be able to choose a career as a highly paid professional, to have family help in buying their first home and so on. The relentless competition of the American elite has been attacked by Daniel Markovits, a professor at Yale Law School, in his 2019 book *The Meritocracy Trap*, for widening the gap between the 1 per cent and the rest.[6]

'Merit,' he writes, 'has become a counterfeit virtue, a false idol . . . A caste order that breeds rancor and division. A new aristocracy, even.'

That is a contentious way of putting it, but most people would accept that there are fissures in US society that damage the country and undermine personal wellbeing. So what will happen?

The challenge comes in three parts. The first two are evident from the above. One will be to protect the disadvantaged. That means more government intervention, and the difficulty there will be to intervene effectively. The second will be to reopen the path that used to exist for the middle class to be able to gain entry to the elite. That will need many detailed changes to American society, from containing the spiralling costs of higher education to improving access to the best-paid professions. None of this will be easy.

But there is also a third element, which will be hardest of all: changing the nation's habits and behaviour in ways that will not only reduce inequalities – that is the negative way of looking at it – but, put positively, increase the wellbeing of all. This raises a string of tough questions. How do you tackle obesity? Should a country try to improve the diet of its people, and if so how? Should it encourage parents to stay together in partnership to bring up their children? How do you discourage people from making lifestyle choices that undermine their health?

Some of these issues are reasonably straightforward. The overall wellbeing of the country would be higher if most people had a cash cushion to tide them over in an emergency. So the difficulty is how to increase personal savings, not whether you should try to do so. Not many people are in favour of drug abuse, but there is a wide spectrum of policy prescriptions to tackle it. At the other extreme there are some third-rail problems – too dangerous for politicians to grasp. What do you do about absent fathers?

In all societies there are tensions between individual freedoms and collective responsibilities. All societies have social problems. But the United States has both grave problems and the resources to tackle them. The scale of the problem has been well charted by the Nobel Prize winner Sir Angus Deaton, who coined the expression 'deaths of despair' to describe the excessive death rates from suicide, accidental drug overdoses and liver damage from alcohol. His most recent book, *Deaths of Despair and the Future of Capitalism*, co-written with Anne Case, argues that the problem is the capitalist system itself.[7] Much of the US economy has 'been captured to serve the wealthy with the connivance of government', the authors argue.

But will the US really make radical changes to its entire economic system, and is that the core of the problem?

The answer, surely, is no in both cases. There will certainly be huge pressure on business and finance to tackle the inequalities that the mixed market economy has generated, and there will be changes in regulation and taxation that will attempt to narrow these down. But it is hard, at least on a thirty-year view, to see radical upheaval. This is, after all, the model that in various forms has worked for the US and Europe and has then been exported to the rest of the world. China will become the world's largest economy because it has adopted substantial elements of the US system. So it will be patched. It will not be overthrown.

In any case, the core of the problem is not so much inequality but exclusion. Too many people are in practice excluded from the benefits that the economy can bring. The pathways are blocked. They are blocked partly by unnecessary entry restrictions on many activities – should you really need a licence to be a hairdresser in Florida? – but they are also blocked by poor educational outcomes. The US education system is great for the elite, but not so good for the masses.

So there is a lot to be done. Gradually, progressively, incrementally, it will be done. Over the next thirty years the US will peck away at its flaws and inefficiencies. It will have some success, as companies see that it is in their interest to support reform. There will be resistance, particularly from unions and professional institutions, and progress will be of a two steps forward, one step back nature. There will still be a sense of frustration and dissatisfaction among many American citizens, which will periodically burst out.

All this is reasonably predictable. There is another way forward. Some time in the next thirty years, probably starting in the 2030s, there is likely to be one of those seismic social movements that periodically sweeps the nation. The big idea behind it will be finding ways of encouraging people to live more orderly lives.

It is impossible to see any of the detail, or even be confident that it will happen, but it is possible to sketch several likely elements of it. Part would be top-down. For example, there could be a government-led drive, ideally a cross-party one, to control prescription-drug abuse. There could be a reform of the judicial system, with more emphasis on rehabilitation. Technology could be used to predict and prevent crime. There could be some version of the people-tracking systems developed in China, maybe with a system of carrots and sticks to nudge people towards more socially positive behaviour.

The problem with top-down initiatives is that there is inevitably some trade-off between privacy and control. Many people resent being told what to do by politicians in distant Washington. So it may be both more palatable and more effective when the initiatives are bottom-up. Expect something more akin to the temperance movements of the nineteenth century rather than the National Prohibition Act of 1919.

The US is not yet ready for this. There are plenty of examples of the effort to bring more order to people's lives. These come from charities, churches, self-help groups, clubs, the wide spectrum of voluntary institutions and so on. But for the time being these movements do not yet have the critical mass to shift the balance of the nation. The mood seems still for people to have greater individual freedom to do what they want, even if that means a diminished collective responsibility for the wellbeing of the country as a whole. But, as noted in Chapter 6, ideas of what is socially acceptable change sharply over time. Listen carefully, and the distant rumbles of what may become a seismic attitudinal shift can already be heard.[8]

So what, then, will the United States feel like in 2050? Writing in early 2021, it feels dissonant, uncomfortable with itself and worried about the future at every level. The bright-eyed young in particular find it hard to come to terms with the fact that all societies are flawed, and that correcting those flaws is a long and difficult task. So to suggest that a generation hence the US will be richer, calmer and more self-confident might seem Panglossian, even absurd. But anyone with a sense of history must acknowledge that the mood of the moment is a poor guide to the mood of the future. There were less than three years between President John F. Kennedy's call for service to the nation in his inaugural address in 1961, 'Ask not what your country can do for you, but what you can do for your country' and Bob Dylan writing his great anti-war protest anthem warning that 'The Times They Are A-Changin'.

The times won't change as fast now. There will be at least a decade of confusion, probably two. The internal divisions will not go away, and the rise of China will cast an inevitable cloud over the US. The tussle between the two great powers may go hideously wrong. America will make mistakes. Other challenges will emerge. But, as argued above, for another generation at least there are many powerful reasons to be confident. Of these three stand out. The US will remain the most powerful magnet for global talent. The rebalancing of the US racial mix will make the country accept its truly multiracial future as it grapples with its past. And it will still be the most technically advanced and innovative society on earth.

There is a final possible twist to this story. By any reasonable assessment, China will be a larger economy than the US in 2050. But look beyond that and consider this. China's population will almost certainly be falling, whereas that of the US will be rising. China may be unable to escape from the 'middle-income trap' and move to fully advanced status. China will face greater environmental challenges than the US and may cope less successfully with them. Pull all this together and something intriguing emerges. It may be that in another thirty years' time the US will be overtaking China in economic size and heading again to become the world's biggest economy some time in the second half of this century. This will be discussed in Chapter 12. The point here is that one should never underrate the capacity of the United States to renew itself. In dark times that capacity remains as bright as ever.

CANADA – A NATION THAT WILL RELISH ITS DIVERSITY

If the US thrives, Canada will thrive. It is difficult to discuss the future of Canada except in terms of its relationship with its neighbour to the south. As noted earlier, 90 per cent of the country's population lives within 100 miles of the US border. There are questions as to the relative attractiveness and availability of Canadian citizenship vis-à-vis US citizenship. Canada needs to take in more migrants than the US for its population to keep stride with America, as, for reasons that are not clear, Canadians have somewhat lower fertility rates. In the eyes of the world it will remain a seductive, more European version of the rambunctious society to the south.

There are two shadows. One is economic. It stems from Canada's reliance on exports of oil and gas, products that in relative terms will become less significant. Natural resources will continue to matter and these will support the economy overall, but at the margin the amounts exported will dwindle. Fortunately, Canada has strength in depth in manufacturing and services, too, but it is vulnerable to tensions with the US. If car assembly is to be run down, as seems likely, a large chunk of Canada's manufacturing industry is vulnerable. It must rebalance its economy by building up service industries – finance, education and so on. It will do so, but its prosperity depends on the speed and success at which it succeeds in this switch.

The other shadow is political. Separatism ebbs and flows, and the idea of an independent Quebec has been in retreat for a generation. But Canada came within a whisker of breaking up at the 1995 referendum, and it would be naïve not to acknowledge the possibility that this could indeed happen. Or maybe French nationalism will revive in a different form. Suppose France were to offer Quebec the status of a full administrative region of France itself? It would become second only to the Île-de-France, the Paris region, in population and importance. It would presumably become a member of the European Union, adopting the euro – assuming both still exist in thirty years' time. To be clear, this is not a likely outcome; indeed, I believe it is an unlikely one. But history has a long pull and it has taught us that nothing should be ruled out. Something that is at the moment unforeseeable could happen in Anglophone Canada that would make this an attractive proposition both for Quebec and for France. The main point here is that the forces that hold Canada together could weaken and Quebec could revisit the dream of independence.

There are, then, challenges. The best way to tackle these will be for Canada to come to celebrate its diversity but also accept its place in the world as a member of the Anglosphere. For it is hard not to be optimistic about the next thirty years for this great nation. It is cultured. It is outward-looking. It is a decent functioning democracy. It has space in abundance. It is and will remain a magnet for talented people. If the balance of the world economy does indeed shift towards Anglophone nations, it will ride on that wave. It will continue to offer the world a softer, more accommodating version of the American dream, a bridge between the US and Europe, that will be useful not only to the US, the UK and Europe, but to the world as a whole.

MEXICO – THE DIFFICULT PATH TO A TOP-TEN ECONOMY

Mexico has the tantalising prospect of a great thirty years ahead of it, escaping from the middle-income trap and becoming one of the top ten economies of the world. But to do so it has to make several successful leaps of policy.

Potentially, Mexico is a huge economic and strategic asset to the US. It is friendly state along the US southern border, posting no military threat whatsoever. It is a lower-wage economy that can supply goods and services that are too expensive for the US to create. It is a ready source of immigrants, enabling the US, if it so chooses, to make goods that it would otherwise have to import. It is also an enormous market for US products, and an entry point in cultural terms to the rest of Latin America. Learn how to sell to Mexico and you get a better feeling of how to deal with Brazil, Argentina and the other lands to the south.

These arguments, however, are not enough to swing the mass of US public opinion into appreciating how lucky the country is to have a land border with a country that can offer all this. Instead, the threat of uncontrolled immigration has dominated political debate. This is quite understandable, given the numbers of undocumented immigrants from Mexico in the US. But it is a pity, because whatever view you take on immigration, the issue has soured relations between the two countries. That makes it harder to cooperate on other issues, such as controlling the illegal drugs trade.

The bumpy relationship will continue, but there are solid reasons for expecting it to become materially easier. One we noted earlier is that the US Hispanic population will increase both in absolute and in proportionate terms. Another is that, as the Mexican economy grows, it will not only narrow the gap in wealth per head with the US, it will also become a more valuable market for US produce. It will inevitably always be very much a junior partner, but it will become a more useful and respected one. For that to happen, though, another massive change has to take place. Mexico has to become a more orderly society in many respects: economically, financially and politically. Most important of all, it must find a way of tackling the scourge of violence.

To ask this of Mexico is not to say it has to become like Switzerland. It is to say that, while the country is home to five of the top ten cities with the highest murder rates in the world, as it was in 2020, it cannot hope to make the transition to becoming a high-income advanced economy.[9] Quite apart from the human aspects of this tragedy, this is an economic disaster. Mexico will remain stuck as a middle-income country, with its people gazing across an unnecessarily hard border to the north.

So the question is whether Mexico will be able to bring in the web of interconnected changes in its governance that will enable it to transform its position. These will include reforming the police, overhauling the courts and financial and political reforms. It is not the place here to give a detailed prescription of what has to be done. That is for the Mexican people. All that outsiders can do is to urge the country along on its path towards becoming a more orderly society. Can it succeed?

Common sense says it will make some progress. It will become richer. Inequalities will be contained and may well decline. Crime will fall. Such success as Mexico achieves will be one of degree, and realistically the next thirty years will be another tale of two steps forward, one step back. But the prize – becoming a calmer, more settled and prosperous nation – is there for Mexico to grasp. It has a good shot at grabbing it.

SOUTH AMERICA – SO MUCH PROMISE, TOO MANY MISSTEPS, A CHANCE TO LIFT ITS GAME

So much depends on what happens to Brazil. It is and will remain the great powerhouse of the region. To focus on Brazil is not to set aside the other countries of the continent, with their different heritages and rich cultures. It is simply a reality, given Brazil's size. In Chapter 1, the sketch of the world as it is now, I posed the question as to whether Latin America would regain the relative prosperity that it had at the end of the nineteenth century, or whether it would continue to slip back as it did in the second half of the last century. The most important single factor determining the answer to that question will be how well Brazil governs itself. It accounts for nearly half of South America's land area and population. It is home to the largest city, São Paulo, and the largest company by revenue, the petrochemical enterprise Petrobras. And while it is not the richest country measured by income per head (an accolade that belongs to Chile), it accounts for more than half the continent's GDP.

Whatever happens, it is hard to imagine that Brazil will not be one of the top ten economies in the world in 2050 – perhaps number seven or eight. It will have made some progress in living standards, health and longevity. But while it will not be a disaster like Venezuela, the danger is that it will still be stuck as a middle-income country, still with shanty towns, still with huge inequalities and still with corruption at many levels. The challenge will be to move from moderate but stumbling progress to something much better: to become a true developed economy offering a sound middle-class lifestyle to most of its people.

The central point here is that South America ought to be doing better. Some countries are. Chile has had a bumpy political ride but in economic terms is a secure, high-income economy as defined by the World Bank. So, too, is Uruguay. But both countries are relatively small in population. Chile stretches more than 2,600 miles north to south, but has fewer than twenty million people. Uruguay has fewer than four million. They are too small to pull the whole region up.

If that is a pity, it is a tragedy that the two countries that might have been beacons of economic development, Argentina and Venezuela, should have squandered their wealth. For Argentina to have gone from being one of the richest nations on earth at the end of the nineteenth century to a disorderly, middle-income country that continually defaults on its debt is a miserable warning for all. It is all the more depressing given the mass of hardworking, talented people who live there. Governance matters, for building the complex, multi-layered fabric of a successful state is difficult. Yet Argentina has so many natural advantages. It is a vibrant society; has high levels of education; a healthy population; and wonderful natural resources. It should be a secure and prosperous country, Latin America's equivalent of Australia. It once was, but now it isn't.

Reason, observing the many unsuccessful attempts to regain its past prowess, says it will continue to bumble along, with each successive effort falling flat. It will be all right in the sense that most of its citizens will continue to be well fed and healthy. But each crisis will suck resources and talented people out of the country and the long, slow decline will continue. However, reason may be a poor guide to the future. It is quite possible that a set of circumstances will come together, where the country breaks from the shadows of the past, embarks on a spurt of growth for a couple of decades and catapults itself into its rightful place as a successful, sophisticated, advanced economy.

For Venezuela the fall has been swifter. It should be one of the richest countries in the world. It once was. In 1950 it was the fourth richest, after the US, Switzerland and New Zealand, and ahead of Canada.[10] Its wealth is largely thanks to oil, for it has the largest proven oil reserves, larger even than Saudi Arabia. But while its GDP per head grew in the 1960s and 1970s, it has flatlined or fallen since then. In 2020, following an economic collapse under the government of President Nicolás Maduro, its people – or at least those who did not join the millions who emigrated – were actually poorer than they had been in 1950.

Collapses on this scale are mercifully most unusual. There is no point here in trekking through the reasons for the progressive mismanagement of the Venezuelan economy over more than half a century. They have been widely reported. It is worth stating one point that is seldom made: with a few years of good governance Venezuela could again become the success story it once was. The world is switching from carbon fuels but, as noted earlier, this will take many years. Venezuela can, meanwhile, generate the revenues to transform its economy. That would not be easy, but it could be done.

The wider point here is that the gap between economic success and relative failure can be quite narrow. This applies to the other key nations of the region, notably Peru and Colombia, respectively the third largest South American country by land area and the third largest by population. Peru has been growing fast and will be a regular, successful, developed economy long before 2050. Colombia has done well, too. Inequality remains high, and it is further back on the development ladder. But if it continues on the path set over the past two decades it, too, should be offering a solid middle-class lifestyle to most of its people by 2050.

This leads to an intriguing possibility. The cruel charge about Latin America is that is always promising but never quite delivering. The earlier comments on Brazil and Argentina that it is just possible that, suddenly, it will burst out and start to achieve its potential really apply to the whole continent, and indeed to Mexico, too. It will start to deliver, after all. The history of the past 100 years would teach us to be cynical. A sustained period of economic success across Latin America will not change the world economy. The region is not big enough to do this. But it would obviously give a much better life for its people and give hope to other nations trying to escape the middle-income trap. It is an evens bet that it will succeed.

8

Europe

THE EUROPEAN DREAM FADES AWAY

Europe will become less important. It will still be objectively one of the best places on the planet to live, at least for the majority of its people. It will be reasonably wealthy, calm and secure. It will remain attractive to migrants of every level – the highly skilled and the less highly skilled – and it will feel its way towards a more comfortable association of nation states than the current form of the European Union. But what happens in Europe will matter less to the rest of the world, for its population will shrink in absolute terms and its economy in relative terms. Accepting this retreat will be difficult for ambitious Europeans who feel their continent could do so much better, and parts of Europe will remain cutting-edge in their knowledge industries. But the continent as a whole will become more a museum of achievements of the past and less a laboratory of ideas for the future.

If this seems a dismal outlook, it need not be seen as such. There is nothing wrong with societies that enjoy settled, quiet comfort. Japan gives the world a glimpse of that outcome. By 2050 Europe will have a similar age structure to Japan in 2020, and will face similar pressures looking after its elderly citizens. There are, however, three ways in which Europe will differ. Huge cultural differences will remain between north and south, between parts of the continent that have accepted large numbers of migrants and parts that have resisted immigration, and between the Anglophone regions and the rest. None of these characteristics of Europe apply to Japan. It is and will remain a homogenous society, whereas Europe is fragmented and likely to become more so.

We'll come to the likely performance of the various parts of the continent in a moment. First, a word about Europe in general. In economic terms Europe has been pulling in different directions since the beginning of the twenty-first century. Until then there was a general convergence. The southern flank – Spain, Italy, Greece – had been closing the gap with the countries to the north, while the Central and Eastern European nations that had joined the EU were closing the gap with Western Europe as a whole. However, since 2000, while the convergence between east and west has continued, the gap between north and south has widened. Italy has stagnated, while Germany has marched forward.

It is easy to explain why the countries of Eastern and Central Europe could narrow the gap with richer Western Europe. It was partly catch-up, as they escaped from the inefficiencies of the communist system and made the initially painful transformation to market economies. And it was partly membership of the EU, which gave free access to richer countries of the West and encouraged inward investment to take advantage of that access.

It is harder to explain what has happened between north and south. There is the caricature of the frugal north and the happy-go-lucky south, with one saving and investing wisely while the other wastes the money and opportunities it has been given. There is usually some truth behind caricatures. It would be silly not to acknowledge that the levels of corruption that exist in Spain, Italy and Greece are higher than those of the Netherlands, Germany or Scandinavia.[1] But that does not explain why in 2000 Italy's GDP per head was roughly the same as that of Germany, whereas by 2020 it was 30 per cent lower. Something else seems to have gone wrong.

We are too close to that period to have a conclusive explanation, but the underperformance seems to have become more serious after the introduction of the euro. The currency union, introduced without a corresponding fiscal union, set a single interest rate for all the countries that signed up to it. But different economies have different structures and need different interest rates. Until the financial crisis of 2008 this did not matter much. Indeed, Southern European nations benefited because they could borrow more cheaply than they would have been able to do had they retained their own currencies. But the crisis forced severe austerity on the south (and on Ireland) and there was no compensating transfer of funds from the north. Instead of pulling the European economies together it drove them apart.

This view is only partly accepted across the EU, and suggestions from Britons or Americans that the eurozone has to break up are not well received in Brussels, Paris or Berlin. (The argument carries more sway in Milan and Rome.) But understanding the paradox that a device designed to bring European nations together, the common currency, has had the effect of driving them apart is central to understanding what is likely to happen to the European project.

For its first half-century, from the Treaty of Rome in 1956 to the financial crisis of 2008, the European Union and its predecessors were on balance a considerable success. For its second half-century, through to 2050 and beyond, it will on balance be a sad failure.

Something called the European Union will in all probability exist in 2050, but it will be a looser association of independent states, rather than the 'ever-closer union' envisaged by its creators. The path will be a bumpy one. Until the 2008 crisis there had been no serious setbacks. Then came two serious reverses.

One was the debt crisis and the near collapse of the euro in 2012. The euro was saved but at the cost of great hardship in the most indebted countries, particularly in Greece, and a rise in questioning of the value of EU membership, particularly in Italy. The glue holding Italy in the union has been weakened.

The other was the decision of the UK to leave, which it finally did in 2020. You can have an argument as to whether this was a wise decision, or indeed an inevitable one. But there can be no argument as to whether losing your second most populous member, second largest economy and second largest contributor to your budget can be regarded from an EU perspective as anything other than a failure.

It is likely that there will be more reverses but, meanwhile, those two issues, eurozone imbalances and Brexit, will hang over the EU. The rigidities of the euro remain. It may be that sufficient reforms can be brought in to secure the currency's future for some years yet, but the costs of doing so would be high. It would require the more prosperous north to subsidise the south to a much greater extent than it has to date. In practice it is the creditworthiness of Germany that stands behind the euro, and hence enables weaker countries to borrow at lower rates than they would otherwise be able to do. There is no direct transfer of taxpayers' funds across the national boundaries. At some stage – and it is hard to predict either the timing or the circumstances – that support will have to become more explicit.[2] That will be a moment of peril for the union.

As for the fallout from Brexit, the more successful the UK is outside the EU the greater the awareness that leaving might create new economic opportunities if a country were, for whatever reasons, to make that political choice. In other words, the fact that the UK has left does not of itself encourage others to do so; given the economic disruption, quite possibly the reverse. But it does show a path which other countries may choose to tread if they too feel that the costs of membership are greater than the benefits.

So what will Europe look like in 2050? It is important to distinguish between the likely form of the European Union and what happens to the continent of Europe as a whole. There will be no final form for Europe. The EU is merely one experiment in a political association that has changed massively over the past and will evolve further in the future. It was a natural and appropriate reaction to the excessive nationalism of the dreadful first half of the twentieth century, but by 2050 it will, so to speak, have done the job.

Getting from here to there, against a background of declining economic importance and ageing populations, will not be easy. Some dissent will come from the east. Nationalism, always lurking in the background, will periodically break out. That may push some

countries to maintain social policies that are deemed unacceptable
by the EU, which in turn may encourage them to leave. Some
Eastern European members may feel increasingly uncomfortable
with the ideology of the EU, which is mostly that of Western
Europe. Other sources of pressure will come from Scandinavia. Two
countries, Iceland and Norway, chose not to join the EU and have
prospered outside it. So there is a model for Sweden, Finland and
Denmark should they choose that route. Or, as suggested above,
the dissent may bubble up in the south, from Italy and Greece,
maybe Spain and Portugal.

And the most likely outcome? There will be no final form for the
EU because whatever the situation is in 2050, it is certain that it will
take on a different form by 2100. One obvious path would be for
the EU to split into a core of countries that are happy with closer
ties and an outer ring that will prefer to be associate members. One
version of this idea, a Continental Partnership, was sketched in
a paper[3] published in 2016 by the Bruegel Institute, a think-tank
based in Brussels. The vision was for a partnership between the UK
and the EU that would allow the two to cooperate on core issues
without the constraints of full membership. This could be attractive
for other countries such as Turkey and conceivably Ukraine. What
was not envisaged was that this might also be attractive to other
full members of the EU who might wish to leave. In the event,
the negotiations between the UK and EU were too ill-tempered to
reach such a partnership, but the model remains.

Actually, the UK and the EU will probably cooperate more
closely over the next thirty years than seemed likely in 2020.
Writing in 2021 as the formal rift has passed into law, it is easy to
be overly influenced by the acrimony of the divorce. On a longer
view UK membership of what became the European Union will
seem a blip – an experiment that lasted less than half a century,
an arrangement that might have worked but didn't. Both sides
will find there are areas where they can successfully work together,
including combating crime and improving public health outcomes.
The crucial point here is that decisions will be taken by Europe,
with the UK having zero influence over them.

Outer ring and inner core is one possibility. A second would be to scramble through to a steady state. The EU would manage to strengthen the glue holding it together and reach a level of cohesion that members were satisfied with, and stop further integration there. The argument against this being achieved is that without the goal of ever-closer union this steady state would actually be unsustainable, as some countries would want to press on and others stay still. So it might actually lead to a core/periphery split on the lines above. But managed carefully, it might work for a while, at least through to 2050.

A third possibility is the big bang – the end of the EU as such and it becoming a union in name only. There are several ways in which this might happen. Maybe the trigger would be the collapse of the euro, with one or more countries defaulting on their sovereign debt and setting up national currencies instead. Maybe mass population movements between different members would lead to some putting up barriers to citizenship, a *de facto* independence from the EU. Maybe mass unemployment in weaker countries would lead to a populist revolution with Brussels seen as the common enemy. Were Italy to leave, the game would be over.

Yet another future for the EU might be somewhere between steady state and big bang: a gradual whittling away of the ever-closer union aim into an acceptance that this was a concept for a time long past. It was to make sure that European nations would never go to war again. In 1950 that was a reasonable concern and a noble cause. During the Cold War and Russia's domination of Eastern Europe that concern remained. After the fall of the Berlin Wall, war in the Balkans rekindled these worries. But by 2000 and certainly by 2020 the very idea of battles for territory in Central and Western Europe had come to seem absurd. There were grave external threats, as Russia's invasion of the Crimean peninsula showed, but there were no internal ones. But the EU was unable to protect its members against external threats. Only NATO, with the might of the US behind it, could do that. The EU model had served its purpose of stopping the possibility of internal warfare between its members, but it was useless against the external threats the continent continued to face. Something else will be needed.

Maybe the attack on Ukraine will pull Europe together, but I think more likely that 'something else' will be the reverse: a looser association, where countries come together when there is a high degree of agreement on what is to be done. This would allow countries to diverge where there is no common view, without divergence becoming a source of tension. Instead of countries seeking the highest degree of cooperation possible, with all the anguish that quest has generated, they would seek the lowest level of cooperation needed for common goals, such as defence and energy security.

For the enthusiasts for the EU model this will seem a dull, lacklustre, utilitarian vision for Europe. But it reflects the reality of different nation states with different ideas of how their societies should be organised. It also reflects the truth that Europe as a whole will inevitably become even less important in 2050 than it is in 2020, and that there are some issues, including immigration, that can only be decided at a national level despite all efforts to form a Europe-wide policy. That the continent should somehow be less than the sum of its parts will trouble many of its citizens. But people have to be comfortable with each other and secure in their different cultures and histories. That means an ever-changing patchwork, and that is just fine.

How will the individual nations cope with this prospect? Well, some will do better than others.

BRITAIN AND IRELAND – A TROUBLED PATH TO A SOLID FUTURE

The British Isles will have a difficult ten years, maybe longer, before they reach a more settled future. But by 2050 the UK will be more confident, more outward-looking and more prosperous as part of a family of nations linked by language and history – the Anglosphere. This will not be any formal group, simply a reflection of the likelihood that culture and language will become a more important glue holding people together than physical proximity.

The idea that there should be a group of countries that think of themselves as linked in this way might seem a romantic illusion: perhaps as a harking back to Britain's imperial past, or an alternative role that it might play in the world after leaving the European Union. At the moment the main specific area where the Anglosphere cooperates is intelligence, the Five Eyes of the US, the UK, Canada, Australia and New Zealand. The agreement dates back to the Atlantic Charter in August 1941, so preceded the entry of the US into the Second World War.[4] It is not really a basis for any wider cooperation, nor was it ever intended to be, though expansion was discussed in 2019. In that sense it is quite unlike the European Coal and Steel Community, founded in 1952 as a precursor to what became the European Union. It survives because it is useful, a bottom-up agreement rather than a top-down vision.

How the Anglosphere is likely to evolve into a wider informal grouping, to include India, Scandinavia, Singapore and much of Africa, is discussed in the final section of this book. The point to make here is that while the UK feels its way towards a new relationship with the rest of the world, having abandoned the forty-seven-year experiment of being a member of the European Union, the unifying factors of language and culture will ease its path. It is always difficult to admit failure. Membership of the EU has been a failure. Questions such as whether it need have been and whether leaving was a mistake are irrelevant. The very fact that the country made the democratic choice to leave, against the advice of the government of the day and the main opposition parties, shows the experiment had failed.

The scars from that experiment and from the humiliation of the country's leadership will take time to heal. For parts of the UK that voted to remain in the EU, notably Scotland, the healing process will be particularly difficult. For some sectors across the UK, notably the universities and much of the business elite, it will be difficult, too. And the fact that younger people on balance voted to remain while older ones voted to leave will exacerbate the tensions that already existed between the age groups. The lack of tolerance towards people of a different opinion – a global phenomenon – will make matters worse.

Perhaps the best way to see what has happened is, in the phrase of Helen Thompson, professor of political economy at Cambridge University,[5] that the UK has gone through 'a constitutional ordeal' for which it was ill-prepared. It will take at least a decade of confusion before a more settled period can emerge. The difficult issues are not so much about the relationship with Europe, which is likely to be a gradual disengagement. That will obviously happen for the various parts of the UK but more surprisingly for many Irish people, the Republic of Ireland will also find itself trading less with Europe and more with the US and the UK. The real challenges will come over the relationships within the UK and between Britain and the island of Ireland.

The more successful the economies of Britain and Ireland, the easier it will be to manage the political relations. Here it is possible to be quite optimistic. There will be a transition, brisk in the case of the UK, more gradual in the case of Ireland, as both economies realign. The 2020s will be particularly disruptive for the UK as trade switches away from Europe, but by the end of the decade new trade patterns will be established with exports to the EU accounting for some 20 per cent of the total, as opposed to a little over 40 per cent in 2020. The UK's population will continue to grow with immigration from the rest of the English-speaking world including Hong Kong, offsetting a decline in migrants arriving from Europe. Migrants will help drive economic growth, particularly from 2030 onwards, so that by 2050 the UK (assuming it retains its present form) will be approaching Germany both in population and in economic size. It is conceivable that the combination of growth of the workforce and strength in parts of the economy that produce goods and services in global demand will lead the UK to become Europe's biggest economy.

For that to happen several things have to go right. Some of these relate to the UK's place in the world after leaving the EU. Obviously it has to remain open to immigration. The intriguing challenge it will have is to use Brexit as a way of attracting migrants that boost the economy. It has to extend its close relationship with the US in diplomacy, security and defence into an equally cooperative relationship in economics. It also has to foster trade relations with Canada, Australia and New Zealand, and, crucially, India. And it has to be useful to both the US in its battle for rivalry with China, and to China in giving a welcome base for legitimate commercial expansion.

Two other things have to go right. It has to find ways to support the areas of global competition where it has a comparative advantage. These include finance, pharmaceuticals, education, the creative industries and high-end manufacturing. It has also to find ways of rebalancing economic growth, bringing the regions closer to the levels of wealth and productivity of London and its hinterland.

All this is easy to write. Can it be done? There should, I suggest, be a broad overarching aim. That is that the UK should see itself as trying to be useful to the world – in other words helping the world cope better with the tensions and troubles it faces. It could become the second member of the Anglosphere, junior to the US but in many ways more outward-looking. It could from that position help the English-speaking world through a difficult period. To do so successfully it must acknowledge that there are several areas where it must raise its game.

One is that it has to dump any residual arrogance about the country's special place in the world. The UK should think of itself more as a big Switzerland, not a small United States. It has to recognise that many of its public services, including healthcare, are not good enough. It has to widen educational opportunity and achievement. It has to grasp the benefits of substantial immigration, and accept that this will mean a society where the rules are defined more by law and less by custom.

This all seems a daunting to-do list. But all developed countries face similar challenges, and the UK is better placed than most. So a reasonable assessment is that by 2050 it will have found a more comfortable place in the world than seemed likely in 2020. It will have forged a secure working relationship with both continental

Europe and the US, and a useful one with India. But all this is predicated on two things: it continues to look outward and it holds together as a nation. They go together. Looking outward will bolster economic success, while economic success will bolster the union.

On balance, the probability is that the UK will still continue as an entity in 2050. But the union between England and Wales on the one hand, and Scotland and Northern Ireland on the other, will become a looser, more federal association. The relationship between England and Wales is reasonably stable and will remain so. Wales will achieve a greater degree of autonomy within the union, as, indeed, will the regions within England. But whatever happens to the relationship with Scotland and Ireland, England and Wales will remain a political entity.

The outcome for Scotland is much less clear. Back in the early 1990s it seemed quite possible that by 2020 Scotland would have chosen and achieved independence. That did not happen, for the 'once in a generation' referendum of 2014 rejected it, with 44.7 per cent in favour of independence and 55.3 per cent against. The pressures from Scotland have ebbed and flowed and will continue to do so. There will almost certainly be a further referendum long before 2050. It is impossible to call the outcome of that, though on balance it is more likely that the union will be retained. But referendums are capricious. The decision by the UK to leave the EU might have gone the other way. Remember that Canada came close to breaking up, with two referendums on independence for Quebec in 1980 and 1995. The first was clearly lost with 40.44 per cent versus 59.56 per cent, but the second was very tight: 49.42 per cent versus 50.58 per cent. The loss first time did not deter the separatists from trying again. Expect Scottish nationalists to follow the Quebec pattern: keep trying.

There will have to be some form of constitutional reform for the UK by 2050. The most likely single outcome would be for the UK to remain as a union, but with some form of 'home rule' for Scotland rather on the lines proposed for Ireland in the late nineteenth and early twentieth centuries, and adopted in some measure for Northern Ireland. Open questions would include these. How many representatives would Scotland send to Westminster? Certainly fewer and maybe none. How much power would it have over taxation and spending? Probably complete control over most taxation, though not VAT, and full control over domestic spending. Would Scotland remain within the union for defence and diplomacy? Almost certainly yes. Would there still be a common travel area between the different parts of the British Isles on the lines of the common travel area between Ireland and the UK so that Scottish people could still live and work in England and vice versa? Certainly yes.

Not complete independence? Such an outcome would be extremely divisive within Scotland, all the more so if the majority in favour were slim. Some parts, such as the Shetland and Orkney islands, might seek separate status akin to that of the Channel Islands and the Isle of Man. There would almost certainly be some movement of population to the south. While an independent Scotland could exist as a perfectly viable state, the transition to independence would be a very difficult one and the outcome might well not be stable, for the unionist movement would remain strong. In short, there is likely in 2050 to be some sort of halfway house between complete Scottish independence and the present partially devolved government. However, history has taught us that more extreme outcomes, either way, are quite possible.

The relationship between Britain and Ireland is even harder to call. The direction of demography in Northern Ireland would suggest that Ireland is likely to be unified, with the minority Catholic and broadly Nationalist community in the north overtaking the majority Protestant and broadly Unionist one some time in the 2020s. The possibility that there might be a majority in favour of unification is provided for in the Good Friday Agreement of 1998.[6] But it is altogether too mechanical (and rather insulting to both communities) to equate religion with tribal identity or political intent. By 2050 there may be a majority for a unified Ireland, but there may also very well not be one. The polls suggest there wasn't in 2020, despite the tensions over Brexit and the underlying threat to the Good Friday Agreement. That will probably have to be redrawn to take into account the change in the relationships post-Brexit, but there is no underlying reason why it should fall apart. The EU had only a minor role in the negotiations that led to the Agreement, much more limited than that of the United States and Canada. While the UK leaving the EU has created practical difficulties in cross-border trade, with goodwill these can be resolved. By 2050 this bumpy time will be a memory.

The economic challenge for Ireland, north and south, is to get from here to there. The economic outlook is easy to sketch, for there will be a gradual shift away from trade with Europe and towards the rest of the world, particularly the English-speaking world. For the Republic this will be more difficult, for it has prospered as an entry point to the EU for US firms. It has created a clever corporate tax structure to encourage this, but equally can offer a well-educated, youthful labour force and a common law environment for inward investors. But Europe will inevitably be a slow-growth region. The two largest export markets for Irish goods are the US and the UK, and it is quite possible that, by about 2040, European trade will account for a quarter or less of the Republic's trade. What will Ireland do?

There is within Ireland a mainstream view and a minority one. The mainstream view is that Ireland has made a choice to define itself as a loyal member of the EU, that this has brought great benefits both in economic and in political terms, and will continue to do so. The model has done well: why change it?

The minority view, unpopular in official circles in Dublin, is that Ireland has made a strategic error and that its future will be best served if it leaves the EU and focuses on its relationship with the Anglosphere. The most forthright exponent of this view is a senior retired civil servant, the former ambassador to Canada Ray Bassett.[7] In *Ireland and the EU Post Brexit* he argues that if you look at the data, the country has very little relationship with Europe and an intimate one with the Anglosphere. Quite aside from investment and trade, both dominated by the US and the UK, if you look at what Irish people actually do, they choose the English-speaking world. Thus the UN Migration report notes there were

600,000 Irish-born people living in the UK in 2013 and 144,000 in the US, but only 10,000 in France and 17,500 in Spain.

Writing in the aftermath of Brexit it is almost unthinkable to suggest that by 2050 Ireland will have left the EU. The Brexit negotiations saw Ireland align with Europe, and from a British perspective take a hostile line against the UK. But the economic logic for Irish EU membership will shift adversely over time, and the emotional mood may well shift, too. If the EU does fragment into a core and a periphery, then Ireland would obviously be more comfortable being part of the periphery – geographical location would be supported by economic argument. If the Nordics were to leave the EU altogether Ireland would surely follow. And if the US were to take an increasingly antagonistic stance against whatever was left of the EU, and the UK were to join with the US in a North Atlantic Free Trade Area, then Ireland would have little choice but to switch to the Anglosphere.

This can all go wrong. The people of Britain and Ireland may continue to allow what the writer and politician Conor Cruise O'Brien called the 'ancestral voices'[8] to disrupt relations not only within the island of Ireland but also between Britain and Ireland, and between England and Scotland, too. Writing as someone who is part-Scottish, part-English and brought up mostly in the Republic of Ireland, this would seem to me to be a dreadful twisting of the richness of our different heritages. Fortunately, the overwhelming probability is that by 2050 the ancestral voices will have become an even more distant echo, and that the people of these islands will be devoting their energy to the opportunities of the present rather than the conflicts of the past. If that is right, then by the 2050s these islands will be more harmonious societies than they have been for much of the past 200 years.

GERMANY AND THE BENELUX NATIONS – THE CORE OF A SMALLER EUROPE

The years to 2050 will be a period of modest success for Germany, for the core strengths of its economy and political society will carry it through what will inevitably be a difficult period. It will retain its dominant position as the largest continental European economy, approximately the same size as that of the UK. It will remain wealthy. But it will be facing three great challenges. The great social challenge for Germany will be to integrate successfully its new immigrant population. The great economic challenge will be to develop new activities to replace the manufacturing activities that will be lost, given that it will have a falling population. And the great diplomatic challenge will be to lead the European Union towards a looser group of cooperating nation states and away from the Brussels vision of an ever-closer union. Some thoughts about each.

The social challenge will be to ensure that immigration successfully offsets the natural decline in the population and the sharper projected decline in the size of the workforce. By 2050 the wave of refugees that arrived largely from the Middle East from 2014 to 2019 will be middle-aged or elderly, and it will be their children who will be helping drive the economy. Assuming that there will be some continued immigration and that the fertility rates of the new immigrants remain somewhat higher than those of the traditional German families, it is plausible that by 2050 people of an immigrant background will comprise somewhere between one-quarter and one-third of the workforce. Despite this, that workforce will be shrinking. So issues such as education, training and access to capital become enormously important. There is no reason why these 'new Germans' should not be as skilled and productive as the 'old Germans'. The point is simply that if the country is to continue to be Europe's economic powerhouse they have to be.

Immigration has been massively contentious in German politics and will continue to be so through the 2020s and 2030s. There has been an enormous and understandable focus on the difficulties of social integration of people who come from a different culture and do not, at least to start with, speak German – despite the contribution of the post-war 'guest workers', most of whom came from Turkey. There has been much less focus on the long-term impact on the economy and on society. Germany will change as a result of the surge in immigration.[9] For a start its population will fall more slowly than it otherwise would. It will grow more rapidly, certainly in overall size, hopefully in output per head. And it would be surprising if there were not some cultural impact, too. By 2050 the debate will have settled down. At some stage before then it is highly likely that Germany will have been led by a government with an anti-immigrant platform, a prospect that would trouble most current mainstream politicians. But that may be helpful in enabling the country to accept that it has become a different place from its old self-image. Countries change, Germany more than most in its rather wonderful transformation to a liberal democracy from the late 1940s onwards. It will change again as its new workforce helps it to cope with a different global economy.

The starting place for the economic challenge is an enviable one. As we saw in Chapter 1 Germany is the world's leading manufacturing nation, particularly in automotive engineering but also in many other sectors including chemicals, machine tools and medical equipment. One problem is that the portion of global consumption devoted to manufactured goods is shrinking inexorably and will continue to do so. Another is that if there is a retreat from globalisation, the trend will be to make products nearer home. Germany, the greatest exporter of manufactured goods, will inevitably suffer. In addition, the markets on its doorstep, the rest of the EU, will be slow growing. Yet another challenge is that the country has been slow to develop new industries to take over the baton from its established commercial giants.

Anyone who has observed and admired the excellence of many aspects of the German economy would have confidence in its ability to tackle these problems. The nation's finances are stronger than those of most other developed economies and its citizens are savers. But the country will be butting into economic headwinds for the next thirty years. It will need all the resilience of its business community to maintain and increase the living standards of its people.

If it fails to increase living standards its diplomatic difficulties will loom all the larger. Germany is the paymaster of Europe. It has long been the largest net contributor to the EU budget, larger even than the UK, but its support for the rest of continental Europe goes far beyond that. It is the anchor of the euro, the de facto guarantor of the eurozone's sovereign debts. Provided that the rest of the European Union is modestly successful, Germany will be prepared to carry on with that burden for a while yet. But whatever the form of the union in 2050, assuming it does still exist in more than name, there will be a moment, probably in the 2030s, when the burden of supporting the EU becomes too great for the German people to bear. Germany will go on paying, until it doesn't.

Some event or series of events will trigger this decision. It could be a surge in inflation. The European Central Bank might refuse to increase interest rates enough to curb price rises for fear of forcing Italy to default. In that case Germany would withdraw from the euro and reinstate the German mark. Or it could be the need for mounting annual payments into the EU budget. If Germany's net payments, running at around 0.5 per cent of GDP a year in 2020, were to rise to 1 per cent a year, that might appear acceptable if German growth were 2 per cent. But if growth were to slow it is conceivable that the country might find all of its annual increase in wealth going to support the rest of the EU. Or there might be some external shock akin to the global Covid-19 pandemic that gravely damages the financial position of Europe, and that will force a rupture in its already weak economies.

Germany will face other diplomatic challenges, particularly over its relationship with Russia. But its key task will be to remain the anchor of Europe. While it remains Europe's largest and most solid economy it will retain its authority to shape the region as it chooses. France has huge influence on the political landscape of Europe as we shall acknowledge in a moment, but ultimately it is the German economy and German finance that will determine the EU's fate.

And that, too, will determine what happens to Belgium, the Netherlands and Luxembourg. If the EU survives in some form, the Belgian economy will be sustained by its European role, though the long-standing tensions between French and Flemish speakers will remain. The Netherlands will be buoyed up by whatever success Germany has in transforming its economy away from manufacturing and into services, for it is an adjunct of the German economy. While Germany remains a strong supporter of the EU the Netherlands will, too, though it is likely to resent the rising cost of membership. If the Northern European economy is adequately strong, the country that has its largest seaport and its second largest airport cannot but benefit. However, if Europe's economy and in particular its exports falter, as at some stage over the next thirty years is quite likely, then the Netherlands will suffer relative decline. As for Luxembourg, as the richest nation on earth thanks to its role as a financial entrepôt centre, the future of the EU is crucial to its prosperity. However, the Luxembourg leadership would surely be nimble enough to find new clients for its financial services were European markets to become more restricted. Luxembourg will no longer be the richest nation on earth in thirty years, but it will be just fine.

FRANCE – THE TROUBLED BEAUTY

France will always be France. By 2050 its cultural power and its ambitions for influence will be as great as ever, though its role both in Europe and in the world will shine less brightly. In economic terms it will still be a global leader, perhaps the leader in luxury goods. In political terms it will seek to continue to use the EU as a platform for projecting its influence within Europe, and the French-language group of countries, La Francophonie,[10] for projecting influence to the rest of the world. It will remain a significant military power. Paris will still be one of the great cities of the planet. Above all, France will continue to offer its people one of the most enviable lifestyles on earth.

If all this sounds a little too good to be true, it is. The strengths noted above are all valid, but there are also several difficulties that the country will struggle to overcome. One will be that its loss of competitiveness in manufacturing, evident in the early part of the twenty-first century, will become a more serious drag on the economy. Another will be the fragility of its public finances. The huge public sector, the largest relative to GDP of any major economy in the world, provides good services, but the burden on it will increase as the French population ages. Revenues will stall with the plateau in the numbers of people at work, even though the total population continues to climb. The transformation of the European Union into some sort of looser federation will undermine French self-confidence as the joint leader, along with Germany, of the continent of Europe. If the EU were to break up in bitter rancour, France would be particularly exposed. Germany's financial strength will protect it. The UK will by 2050 have rethought its place in the world, accepting that its future is within the Anglosphere. La Francophonie does not offer France a similar option. It is helpful to France in cultural terms but too small in economic terms to matter.

France has to confront a further difficulty, similar in some ways to that faced by Germany. It has to integrate its immigrant population so that they become a more powerful driver of growth. No one should underrate France's ability to do this, once its political leadership makes the decision to do so. But it is a huge task – and it will have to be done alongside the reconfiguring of the role of the state. Successive governments have attempted substantial financial and economic reforms, but have been pushed back. What on the surface appears to be a powerful centre has to cope with a deeply conservative, hard-to-move mass of voters. Change is difficult in France.

So France will have a bumpy ride through the next thirty years. Social tensions are already evident and will get worse. There will be more riots in the streets. It is highly likely that at some stage France will have a right-wing government, perhaps the National Front or some development of it, perhaps a new political grouping. Paradoxically, it may be better at integrating the immigrant communities than the more liberal governments of the past decades. But whoever does it, the job has to be done. The French writer Jean Fourastié coined the phrase *Les Trente Glorieuses* as the title of his 1979 book describing the thirty-year period from the end of the Second World War to 1975.¹¹ It was one of huge political upheaval, with the creation and fall of the Fourth Republic (which had twenty-one prime ministers in ten years), and the return of General de Gaulle to lead the Fifth Republic in 1958. But despite the politics and despite the loss of the colonies, including Algeria, in economic terms it was a period of steady and impressive progress as France managed to catch up with the rest of Europe after the devastation of war. The coming thirty years will not be glorious, but if France can do three things – come to terms with the decline of the EU, cut back the size of the state and give a better deal to immigrants – then they will be thirty years of decent progress, too.

ITALY – THE QUEST FOR LEADERSHIP

Can Italy hold together? And will Italy leave the European Union?

These are such enormous questions, both of which vex many Italians, that it seems presumptive for a non-Italian writer to claim to be able to answer either in any convincing way. To suggest that it might split into two countries would seem to many people outrageous, even absurd. But if the past fifty years have taught us anything it is that the seemingly settled constitutional arrangements of one era can be overturned in a flash. After the collapse of the Soviet Union's empire, Czechoslovakia split amicably into the Czech Republic, now called Czechia, and Slovakia. Yugoslavia, sadly much less amicably, broke up in a series of conflicts, the scars of which the region still bears today. As for leaving the EU, Italy was one of the key founder members, and to leave would be a far bigger signal of the EU's failure than the loss of the UK.

Both are hotly debated, and writing in 2021 both might seem realistic probabilities. There is great tension between north and south and some opinion polls suggest a majority in favour of leaving the EU. Yet while both outcomes are conceivable, it is important to be cautious in predicting them. The cultural glue holding Italy together would take a lot to break, and the EU will strive to keep Italy on board in a way that it was not really interested in doing in the case of the UK. Besides, leaving the EU would not really help.

A currency devaluation – via a two-tier euro perhaps – would bring economic benefits and that might in turn lead to a partial breakup of the EU. But that outcome would, so to speak, be a by-product of Italy's financial weakness, rather than Italy making the decision to leave for economic reasons.

The great challenge to Italy is its demography. How does it increase its birth rate and how does it stop its young people leaving? It is one of the fastest-shrinking countries in the world. While it is mathematically possible that it could rebuild its population by immigration, and while there are certainly millions of people, mostly from North Africa, who would like to migrate, it is unlikely. The country would need to take at least five million immigrants, maybe more, to maintain the population at the 2020 level of sixty million. It is hard to see that taking place without huge social and political tension.

So what will happen? Italy has to improve the quality of its administration. There will be great populist pressure for a strong leader, someone who will do so – who will, like Benito Mussolini, 'make the trains run on time'. That could even be his grand-daughter Alessandra or his great-grandson Caio, for both have political careers. But on a thirty-year view it is impossible to predict the personalities of the next generation of political leaders. My point is simply that some event or series of events will happen that will push Italy into electing a strong populist leader. That will in all probability happen within the political system. This is not a prediction of a coup. Whether that leader is effective in changing the way the country truly works will determine whether Italy is a contented and stable democracy in 2050, or something more unsettled and troubling.

THE IBERIAN PENINSULA – LOOKING WEST AS WELL AS EAST

Both Spain and Portugal will face headwinds over the next thirty years, for both face a decline in population of around 10 per cent, a similar order of magnitude to Italy. But the prospects for Portugal, smaller and poorer than Spain, are likely to turn out to be brighter than those for its larger neighbour. There are several reasons why. These include Spain's overdependence on tourism and tensions over the status of Catalonia, and, as noted in Chapter 1, Portugal's particular advantage of being the entry point to Europe for Brazil. Spanish-speaking Latin America does not bring a similar benefit to Spain.

There is also the possibility that Portugal will be better governed than Spain over the next thirty years. That might seem a harsh comment on Spain and perhaps it is. But political preoccupations of successive governments have been to focus on matters of territory rather than quality of governance. The issues here are the status of Catalonia and the Basque region, obviously, but also of Gibraltar and the two Spanish enclaves in North Africa, the cities of Ceuta and Melilla. The better the quality of governance that Spain can offer Catalonia, the less the pressure for the latter to secede. As for the Basque country, some form of federal relationship for Catalonia would be a trigger for a new attempt at full sovereignty by the Basque people. On Gibraltar, it would be more sensible for Spain to see it as a useful economic partner for one of its poorer regions, rather than an issue of great national pride. The dispute over Gibraltar will continue to sour relations with the UK for the foreseeable future. With regard to the two enclaves in Africa, Morocco, while seeking to gain control of Ceuta and Melilla, currently does not have much leverage in the dispute. But that will gradually increase as it closes the gap with Spain in terms of population, passing Spain around 2050, and narrowing the gap in GDP, too.

The real challenge for Spain will be how to use its scarce young people better: what to do about youth unemployment and how to stop its best and brightest leaving. It will struggle to meet the challenge, with the result that there is likely to be some kind of rupture in Spanish governance long before 2050. This could take the form of the evolution of the 1978 constitution to something less rigid, or it could go in the other direction to a more authoritarian system, though of course not to another General Franco. Either way, it will be bumpy.

By contrast, Portugal may become calmer. As noted above, it is a key entry point into the EU for Brazil, but, more than that, the Portuguese leadership understands the need to look outwards from Europe as well as playing its part within it. It will seek to become more of a magnet for both capital and talent from the rest of the world. If successful, it will cease to be one of the poorer countries of Western Europe and gain greater global influence. Portugal is a small country and will have to work hard to offer better attractions to its own people to slow the decline in population. But it has an interesting hand to play, and, if played skilfully, the next thirty years could be a period of modest success.

SCANDINAVIA AND SWITZERLAND – CALM PROSPERITY

The five main Nordic countries – Sweden, Denmark, Finland, Norway and Iceland – will continue to be prosperous and secure in 2050. So, too, will Switzerland, grouped here with the Nordic lands because, though physically separate from them, its world vision is broadly similar. These countries all deal with Europe because physical proximity does matter, and three are members of the EU. But they have never been part of the European project, the ever-closer union. Rather, they are all natural members of the European Free Trade Area, and Switzerland, Norway and Iceland still are.

They will continue to be envied for the quality of their governance, their decency and their quality of life. The EU members will gradually disengage from Europe and look outwards to the world beyond. That will be an easy process for Norway and Iceland, as they decided not to join in the first place. It will be more difficult for Finland since it adopted the euro as its currency, and for Denmark as its economy is more closely linked with the rest of continental Europe. As for Switzerland, it will continue in its idiosyncratic way to be an island of individualism, sometimes cussed but always canny, staunch and ultimately successful.

All will, in their different ways, gradually find themselves slipping away from the core of Europe, even if that idea seems strange for landlocked Switzerland.[12] The common theme will be economic imperative: their largest markets will be outside the EU, so they will have to adopt the standards of those markets rather than those of the EU. This would have happened anyway but the decision of the UK to leave the EU will speed this gradual disengagement. There probably will not be a sudden rupture, because there won't need to be one. Scandinavia and Switzerland will simply be part of the outer ring of Europe, whatever happens elsewhere. There will be bumps, for example were Finland to drop the euro and revert to its own currency. The broad direction of Scandinavia will be to move towards becoming de facto members of the Anglosphere, trading more with the US and UK and less with continental Europe. As for Switzerland, it will look more to the emerging world, building on the fact that already in 2019 its largest export market was China and its third largest India.

The tough question is whether any of this matters. The combined population of the Nordic countries and Switzerland is some thirty-six million. By 2050 it will be about the same, half that of the UK, France or Germany. However, the importance of these countries to the world goes far beyond their economic size. They matter because they are all in different ways beacons of excellence. They are not perfect; no community of human beings ever could be. But if you want a snapshot of how prosperous, well-ordered, socially and environmentally responsible societies should look, this is a good place to start. They will continue to be serene islands in a stormy world.

CENTRAL AND EASTERN EUROPE – LOOKING TO RUSSIA AS WELL AS THE WEST

It may seem monstrous to lump together the arc of countries that stretch east of what Winston Churchill memorably called the Iron Curtain from the Baltic to the Mediterranean. In many ways it is. They are different in so many ways: religion, culture, economic development, ideas of how societies should be ordered and so on. But there is a common theme. With the exceptions of Austria and Greece they were all members or associate members of Comecon, the Soviet Union's brief Eastern European empire. The economic fallout from that period is described in Chapter 1. Comecon broke up in 1991, so we are already thirty years on. By 2050 we will be another thirty years ahead. Yet that legacy seems stronger now than at any period since 1991, for a yearning for more authoritarian governance is evident across many of these countries. This is now grounded in democratic support rather than being imposed by a foreign power, but that legitimacy gives it all the more drive. Expect the mood to swing, but on balance it is more likely to stiffen in the three decades to 2050.

Much will depend on Russia. The more successful Russia is perceived as being, the more Central and Eastern Europe will be drawn towards it. It is most unlikely that Russia will seek to reimpose its empire by force, though there is an awkward question as to where the real border of NATO really is. Would NATO defend Germany from a Russian attack? Absolutely. Would it defend Poland? Almost certainly yes. What about the Baltic states of Estonia, Latvia and Lithuania? It is not a thought that is welcome in polite company, but maybe not. This is not to suggest that Russia is likely to invade the Baltic states, as it did Ukraine, though that cannot be completely ruled out. More likely, it will seek to increase its influence over them using the Russian-speaking minorities as a lever. Sometimes it will be successful in doing so.

Geography matters. The continent of Europe has to live with Russia, and those parts closest to it will have to acknowledge that. There will be a tug of war between the attractions of the wealth and liberal ideas of Western Europe on the one hand and the no-nonsense populist ideology of Russia on the other. If this were a straight fight, an either/or situation, of course the West would win. The EU's relative economic weight in the world will decline, but Russia's will decline faster. Indeed, by 2050 Russia is likely to be a smaller economy than Turkey, the other great part-European, part-Asian power. But this isn't solely or indeed mainly about economics. It is a tussle about ideas: how should societies be organised? The magnet of the EU market has attracted most of the former Comecon countries into its orbit, but the price has been high in terms of accepting onerous EU regulation, and losing many of their brightest young people to the richer pastures of the West.

So by 2050 Central and Eastern Europe will be even more of a patchwork than it is now. Some countries, including Austria and Slovenia, will be embedded as core Europe. Greece will remain an anomaly, impoverished by the debts incurred after it adopted the euro. But given its history and its difficult relationship with Turkey, it will still lean to the West. Others will reach an accommodation with Russia and abandon efforts to align with the EU. Ukraine will be forced to do so. Romania may switch to the East, if it perceives that Russia could offer a better deal, though that seems most unlikely now.

The most important question will be the decisions taken by the Visegrad Four: Poland, Hungary, Czechia and Slovakia. They will not move as a bloc, for they have such different historical and cultural links with Russia. Those links have not, to put it mildly, been happy ones. But they were the core of Russia's European empire, and the extent to which they choose to align more towards Russia will determine the balance of the entire region. It will be a messy thirty years but by 2050 it seems realistic to think that the relationship between Russia and the rest of Europe will have settled into a steady state. That would require an acceptance in the West of the importance of Russia and its sphere of influence in Eastern Europe. And it would require Russia to feel comfortable that its importance is recognised and respected, and for it to abide by the normal rules of acceptable international behaviour. Can Russia do that?

RUSSIA – THE DIFFICULT PATHS FOR THE WORLD'S LARGEST COUNTRY

The extraordinary, complex, rich, wonderful yet tragic tale of Russia will continue for the next thirty years and beyond. It would be nice to be able to predict that it will become something akin to a normal Western democracy, with an orderly government, an effective opposition that can take over if the people choose to elect it to do so, independent courts, a free press and so on. It would then throw itself into tackling the problems noted in Chapter 1, including overdependence on exports of energy and raw materials, public health and social challenges, an ageing and declining population, and the practical difficulties of running the world's largest country in terms of landmass with relatively few people to do it. It would also be able to have friendly and cooperative relations with its neighbours in Europe, perhaps becoming some sort of associate member of a reformed EU.

Nice to predict, and let's cling to hopes that this will indeed happen – particularly as the need for good neighbourly relations will increase as environmental threats mount. But no one should assume that this will be the case. While it is certainly possible that Russia will have become more 'normal' by 2050, the path from here to there is extraordinarily difficult. It is always difficult to reform de facto dictatorships in an orderly and peaceful way, and in Russia particularly so. There will be some moment in the future when there is a break with the past, an upheaval when the current autocracy is challenged and replaced by another form of government. Writing now, it is tempting to think in terms of the ending of the regime of Vladimir Putin; that the break will happen when he steps down or dies. It may. But it is equally plausible that Russia will continue for a while with autocratic governance under a successor, with the break coming later. Or it is possible that some disaster or other event – maybe the invasion of Ukraine – will end his regime prematurely.

Thinking thirty years ahead, it is most probable that Russia will be functioning as a rough democracy that accepts political opposition, rather than an autocracy that tries to kill people who oppose it. But the path from here to there is impossible to predict.

What is easier to predict is that by 2050 Russia will be struggling to police and protect its borders. It will be too big a country for its population, particularly for the population of working age, and particularly if large numbers of its young people choose to emigrate. We don't know for sure how quickly Russia's population will decline, though the forecasts that it will be below 100 million by 2100 should be taken seriously. But long before that Russia will seem an anomaly, an empty space in an increasingly crowded world.

So what will happen? Russia will draw some strength from some of the former USSR members, notably Kazakhstan and the other countries round the Caspian Sea. They have natural resources, but, more important, they have been a source of young immigrants, as noted in Chapter 1. Western commentators tend to focus on the uneven governance of these countries and overlook the vigour, intelligence and decency of their young people. Indeed, I feel the West in general tends to underrate the wonderful resource that Russia has in its next generation of citizens. But there is a lot of space to fill.

China and Mongolia, with which Russia shares a land border 2,600 miles long, need space. That will continue to be an inevitable source of tension, as it has been in the past. There will be tensions on its European borders for all the reasons noted above, though here the most likely will be for emigration, not immigration. There will certainly be a huge drive for Russian families to have more children, but even if moderately successful that would not be enough to make a radical difference. The only policy that would really move the dial would be for Russia to seek to make itself attractive to immigrants, in much the same way as the US, Canada, Australia and the UK have managed to do. But that is a tall order.

The most likely outcome is that Russia will continue to maintain its borders for another thirty years, maybe longer. It will certainly try to do so. But it is likely that some sort of discontinuity will occur in the second half of this century. That is beyond the timescale of this book, but it is worth trying to envisage what this break might entail. In its most extreme form that could be the loss of Siberia, so that Russia returned to being a purely European nation. If that seems improbable, note that currently more than three-quarters of the Russian population lives in Europe, while more than three-quarters of the country's land area is east of the Urals, in Asia. Were that to happen, Russia would still control 40 per cent of Europe's land. What might happen to Siberia then? It would become a new sovereign nation, seeking people from anywhere and everywhere (but realistically from Africa, China and the Indian subcontinent) to help it exploit its massive natural resources.

There are, of course, many other possibilities. There could be a federation of two Russian countries, with different laws and customs and different political systems. There could be a sale of Russian territory to China or even the US, rather as Alaska was sold to the latter in 1867. There are other outcomes that don't bear thinking about, for these territorial tensions could lead to war. But while it is not helpful to try to guess at what Russia might look like eighty or more years into the future, we can be reasonably sure that, come 2050, the difficulties of running Russia will be even more evident than they are now. The world's fifteenth largest economy cannot control the world's largest land area for ever. Something, sometime, will have to give.

TURKEY – HUGE OPPORTUNITIES, TROUBLED GOVERNANCE

Some thoughts about that other great part-European, part-Asian power, Turkey. Like Russia, it is a rough democracy that is coping with inherent political instability by having an authoritarian regime led by a strong leader. Like Russia, it has bumpy relations with some European countries, particularly its neighbour Greece. But aside from the obvious physical distinction that Russia's population is mostly in Europe while Turkey's is mostly in Asia,[13] there is the crucial difference that Turkey's weight in the world is increasing, while Russia's is in decline. By 2050 it is likely to be around the tenth largest economy, well ahead of Russia, and thanks to its relative youth, with a larger working population, too. It could also, if it so chose, build a more powerful military machine.

Back in the early 2000s the general expectation was that Turkey would by 2020 have long been a full member of the EU. It had applied back in 1987, only a year after the applications of Spain and Portugal, and when Warsaw Pact members such as Hungary and Poland were still Soviet satellites. Now membership is most unlikely, whatever happens to the EU, partly because Turkey would struggle to meet the EU's standards of political diversity, but more because to Turkey there no longer seems any point in joining. Any marginal economic advantages are more than offset by political disadvantages. So Turkey will move further away from Europe, not towards it.

It will, however, work more closely with Russia, forming part of the outer ring of countries that sometimes look inwards to Europe, sometimes outwards to their other regional interests. For example, both Turkey and Russia very much want stability in the Middle East. Turkey will veer between hard-line populist governments and more cooperative liberal ones, but whatever the political tone of the government its nationalist path is set.

A FINAL WORD ABOUT EUROPE

By 2050 the continent of Europe will be less important in economic terms than at any stage for the previous 250 years. It will generate less than 15 per cent of global GDP, even including the offshore islands of Britain and Ireland. That will be a smaller proportion of world output than at any time since the early 1800s. It will continue to contain pockets of great wealth. It will continue to be a store of cultural activities and a leader in some technologies. It will continue to offer a reasonably good lifestyle for most of its people. But it will not be able to do much to shape the world. That is not because of politics, whether or not the EU survives, or the form that a successor body might take. It is to do with demography and economics. Europe will be too old and too small to matter much.

For many Europeans this will be a troubling prospect. It is not the story told by the bureaucrats in Brussels, or the pro-EU politicians across its member states. Anyone who points to the mathematics of global growth is unlikely to receive a warm welcome. The story will become all the more dispiriting if many ambitious and well-educated young Europeans decide to seek their careers elsewhere. The brain drain evident now in southern Italy could spread across the continent, thereby speeding up the decline.

But once people accept that Europe will become somewhat less important, then the clouds begin to lift. As argued earlier, the continent has a huge range of activities in which it excels. It can offer a fine lifestyle. It can offer peace and security. It can in modest ways help to make the world a better place. As long as Europeans can drop any sense of entitlement, adjust to relative decline and accept that for the next thirty years the big decisions in the world will be taken elsewhere, the continent can have a settled and progressive period. And those decisions? Many will be taken in Asia, to which this story now turns.

9

Asia

ASIA'S CENTURY

Asia is so important to the future of our planet that it seems unbalanced to treat the world's largest landmass in a single chapter. But the conventional concept of the six continents is a useful shorthand to take those continents (minus Antarctica) as a framework for this book – just as it is a useful shorthand to call this 'Asia's Century'. That phrase captures its importance, to be set against the nineteenth century when Europe dominated the world and the twentieth when the United States did. But it is a shorthand that ignores three crucial points.

One, noted in the Introduction, is that until the Industrial Revolution the economies of the civilisations of Asia were much larger than those of the rest of the world. In economic terms *all* the centuries that came before were Asia's. The nineteenth and twentieth centuries were aberrations. We are now reverting to the normal state of affairs, one that will run far into the future, where the largest chunk of human economic activity will continue to take place on the Asian landmass. It will indeed be Asia's century, but no more than, say, the tenth century was or doubtless the twenty-third century will be.

The second is that this landmass is so varied, so diverse in every possible way, that using one single four-letter word to describe it is quite inadequate. To write about what Asia might be like thirty years hence means inevitably lumping together the paths of regions as different as the Arctic tundra and the equatorial forests. The different parts of Asia and its different cultures face totally different challenges and will do so in totally different ways. The better they cooperate, the more successful they are likely to be in those efforts. What is essential is that they continue to manage the inevitable tensions that arise.

That leads to the third point. Asian nations will face less interference from the West. Of course the leadership of the United States will remain crucial, certainly in military terms but in economic and cultural ones, too. Europe will matter to some extent as well. But the legacy of European nineteenth-century dominance has been much eroded and the impact of the US has started to wane. The technology and ideas of the West will continue to influence the peoples of Asia, but to a lesser extent than at any stage in the past 200 years. For better or for worse – probably for better – the Asian peoples will be master of their own futures. The West should accept that with grace and respect.

GREATER CHINA – BACK TO ITS PROPER PLACE IN THE WORLD

We must start with China. In 2050 it will have become unquestionably the world's largest economy. That very fact will have made it a more self-confident, calmer nation, one that will be easier for the rest of the world to live with. It will be master of the landmass it considers to be its traditional territories. It will have reached a reasonable working relationship with its great rival for global leadership, the United States. It will in general command the respect that it feels it deserves, reversing the 'century of humiliation',[1] what it sees as the subjugation by other major nations from 1839 to 1949. In short, it will again have attained its proper place in the world.

Or at least this is what *should* happen. That China will become the largest economy is more or less inevitable. But there are many missteps it may make on that path, many challenges it will have to overcome. Even if it is broadly successful both at avoiding missteps and at meeting challenges, by 2050 it will be looking towards a retreat, a relative decline in its importance vis-à-vis the resurgent United States and an increasingly self-confident India. If it is less successful the retreat will start earlier. There will be some sort of crunch point in the 2030s or 2040s, a moment when the country will change direction.

We will come to that in a moment; first the challenges. There are three main ones: the environment, technical leadership and internal stability.

For the past forty years China has been the hungry teenager. It has grown at astounding speed, scooped up resources from all over world, concreted over large swathes of its own lands and inevitably done damage to its own environment. As growth slows it will become less hungry, and as it becomes richer it will be able to devote more resources to protecting the environment. This is already happening. But damage has been done and it will be a thirty-year task to correct those mistakes. The country's leadership is very well aware of this, hence its commitment to becoming carbon neutral by 2060.[2] But China is particularly threatened by climate change, as well as the burdens it has put on its own environment from headlong economic growth. In 2050 China will be short of water, short of arable land and short of sources of energy.

Some problems will be tackled successfully. Local air and water pollution will be much improved. China's megacities will have stopped growing. Population pressure will be a thing of the past. The move off the land will have stopped and may have reversed, and despite the shift to a three-child policy the country's population will be falling fast, possibly dropping below one billion in the 2070s.[3] But the problems will demand resources to fix, for factories will have to be closed, unwanted city apartments pulled down and empty office blocks dismantled. This will suck resources from other forms of investment, but the older citizenry will want these problems dealt with.

The bigger worry will be that there will be some kind of environmental catastrophe. That could be a global disaster that affects China more severely than other countries, or it could be something specific to China itself. The Covid-19 pandemic demonstrated to the world that viruses and bacteria know no borders, but it also reminded us that China is where such pandemics have historically come from. The Black Death originated in China.[4] The Chinese authorities are very well aware of the environmental threats their country faces and it is reasonable to hope that they will be both alert and competent in their responses. But they could be overwhelmed. It is neither possible nor helpful to try to list the dangers in some order of magnitude. What we do have to acknowledge is that China, along with the Indian subcontinent and much of sub-Saharan Africa, is in an environmentally fragile place – and it will become more, not less, vulnerable over the next thirty years.

The technological challenge is simple: can China continue to catch up with the West, or will it fall behind? Russia seemed in the 1950s and 1960s to be rivalling the US in technical achievement, but that proved to be a mirage, partly because it failed to develop effective computers. Japan dominated many areas of industrial production in the 1970s and 1980s, but then lost ground from the 1990s onwards, partly because its electronic consumer products were outclassed by the US and Korea.

Right now the prospect is rosy. Quite apart from its general competence in manufacturing and construction, China appears to be either level with the US or ahead in several technologies, including battery development. But the experience of Russia and Japan teaches us that China will find it hard to maintain technical dominance for long. It shares with those two countries one key characteristic: it finds it hard to attract foreign talent, so it has to rely on its nationals. In the case of China that pool is huge. No one should disparage the quality, education and drive of the millions of young people who leave its schools and universities each year. Unlike Russia and Japan, China also sends many students to study abroad, so the pool of talent it can draw on is wide, and its universities cooperate with others around the globe. If it wants to build a new airport or sports stadium, it can hire the best architects in the world. Pay enough and anyone will come and do a job for you. Nevertheless, it will remain at a disadvantage if the broader mass of clever people from elsewhere in the world do not want to work there on a more permanent basis.

This is not only about talent and the ability to develop new cutting-edge technologies, vital though these are. Nor is it only about paying celebrities for their services. It is also about the personal connections, the cultural links and the intuitive understanding of other markets that open societies bring. No country, not even China, not even the US, can do everything best. The danger for China is that, while it will certainly be able to continue to develop its own successful industries, its economy will increasingly find itself cut off from the rest of the world, led by the US. Its products and services will be fine, but they will not be the most successful in terms of global appeal. So China will be stuck. In terms of absolute output its economy will be huge, the largest in the world. But in terms of quality it will be second-rank. The result will be that even the richest parts of mainland China will not achieve the standard of living that has been reached in Hong Kong, still less that of Singapore.

The escape route for China is obvious. It must create the sort of lifestyle that attracts ambitious non-Chinese people to Singapore. It is a mix of business opportunities, cultural activities, public safety and the practical amenities and attitudes that make life enjoyable for people successful enough to have a choice. That mix is the 'Life, Liberty and the pursuit of Happiness' in the US Declaration of Independence. Hong Kong could have been a model for mainland China's great cities to follow, but, as we shall see in a moment, that is most unlikely to happen. If China remains stable socially and politically maybe the country's leadership will feel relaxed and able to open up its society, allowing it to become a true global leader. As of now that does not look likely.

Can Chinese society remain stable? It is difficult to form a judgement. It would have been impossible in the chaos of the Cultural Revolution in the 1970s to envisage that within thirty years China would have transformed itself into a successful market economy, or that within sixty years it would be challenging the US to become the biggest economy in the world.

It is easy to see lots of reasons why Chinese society might *not* remain stable. At the top must come some sort of strategic failure by the country's leadership. This could be an overreach in international relations. The present bout of excessive nationalism could find the country diplomatically isolated: a huge economy but with no true friends. It is conceivable, though unlikely, that there could be a military adventure that went wrong, and the leadership would be unseated. A clumsy attempt to reintegrate Taiwan into the political system of mainland China could turn into disaster. Or there could be a more general middle-class revolt against the political system. With more than half its population made up of the educated middle class, it is easy to see how resentment against the system might mount.

A second cause of instability might be economic stagnation. If the Chinese economy becomes stuck in the middle-income trap as its population ages, it is plausible that the Chinese young will seek to move abroad for the better opportunities of the West. A large-scale brain drain would be not only an economic blow; it would also be a symbol of political failure.

Or there may be some kind of financial upheaval, the banking system being overwhelmed by bad debts, and the authorities making some mistake in their response. China is carrying a huge load of debt, much of which cannot be repaid. While you are growing swiftly you can, so to speak, grow your way out of the debt load. If your economy stagnates and that load becomes too great to service there has to be some kind of reconstruction. But reconstruction is no more than a nice word for lenders not being repaid in full. Is China in more of a danger here than, for instance, Japan? The answer is probably not. Certainly China will seek to learn from Japan's mistakes. The point here is simply that the Chinese financial system is not inherently robust and will need to be managed carefully if it is not to become unstable.

There are also obvious internal tensions: town versus country, young versus old, ethnic minorities versus the Han majority, Hong Kong versus the mainland, Cantonese versus Mandarin and so on. It is not helpful to dwell on these or to try to make judgements of the risks from afar. The point to be aware of is that internal stability will be a continuing concern for the Chinese authorities, as it has been in the past. At some stage in the next thirty years there will probably be more than one serious challenge to the leadership of the Chinese Communist Party. The balance of probability is certainly that the Party will retain power, but no one can be certain of that. China in 2020 is not the Soviet Union c. 1970, with a seemingly dominant regime that actually would be overthrown in little more than twenty years' time. The historical glue is much stronger. The USSR was a twentieth-century vision, not the civilisation with the longest continuous history on earth. But the next thirty years will see a radical change in direction for China. It will meet that crunch point. Its future, maybe, too, the future of the world, will depend on how it copes with that crisis.

Here is a scenario. The economy continues through the 2020s and 2030s to grow solidly, though not at the helter-skelter pace of the first two decades of this century. Then there is some searing event in the 2030s or 2040s that leads to a serious economic downturn. The most likely candidate would be the financial crash noted above, but there could be others. Recovery will be slow and there will be periodic reverses. As a result the 2040s will in economic terms turn out to be a lost decade. The US, though still number two, will start to close the gap with China and be on the path to overhauling it some time in the second half of the century.[5] The Chinese leadership will make efforts to restore financial stability and rebuild growth, but these will be only partly successful. As China's population declines, and the size of the workforce declines even faster, the only option will be to accept relative stagnation and adapt to it. Initially this will be a fraught period. As Britain and Japan have experienced, accepting relative decline is uncomfortable. But by 2050 China will have started to accept that the peak of its power is coming to an end. It will be the secure master of its landmass and one way or another will have reached a stable relationship with Taiwan. It will be respected for what it has achieved – lifting its people from poverty to secure middle-class status – but it will retreat from its overseas expansionist endeavours. It will try to run China better; it will not try to dominate the world.

Will it be what the West would see as an open and democratic society? Well, it really has to become so because its future prosperity and economic growth depends on that happening. The danger is that it will reach a plateau of development and not be able to move further forward. So there will, as a response to the 2030s stagnation, be some sort of transition in its governance. It will not be a carbon copy of the US or Western European political models, but it will build its own form of democratic governance.

This is a relatively optimistic scenario, a best reasonable case. It is easy to sketch less optimistic ones. These include the US and China being unable to manage their relationship and a new cold war emerging between the two. China could become involved in armed conflict on the Indian subcontinent. It could mishandle its relationship with Taiwan. Its attempts to extend military control over the South China Sea could equally trigger conflict. The transition it has to make towards a more democratic form of government might be mishandled and result in another political revolution. There are other outcomes, other flashpoints, that don't bear thinking about. The balance of probability, however, is that the more dreadful outcomes will be avoided and that China will indeed secure its proper place as the great nation and great people it truly is.

HONG KONG AND TAIWAN – A TROUBLED FUTURE

Before moving on to those other great nations of the Indian subcontinent, some words about Hong Kong and Taiwan. As argued earlier the 'one country, two systems' agreement over the governance of Hong Kong might have become the model for China's relationship with Taiwan. It won't now. Maybe it was unrealistic to expect the system to last for the full fifty years to 2047, but in the event it has lasted for nearly twenty-five years and that is an achievement. But now it is clear that Hong Kong will swiftly be absorbed into the

Chinese political system, though perhaps retaining some aspects of
its earlier status. By 2050 it will almost certainly be barely distinct
from the other great cities of China. But the pull of history is long.
As social and political attitudes shift in China it is plausible that
some of the characteristics that drove Hong Kong's development
from a small fishing village to one of the great financial centres of
the world in less than 100 years will reassert themselves. It is possible,
too, that it will suit the mainland leadership to encourage Hong
Kong to retain some sort of special role, something that is useful
for the country as a whole. Meanwhile, the rest of the world will
welcome the talented and resilient people who have made Hong
Kong the great city it still is but who have chosen to deploy their
skills elsewhere. The legacy of Hong Kong will be alive and kicking
in 2050, but will be evident in other cities around the world.

Taiwan is different. It is easy to see the broad outlines of Hong
Kong's future, much harder to be confident about that of Taiwan.
As far as its economy is concerned it will continue to be one of
the most successful of its region. Its next thirty years will not be
as vibrant as its past seventy years for demographic reasons, but
it will make solid progress. Its future will not be determined by
economics but by politics. The present relationship, with China
claiming its territory but it operating in practice as an independent
country, actually works quite well. But it is not stable. What has
happened in Hong Kong has destabilised it further, for Taiwan has
become the first-choice destination[6] for Hong Kong people seeking
to emigrate. Reason says this relationship should continue –
de facto independence but not de jure – for it works well. But as
China's economic power increases there is a danger that it may seek
to pressure other countries not to deal with Taiwan. It could point
to a precedent. The US has after all used this weapon to prevent
countries from dealing with Iran.

Economic pressure would be a more effective way of undermining
Taiwan's independence than military action. Quite aside from the
human cost of the latter (not to mention the possibility of defeat),
were China to invade Taiwan the US would strive to make sure it
became an economic pariah. The rest of the world would have to

choose which side it was on. Few significant countries would pick China over the US, Europe and the rest of the developed world. China would be the big loser. It would be forced back into itself, having to abandon its global aspirations.

It is for political scientists to assess how China and Taiwan are likely to manage their relationship over the next thirty years, and for military experts to assess the likely outcomes of an invasion. From an economist's perspective any relationship other than the status quo makes little sense. If this awkward stand-off has been maintained for more than seventy years, common sense says it can be maintained for another thirty. The rest of the world has to hope that this will indeed be the case.

INDIA AND THE INDIAN SUBCONTINENT – THE EXCITING BUT BUMPY RIDE AHEAD

India is as important to the world as China. As noted in the Introduction, at the time of the Roman Empire it was the world's largest economy. In 1500 it was approximately the same size as China, and in 1820 it was still second only to it. So its position in 2050 as number three economy in the world, after China and the US, should really be seen as a natural and correct return of the country, and indeed the rest of the subcontinent, to its true status in the world. By 2100 I expect that its share of global GDP will have increased yet further.

To Indian nationalists this may sound triumphalist – India not just as number three to China and America, but probably larger than the European Union, too. For those of us who know and like India, and have witnessed its progress for many of its years as an independent nation, it is certainly a story of massive progress. That should be celebrated. But in that celebration it would be right to sound a note of caution, for the path to 2050 will be strewn with obstacles and dangers. India has to surmount these and be aware of the dangers. This journey will probably turn out fine, but it could conceivably turn out to be a disaster.

Four obstacles loom.

First, India has to improve its infrastructure. The need is widely accepted, with the contrast with China particularly evident. The scale of the challenge is enormous. Roads, water and sanitation, housing, commuter rail networks, hospitals, schools, telecom networks, healthcare, electricity supplies – the list goes on and on. Much progress has been made over the past thirty years, for people comparing India with China tend to underestimate how much has been achieved. That investment is continuing and by 2050 Indian infrastructure will be much better in every way. The question is whether it will be good enough to enable Indian people to be as competitive in their jobs and as happy in their home lives as they could and should be. The answer will be, for many people, not really. The wealthiest cities, including Delhi, Mumbai and Bengaluru (Bangalore), will be easier and more comfortable places to live and work. Much of the countryside will lag behind. The progress will therefore be uneven and the question will be to what extent inadequate infrastructure holds back the spread of prosperity and the general levels of health and wellbeing. The answer to that depends on the gravity of and the response to the next challenge, the subcontinent's environment.

Much of what happens to India's environment is beyond the country's control, for the subcontinent is particularly vulnerable to climate change. Rising sea levels threaten coastal communities, and though that should be manageable on a thirty-year time horizon, by 2050 large parts of cities such as Mumbai and Kolkata will be in danger. Perhaps even more serious, and certainly more immediate, will be rising temperatures because these will affect the entire subcontinent, not merely the coastal areas. Food production is particularly vulnerable, and India alone will be feeding more than 1.6 billion people. It is not helpful to predict catastrophic famines. It is, however, right to call for a thoughtful and measured response to minimise the dangers. By itself India can only have a marginal impact on climate change. But the most populous country in the world will have a special interest in leading the movement to try to hold down the pace at which carbon dioxide emissions climb.

It also has to tackle the things that are within its control, including land use, agricultural practices and, especially, water consumption. None of this will be easy, and a reasonable assumption must be that India faces a period of increasing economic and social disruption as a direct result of environmental pressures. Central government will be seen as failing, and people will turn to regional and local government for solutions. India will muddle through, but at a serious cost to human welfare.

The third obstacle is education. Middle-class lifestyles can only be supported by a skilled workforce. There will be no shortage of labour in India for at least the first half of this century, but that steady supply of young people entering the workforce every year needs jobs. India can only create those fast enough if it educates its workforce better, for the job opportunities are for the skilled. The young people of India's huge middle class are competing in global markets against their peers around the globe. So they must be competitive if they are not to be disappointed, and find themselves in dead-end jobs. India's education system has pinnacles of excellence, but too many mediocre performers at lower levels. It is a mammoth challenge.

Finally, and associated with education, if India is to have a harmonious future it will have to tackle inequality. It is gradually doing so, and probably does not receive sufficient credit for that.[7] Indian society is helped by the ways in which its families, especially poorer ones, support each other through difficult times. The safety net is family, not the state. Overall wealth will rise and it is reasonable to expect that by 2050 more than half the country will be middle class. That is enormously welcome, of course, but it will make harsher the gap between these newly comfortable families and those that are left behind. Central government will not manage this well. It can't. Top-down social welfare policies, even if affordable, are impossible to administer across a nation of more than 1.6 billion people. So state and local governments will step in, or at least be under political pressure to do so. As noted in Chapter 1 some states are vastly wealthier than others, with the effect that different levels of wealth and inequality will tend to drive the country apart. India

252 THE WORLD IN 2050

will hold together as a country, but the effectiveness or otherwise of the way it tackles inequalities will be one of the factors that will determine how loose or how strong the glue that holds it together will be.

The dangers: there are three obvious ones, as well as more that we cannot yet see.

The first two pull against each other and it is not clear which is more likely to dominate. One is fragmentation, the other nationalism. Unless there is some catastrophe India will retain its territorial integrity. But it is likely to become a looser federation of states as their interests diverge. This will have to be managed and there is plenty of potential for miscalculation. Countering this will be Hindu nationalism, a single identity imposed from on top. Currently nationalism is the prevailing force, and it is quite possible that it will remain so through much of the 2020s and beyond. But at some stage the wind may shift and nationalism be pushed aside by regionalism. While no one can hope to call how this tussle will be resolved, there is a real danger that it might break out into active internal conflict. It is a profoundly uncomfortable possibility.

The third danger is an external conflict that escalates into war. It makes no sense to predict war. All we can do is to observe the tensions between India and its two great neighbours, China and Pakistan. Those tensions have risen and fallen over the past seventy or so years. The balance of probability is that they will continue to do just that: periods of near-open conflict, three nuclear-armed powers that periodically assert their political positions by initiating modest clashes but never using anything like their full conventional arsenal, let alone using nuclear weapons. For there to be a nuclear war over what would in the broader scheme of things be a quite small territorial dispute is mercifully not only utterly irrational; it is almost unthinkable.

However, the unthinkable, the unbearable, can occur. The history of the twentieth century tells us that. We can make judgements about the likelihood of catastrophe; my point here is simply to acknowledge the possible outcomes, however unlikely I think they may be. India and China will inevitably be rivals. In a sense they should be rivals. For centuries they were unquestionably the two largest economies and arguably the two greatest civilisations on earth. In the next thirty years that relationship to some extent resumes – the largest and the third largest economies. We, and they, have to rely on the judgement of their leadership to ensure that the reasonable working relationship that has characterised their dealings over the past centuries continues through this one.

INDIA'S NEIGHBOURS – PAKISTAN, BANGLADESH, SRI LANKA

Because India dominates so much of the landmass of the subcontinent there is a tendency to neglect the importance of Pakistan and Bangladesh, two countries that might, had history taken a different turn, have been part of India now. The simmering tensions between India and Pakistan over the past seventy years, coupled with the separation of Bangladesh, tend to obscure the potential benefits that closer economic cooperation might bring to the subcontinent. The acrimonious noise from the politics drowns out the positive signals from the economics. There may at some moment in the distant future be a way of bringing Pakistan and Bangladesh into some kind of federation with India, but that is not going to happen in the timescale of this book. More likely, the acrimony will continue, cooperation will be minimal and in the case of India and Pakistan armed conflict may break out.

Providing – a big proviso – a reasonable working relationship is maintained between the three countries, both Pakistan and Bangladesh can hope to make real progress to a more prosperous future. They will be substantial economies, both around number thirty in the world. Pakistan will have a population of some 275 million, Bangladesh around 200 million. Both will be on the brink of becoming middle-class economies. Though their overall GDP per head will remain relatively low by developed world standards, somewhat lower than in India and quite a lot lower than

Sri Lanka, their people will be much richer than they are today. They will also have before them a path to greater prosperity in the future.

For Pakistan, the challenge will be one of governance. How can the country move to a society that gives greater priority to the wealth and wellbeing of all its people rather than that of its elite? For Bangladesh that challenge also matters but may come to take second place behind the environmental difficulties the country faces. Nearly a quarter of its land area is less than seven feet above sea level. True, the sea is not going to rise by seven feet in the next thirty years, but it does seem likely that a large proportion of its population will have to cope with more frequent flooding. Environmental issues will increasingly dominate the entire subcontinent, but one of the most troubling flashpoints will be at the delta of those three great rivers the Brahmaputra, the Ganges and the Meghna, as they flow into the Bay of Bengal.

For the whole of the subcontinent, Sri Lanka stands out as an example of reasonable economic progress. The difficult, often vicious, war with the Tamil minority has deflected attention from the modest economic progress of the island state. This is not the place to comment on that conflict, horrific though it has been. My point is a different one. It is simply that by the standards of India, Sri Lanka is a considerable success story. It is richer per head than most of the subcontinent. But by the standards of East Asia it has been a laggard.

That leads to a wider question about the entire subcontinent. Might South Asia achieve a take-off similar to that of mainland China? The starting point in the 1950s was certainly that. In 1950 India's GDP per head was actually a little higher than that of China. China did not overtake India on that measure until the latter 1970s, but as we have seen has raced ahead since then. It is a massive, tantalising, soaring prospect: that India and its neighbours might 'do a China'.

It is certainly possible. The subcontinent has many of the characteristics of China in 1978, when Deng Xiaoping took over, including huge untapped human resources. All the things that hold back India now were evident in China then. As argued above, India will grow at a decent pace over the next thirty years. But might it sustain the headlong gallop that China has achieved? If that were to happen, its role in the world of 2050 would be transformative. It would still be the third largest economy, but instead of being well behind China and the US it would be hard on their heels. There would be the possibility that by the end of this century an Indian federation might be back to the position it was in 1,000 years earlier: the largest economy in the world.

Possible? Certainly. Plausible? Well, there would have to be some sort of sea change in Indian political life akin to the changes that Deng Xiaoping set in train in China – a group of people who saw that the world's most populous country should also seek to be the world's largest economy. They would then have to set about using the experience of other countries to create a path to that goal. They would have to use nationalism in a positive way to support wealth creation. They would have to show that as wealth was being generated it was also being spread. Some of the regional tensions noted above would have to be tackled in a sensitive way. Religious barriers would have to be dismantled. And if there were to be even the loosest federation of the subcontinent, Pakistan and Bangladesh would have to see the ways in which this benefited their own controlling elites. This is all doable. The question is whether it is likely to be done.

Probable? The rational answer must be no. It is not easy to see a sequence of events, not only in India but also in Pakistan and Bangladesh, that might lead to a Greater India becoming the world's largest economy by the end of this century. For it to happen it needs too many things to go right, and very few things to go wrong. So let's call it a realistic possibility that India will indeed become the world's largest economy at some stage in the future, but it is probably not something that will happen within the next 100 years. What is, however, almost certain is that by 2050 India will again have become the global economic power that it has been for most of recorded history, and there will be everything to play for in the years beyond.

JAPAN – THE ELDERLY PIONEER

Japan is the pioneer of the ageing developed world. As we saw in the Introduction, it is already the oldest society on earth. It will become even older, with the population falling to around 100 million by 2050. It will remain wealthy, but with the size of the workforce falling even faster than the total population it will become a nation of elderly people looking after even more elderly ones. Many of the smaller towns will be abandoned, fields will go back to forest, factories will be replaced by retirement communities. Japan will become even cleaner and even calmer than it is now. In theory demographic decline could be slowed by large-scale immigration. In practice that will not happen. The more chaotic the rest of the world becomes, the more confident Japanese people will be that they have made the right choice to seal the country's borders. The social contract that has glued its society together – that people help each other through difficult times but acknowledge that such help should be repaid in kind – will hold.

In short, Japan will not simply remain Japan as it is now. The characteristics that currently distinguish it from the rest of the world will intensify. It will become more Japanese, more special, more different from the rest of the world, even more cut off from outside ideas as to how societies should organise themselves, more certain that its way of organising society is the right one for the Japanese people. An older Japanese population will want to create a Japan that satisfies its particular needs. That will mean looking in, not looking out, as indeed Japan has increasingly done during the past thirty years.[8]

Does this matter? That depends on what the rest of the world hopes and expects of Japan. Remember, despite its relative decline in economic size it will still indubitably be the world's fourth largest economy. It will still be part of what might be called the Western Alliance, a solid ally of the United States. It will still be a manufacturing nation of great competence. It will still own many physical and financial assets around the world. It will still have a strong cultural influence on other countries. And it will still be the go-to place that other ageing societies will look for guidance on how best to manage the transition they too face.

All this is a huge achievement. But there are real concerns that must be acknowledged, hard though it is for anyone who knows and likes Japan to do so.

One is the structure of the economy. The question is whether Japan can manage to remain a true technological leader. Its present prowess is based on skills built up a generation ago. To put the problem harshly, the country is better at hardware than software, better at creating exportable goods than exportable services. It no longer leads in consumer electronics. Its automotive companies do remain technical leaders, but that sector will become less important at least in relative terms. Its universities are excellent on their own terms, but few foreigners go there to study. Japan will still be a powerhouse in 2050, providing a decent life for its people, but its economy will no longer be cutting edge in most sectors.

A second concern is the state of national finances. Japan already has the largest public debt relative to GDP of any major economy. That will continue to grow. It is unsustainable. At some stage in the next thirty years the debts will have to be renegotiated. No one can know when this will happen or the form the default – for that is what it will be – will take. Maybe there will be some external trigger, a rise in interest rates worldwide, perhaps. Maybe the source of tension will be some internal political event. But the largest national debt in the world relative to the size of the economy cannot be sustained by a fast-shrinking workforce. The situation is mathematically unsustainable. Japanese society is immensely resilient, but it is hard to see the nation's debt burden being resolved without disruption and without pain.

A third concern is geopolitical. Japan will be too inward-looking to be an effective counterbalance to the rising power of China. It will defend its territory – that is not an issue – but it will not be part of a shield seeking to contain Chinese territorial expansion. Maybe there is no need for a shield, for once China has control over the area that it sees as its own, it will check itself. In any case one of the key themes of this book is that eventually China's expansionist zeal is likely to wither away. But it is hard not to feel uncomfortable about Japan as a passive, uninterested observer of the tensions between its neighbours in South East Asia.

Japan in 2050 will, in short, remain a cohesive, settled society that is not very interested in the rest of the world. Its priorities will be to look after its own people and manage its difficult financial problems. It will not try to cut itself off – how could it? – but it will cherish its relatively crime-free environment, its cleanliness and its order. The more chaos there is among the countries on its periphery the more confident the Japanese people will be that their way is a better one. Island nations can choose either to look out to the world and seek, if not to dominate it, at least to influence it; or they can try as far as is practicable to shut the world out. For some forty years from the 1950s to the 1990s Japan chose the first path. The legacy of that is the worldwide commercial success of its great corporations such as Toyota and Mitsubishi and that legacy will remain. But during this century it has chosen the second. Japan will tread that latter path with even more intensity in the years to 2050.

SOUTH EAST ASIA – THE FRAGILE SUCCESS STORY

South East Asia has been one of the great success stories of the past seventy years. It will in all probability continue to be so, but it is also a fragile region in many different ways. The worry is that the underlying fragilities will push to the surface and undermine the enormous social and economic progress that the region has sustained.

South East Asia is a convenient geographic phrase for an extraordinarily diverse region in every regard. Inevitably, the performance that the different countries have made varies enormously. But if you take a broad overview of the arc of nations that swing down from the Koreas through Taiwan to Thailand, Cambodia, Vietnam and the Malaysian peninsula, add the Philippines and the huge nation of Indonesia, this region has been the most successful on earth. As noted in Chapter 1 its star performer, Singapore, is one of the richest countries in the world. It also scored top on the 2020 World Bank's Human Development Index.[9] After the bitter civil war, South Korea had in the early 1950s a GDP per head that was lower than Liberia or Ghana. Now it is roughly the same as that of Italy. Even the laggards, notably Myanmar, show some signs of catching up.

So will this run of success continue through to 2050? To some extent of course it will, or at least it will barring some environmental or political catastrophe. But it would be right to sound a note of caution. This is an area where things have, at least since the end of the Vietnam War, gone broadly right. It is, by the same token, one where things could go wrong.

There is one general overarching global issue, and several specific national ones.

The general issue is the future of globalisation. South East Asia has been a great beneficiary of the ever more global trading environment that has, at least up to the middle 2010s, dominated the world economy. The most spectacular beneficiary has been Singapore, which until it was passed by Shanghai in 2011 was the greatest seaport in the world. But others have triumphed in the global marketplace. Thus South Korea's Samsung was the largest phone manufacturer until 2020, when it was passed by China's Huawei. In a quite different market, Thailand is a top ten tourist destination, ahead of the UK. Indonesia, the world's fourth most populous country and the seventh in GDP measured at purchasing power parity, has a large, diversified economy that has lifted the living standards of most of its people to middle-class status. Vietnam has recovered from war and been one of the world's fastest-growing economies this century. This growth, driven by exports, helped it cut its poverty rate from over 70 per cent in 2002 to below 6 per cent in 2019. The World Bank describes this progress as remarkable and it is right.[10]

One could go on pointing to regional success stories, acknowledging, too, that rapid growth has brought costs in terms of environmental damage. There is always a darker side to economic success. The basic point here is that since the region has been

the greatest beneficiary of the growth of global trade it will also
potentially become the greatest victim should the world increase
the barriers on international trade. The Covid-19 emergency gives a
glimpse of the damage that might occur, though the relatively rapid
recovery in China blunted the fall. If the world were to shift to two
distinct trading blocs, one led by the US and the other by China,
South East Asia would be faced with an impossible choice. More
likely, though, than such a breach of multilateralism would be a
gradual squeezing down of supply chains. Products currently made
in East Asia would be manufactured nearer the markets in which
they were sold. Rising real wages in the region, in themselves most
welcome, narrow the cost advantage. The way forward may well be
for South East Asia to boost its service exports, but its comparative
advantage in services may not be as big as its advantage in goods.
Finally, ask the tough question: what can a country like Thailand
or Malaysia do that China can't do more cheaply? The answer may
turn out to be not a great deal.

There are many national challenges. Some inevitably brief words
about those for six countries of the region, Korea, Indonesia, the
Philippines, Thailand, Malaysia and Vietnam, plus some more
general final thoughts about the region.

For some the key issue is political. Take Korea. South Korea has
been one of the world's great success stories; North Korea has been
one of its greatest human and economic catastrophes. Rationally
there must be a strong probability that the two Koreas will be
unified by 2050. But reason does not determine political outcomes.
It seemed in the early 1990s, after the fall of the Berlin Wall and
the unification of the two Germanys, that this similar fissure would
have been closed by now. It hasn't. Quite the reverse, with North
Korea becoming even less predictable and even more shut off from
the rest of the world. Rationally, at some time in the next thirty
years unification will take place, but with every year that passes
the two Koreas grow further apart. At some stage in the next thirty
years it may become clear to the North Korean ruling class that it
is in their self-interest to have a rapprochement with the South. Or
there may be some external trigger that brings them together.

So unification *may* happen, but there may equally be a miscalculation that plunges the Koreas into armed conflict. It is unbearable to think about that, and it is not helpful to try to game the different ways in which such a conflict might play out. What is worth saying is that this is one of the world's most dangerous situations and the fact that the two Koreas have been able to avoid armed conflict since the creation of the demilitarized zone in 1953 does not mean they will continue to do so. No peace treaty was ever signed. Technically, they are still at war.

To be clear: the balance of probability is that the status quo of the two Koreas will persist. But that is merely the most likely outcome; the fragility remains.

Indonesia, whose future is massively important to the world, faces a multitude of issues. One is environmental. Indonesia is one of the countries most at risk from climate change. It encompasses the world's largest archipelago, more than 17,000 islands, some of the most threatened rainforests, and a capital city part of which may have to be abandoned to rising waters. Another is political, for it has had a bumpy ride for the past half-century. Still another is religion, with the largest Muslim population in the world, but with a significant Christian minority. Finally, there has been since independence in 1945 the threat of the country splitting into several entities.

So what will Indonesia look like in 2050? It will be a messy giant. It will manage to scramble through one set of crises and then on to the next. It will succeed in providing a better quality of life for the majority of its people, but it will trail behind its neighbours to the north, notably Malaysia. It will cope to some extent with environmental degradation but only to some extent. It will remain a single country, for that is clear. But its more disadvantaged groups, and regions, will make little progress. Its 330 million people will wonder whether their futures might be better.

The Philippines poses the similar, tantalising question that faces Indonesia: how could it do better? There has been a governance issue since independence. There are environmental concerns. It is an archipelago with tensions between the different islands and the different ethnic groups that live there. By 2050 it will have a population of some 150 million, the second largest of the region. But it will not be offering a standard of living that compares with, for example, Malaysia or Thailand. Why? It is a puzzle and a worry. The Philippines will be fine – but they could be more successful than they have been, and will be. They benefit from their location, from their close connections with the United States, and from their positive demography. But somehow the country has been less than the sum of its parts, and will continue to be so.

The puzzle is all the more evident when set against the success of Thailand, Malaysia and Vietnam. Thailand and Malaysia have been beacons of progress. Vietnam has been fascinating in its recovery from the most difficult of circumstances, and while it is further down the development ladder, it has demonstrated that there is such a thing as a ladder that most of the region is climbing. Those three economies have different economic approaches, but they have moved along a similar path.

By 2050, then, it is easy to predict that Thailand and Malaysia will be prosperous, developed countries. They will have similar standards of living and similar health and welfare outcomes as South Korea in 2020. Vietnam may lag a little behind, with its neighbours, Laos and Cambodia, a bit further behind, too. It would be nice to be confident that a calmer Myanmar would be paying more attention to human rights, a precondition for closer integration into the world economy and greater economic and social progress. On that, however, it is impossible to frame a view.

However, the region, taken as a whole, will find it harder to match the rapid growth rates that it has had for much of the past fifty years. Catch-up drove that growth. But now most countries have pretty much caught up. Only stunning Singapore has succeeded in propelling itself to the pinnacle of economic development, and there is only room for one Singapore in the East Asian time zone. Besides, the region is getting older. Its people will want comfort and security rather than pure growth. It will face difficult political choices as to how to play its relations with a China intent on controlling the South China Sea.[11] Should it side with the US or

China if the world does slide into two antagonistic trading blocs? Does it suit China to have a successful region to its south?

The answer to that last question is surely yes, if China continues to act in its own self-interest. But global trade tensions are dangerous for South East Asia, and a trade war would be disastrous. The more your success is based on globalisation, the more exposed you are if that falters. So the difficult periods that will inevitably occur between now and 2050 will be particularly tough on South East Asia. It is one of the most resilient parts of the world. It will need that resilience over the next thirty years.

Africa and the Middle East

THE WORLD'S FASTEST-GROWING REGIONS

Africa faces huge challenges, but also offers the world huge hope. By 2050 it will be home to some 2.5 billion people, a quarter of the world's population. It will still be the poorest continent, but it will also be the fastest-growing in terms both of living standards and of human welfare. It will be the youngest continent, too, vigorous, full of drive. But the problems those people have to tackle and the pressures they will face as they do so will make the next thirty years a terrifying ride. It is fashionable in the West to despair. Part of the reason for that, as argued in the Introduction, is the negativity bias of the aid agencies. If Africa was doing fine they would have no role, so they highlight what is going wrong rather than what is going right. But the stream of migrants from across the Mediterranean seeking to escape the continent is testament to the fact that much of Africa is not doing fine at all. Or at least it is not doing well enough to give satisfying life opportunities for many of its people. That is something that anyone peering into the future must acknowledge.

It would be easy to look at the dissonance now and argue that Africa will continue to stumble from one disaster to another. If the current situation is grave, how much worse will it be with nearly double the population and a world that is 2° warmer? But hand-wringing gets us nowhere, and actually is almost insulting for it ignores the resilience and energy of African people. It is their continent. They know the challenges, and it is they who will have to manage them.

So how will Africa develop? The easiest way to get a grip on this is to take the two conventional geographic areas of sub-Saharan Africa and North Africa and then to look at the region that shares the key characteristic with Africa – the rapid growth of its population – the Middle East.

SUB-SAHARAN AFRICA – CREATE THOSE JOBS

There are four main challenges: finding jobs for the surge in the numbers of young people, coping with the many threats that result from climate change, improving weak governance and containing religious tensions.

Jobs, jobs, jobs. The median age in Nigeria is 18.1 years.[1] It is the most populous country in Africa, with a projected 400 million inhabitants in 2050. The median age of Africa as a whole is under twenty. What will these people do? There is the economist's classic answer that the market will decide. In the case of Nigeria there is, as we saw in Chapter 1, massive entrepreneurial zeal. The very fact that the population is expanding so fast will of itself create tasks that have to be done. The growing millions have to be fed and clothed. Homes have to be built. Demand for education and healthcare will continue to climb. All this creates jobs.

But supplying services to the domestic market is not enough. All countries must have, so to speak, a cash crop. Africa needs goods and services it can export to the world at a competitive rate. Right now these are principally primary goods: oil and gas in the case of Nigeria, minerals and gold in South Africa and Tanzania, food crops in the Congo and so on. A still-growing world population will go on needing raw materials, and will very much need to be fed. But the danger for sub-Saharan Africa is that its competitive advantage in these areas will be eroded. China will go on wanting to scoop up the continent's resources but as its own population declines its demands will wane. The mature adult of the future won't have as much appetite as the hungry teenager of the present.

So how will the booming number of African people respond? The answer is that there is no shortage of entrepreneurship. So they will find ways of pushing their economies upmarket into higher value-added goods and services, using technology in innovative ways rather as they have used mobile telephony. It will be catch-up growth rather than frontier growth, and there will be countries and regions where too many people are underemployed. But it is reasonable to expect that living standards will climb to two to three times their present level. That is an average and, like all averages, should be viewed carefully. There will, sadly, be pockets of extreme poverty, and overall the majority of African people will not be as rich as the majority of people, for example, on the Indian subcontinent. But there is a very good chance that most children alive now will be brought up with better education, better health, a better diet, and with better employment prospects than their parents. Providing it meets the next three challenges Africa will go forward, not back.

Climate change. Sub-Saharan Africa is generally vulnerable, and some regions particularly so. In the very long term, Africa's future depends on how effectively – or not – the world as a whole tackles climate change, but on a thirty-year view African countries have to adapt. In a way it is monstrously unfair. Africa, for all the shortcomings of regional and national policies and despite its surging population, contributes relatively little either to global emissions or to habitat destruction. Yet it will suffer more than most, partly because it is the hottest continent, and partly because it lacks the financial resources to mitigate the changes that are likely to take place.

Thus Africa has to live with a complex series of problems that are not largely of its own making. The legacy of colonialism is gradually receding but the impact of the rest of the world on the environment will intensify. What will happen?

It is absurd to generalise. The challenges faced by, for example, Ethiopia are utterly different from those facing Equatorial Guinea. However, it is possible to pick the two broad themes that will overlay the continent's response to environmental challenge. One starts from the fact that there will be a sense of guilt in the West about the impact of climate change on Africa. That will lead to a string of initiatives that seek to compensate for and/or slow down the damage. The other theme is that the people who live in Africa will feel, with justification, that they know more about how to live with their environment and the issues raised than the people who run some aid agency on the other side of the world.

So there will be tension between what much of the world would like African governments to do and what the people of Africa choose to do. The positive feature is that any technology that helps mitigate the impact of climate change will be universally available. If there are fixes, Africa will have access to them.

That leads to challenge number two: improving the quality of governance across the continent. It may seem arrogant for outsiders to express blanket criticism of how other countries manage themselves, but it is inescapable that, with a few exceptions, governance has been weak. This will change. It is already changing. As their economies grow and the continent carries a greater weight, there will be a rebalancing of power between the countries of sub-Saharan Africa and the rest of the world. The concept of African countries as supplicants, beholden to Western aid agencies and Chinese investors, will gradually wane.

Is that too optimistic? It may be. It is certainly difficult to measure quality of governance, for any attempt to do so is inevitably shaped by the choice of data that is chosen and the weights attributed to different outcomes. But take just one number that gives a crude proxy for governance, life expectancy.[2] It rose steadily across most of sub-Saharan Africa until the late 1980s. It then fell, partly as a result of the spread of AIDS and partly because of conflicts, until the early 2000s. But since then it has again been climbing steadily. Too many lives have been lost too early, but now viewed overall the lost ground is being recovered. Cast forward and the World Bank projects that life expectancy will continue to increase, narrowing the gap with the developed world. If that is right, it would be implicit that overall levels of governance will improve, too.

Religious tensions? It is difficult to be positive, writing at a time when the clash between the Muslim populations of North Africa and the fast-growing Christian communities has resulted in many terrible atrocities. The Sahel, that great band stretching across the southern reaches of the Sahara from the Atlantic to the Red Sea, is one of the frontiers between the world's two largest religions. There are many Muslim communities down the east coast of Africa, too – Tanzania is roughly a quarter Muslim – but the key to a more peaceable relationship will be what happens in the Sahel. It is possible that religious and social tensions may lead to Nigeria becoming a looser federation, and conceivable that it might break up.

The relationship between the world's largest and second largest religions was noted in Chapter 6. Africa is one of the areas of religious tension, but only one, and this is something the world will have to live with for the foreseeable future. What is worth saying is that people of different faiths have lived together in Africa for a very long time and that it is quite plausible that the African people will manage things better than others elsewhere in the world. Eventually the tensions will ease, probably within a generation. As we have seen, over the centuries, there are cycles in religious fervour that wax and wane. Our hope must be that not too much damage will be done and not too many lives lost before a more harmonious period emerges.

It would not be credible to argue that by 2050 sub-Saharan Africa is likely to be a calm and prosperous region. It would be easy to predict that the combination of rapid population growth and relative poverty will be explosive. It would be easy, too, to argue that the present trickle of refugees across the Mediterranean is likely to increase massively as people seek to escape the worst effects of climate change and conflict. But there is a much more hopeful outcome that would run like this.

Nigeria and South Africa come right. Together they dominate sub-Saharan Africa, the most populous nation and the largest economy. By 2050 the two economies will be roughly the same size. Nigeria will be massively the most populous country in Africa, and with some 400 million people probably number three in the world after

India and China. South Africa's population will be around seventy-five million but its higher GDP per head will offer a middle-class lifestyle to the majority of its people. Both will have made solid economic progress, and that progress will anchor their respective regions.

Success breeds success. In simple trading terms one country's success helps its neighbours, provided local communications are functioning. Often they aren't. Accra, capital of Ghana, is less than 300 miles from Lagos, commercial capital of Nigeria. Yet it takes the best part of twelve hours to drive it, assuming you are not held up at the border crossings of Togo and Benin. So trade is much more difficult than it need be. Kofi Annan, former secretary-general of the UN, argued that inter-regional communications were a key to African growth and that is surely right. These will inevitably improve, though equally inevitably not fast enough. But by 2050 communications will be much better.

This is, however, not just about trade. It is about attitudes to governance. One of the striking things about Nigeria is its vigorous open political debate. People do demand more efficient administration. Gradually pressure to do better will deliver that, and when it does Nigeria will become a beacon of hope to its neighbours in West Africa.

This admittedly optimistic vision of Nigeria's future can be mirrored in a vision of how South Africa might develop. It is impossible not to acknowledge the many problems there, mostly inherited from the apartheid era, but quite a few made worse by uneven governance since then. However, as explained in Chapter 1, it is the great economic powerhouse of the continent. It will remain so. As the legacy of apartheid fades, the balance of probability is that race relations will become more harmonious, inequalities will decrease and internal security will improve.

If all this is even half right, then the effects will be continent-wide. Once a set of political or economic ideas take hold they spread far beyond the place where they began. We have seen that many times. Often the spark is political: examples include the bursting out of Eastern Europe from the Soviet empire at the end of the 1990s, and less happily the so-called Arab Spring in the early 2010s. But sometimes it is economic, with perhaps the best example being the way in which Japan's growth inspired South Korea, and the clutch of smaller East Asian 'Tiger Club' economies, Indonesia, Malaysia, Philippines, Thailand and Vietnam, pulled each other along.

It is plausible that at some stage in the next thirty years there will be an African take-off. If this happens it won't be organised or planned, and it will be regional rather than continental. Of course, it may not happen, in which case muddle through will prevail. But consider this.

One possibility is that South African growth would spread northwards through Mozambique and Zambia to Zimbabwe, Tanzania and Kenya. East Africa could do very well over the next thirty years because the basis for a better performance is already there: a competent middle class, improving education, notably in Kenya, the legacy of Zimbabwe's catastrophic period under Robert Mugabe fading, and more.

Another possibility is that Francophone West Africa could jump forward in a burst of growth alongside Nigeria and Ghana's better performance. The great civilisation of Ethiopia may move to a more settled period as wealth increases and it moves its economy away from agriculture and up the value chain. Or maybe, though this is harder to be confident about, the natural resources of the Democratic Republic of Congo will be more equitably shared and drive up central African living standards. That natural wealth, as noted in Chapter 1, is stunning. For example, the DRC produces some 60 per cent of the world's cobalt, one of the key minerals for batteries. Mining conditions will improve, as they need to, for the pressure on companies that use these minerals will continue to mount. Is it reasonable to hope that these pressures will make a material difference to welfare standards across the continent? Surely the answer is yes. You have to be profoundly cynical to think that they won't have *any* impact, so the question is one of degree. A larger proportion of the wealth of Africa will stay in the continent in the future than it has in the past.

There are parts of sub-Saharan Africa where it is difficult to feel confident, or indeed comfortable about what might happen over the next thirty years. Small, poor, land-locked countries with equally poor neighbours will continue to struggle to provide a decent minimum lifestyle for their people. Countries that through either their history or location face ethnic strife will continue to do so. There will be growth, but it will continue to be unequally shared. Technology can help – witness the way in which Africa has pioneered new uses for mobile telephony – but only up to a point. By the standards of the world as a whole, a quarter of humankind in Africa will remain poorer than their counterparts in India and China, let alone the people of the developed world. But it is important, while accepting all this, not to lose sight of the probability that overall living conditions and life opportunities in sub-Saharan Africa will be sounder in 2050 than in 2020. Put another way, children born now will have a better shot at life than their parents. That surely is something worth celebrating.

NORTH AFRICA AND THE MIDDLE EAST – THE ARAB WORLD

North Africa and the Middle East face a different set of issues from the rest of Africa. It makes sense to take this as one region because of the cultural identities across the Arab world. The governing regimes are utterly different, ranging from dictatorships, through more or less constitutional monarchies, to the whole gamut of different forms of democracy. There are also many different ethnic and religious groups that have for millennia lived here, for much of the time in harmony. This is where what we now think of as Western civilisation began. But while it is really important to recognise the key role that other cultures will play in the future of the region, the glue is the language of Arabic and the Muslim faith of the majority of its people.

The latter years of the twentieth century and the early years of the twenty-first have not been kind. Two Gulf wars, the conflict in Syria, the catastrophe in Libya, political unrest in Lebanon, the continuing misery of Palestinian people – the inherent fragility of the whole region has been manifest. So the overarching question when thinking about the next thirty years is whether these are likely to be some sort of rerun of the past sixty, or whether it will settle down to a period more like the peaceful interludes of the past several hundred.

There can be no answer, but there are clues, things we can look for that will give us a feeling for how these years will develop. Of course, politics will dominate and it is for the specialist regional analysts to give their opinions about that. The trouble is that few predictions are any help.

A personal perspective. When I visited Libya with my spouse and some Arabic-speaking American friends for New Year 2005, the mood was one of the country opening up to the West, and, incidentally, to tourists such as ourselves. It was a wonderful moment and a great privilege to be there. Tony Blair had recently welcomed Muammar Gaddafi back into the fold of the Western nations, visiting him in March 2004.[3] His second son Saif al-Islam Gaddafi was set to study for a PhD at the London School of Economics. British Airways was flying to Tripoli. The worry was who might succeed when Muammar Gaddafi died. It was unthinkable that just six years later he might be deposed and be shot, begging for mercy, in a roadside ditch. The experts, including most of the academics who had welcomed Saif al-Islam at the LSE, were proved utterly wrong.[4]

This is not to get in a dig at Tony Blair, the LSE or political analysis in general. Economists get things very wrong, too. The Queen, visiting, by one of those twists of fate, the LSE in November 2008 asked about the financial crash: 'It's awful. Why did nobody see it coming?'

The Libyan story simply shows how hard it is to predict seismic political shifts, and this region is particularly exposed to these. What *is* possible to predict with some confidence is the economic factors that will affect it. Two stand out: a surging youthful population and a gradual move away from reliance on oil and gas. They affect different countries in different ways. For Egypt the challenge will be how to give a good life to 160 million people. For Saudi Arabia and the Gulf emirates it will be how to rely less on oil and gas exports and follow the path pioneered by Dubai to become entrepôt trading and service centres as well as primary producers.

North Africa's proximity to Europe adds a further dimension to the demographic challenge. Southern Europe has its share of young people struggling to find work, but there is some protection thanks to the welfare systems and there is the option of moving north. For most people across the southern coast of the Mediterranean neither of those features apply. For much of the past 2,000 years the Mediterranean has been a unified economy. It no longer is. That is bound to cause resentment.

There are two ways that such resentment can be met and we are likely to see both over the next thirty years. One will be that Europe will redouble its efforts to isolate itself from immigration from North Africa. There will inevitably be more migration, but the politics in Europe are such that governments will have no option but to resist it. The other development will be efforts to recreate a Mediterranean economy, with Europe buying more from North African countries and taking advantage of their lower production and energy costs. It would be fanciful to suggest that Egypt will again become the breadbasket of Italy, as it was at the height of the Roman Empire. It is not, however fanciful to expect trade both in goods and in services to boom, because North Africa has two things that Europe lacks: a ready supply of young labour and rapid economic growth.

So there will be a tug of war between the benign elements of this relationship and the malign ones. The outcomes will vary from country to country. It is easy to be reasonably positive about Morocco, Algeria and Tunisia, and inevitably less easy to be so about Libya. But the past thirty years have taught us to be wary of generalisations and aware of the potential surprises. We should not rule out hard-to-envisage disasters, or conversely the possibility of surprise success. Libya could come right, and its people deserve it to.

What happens in Egypt is enormously important to the entire region, west and east. It is so huge, so vigorous, so steeped in history and ambition. By 2050 it will be home to some 160 million people, crammed along the banks of the Nile and into the triangle of its delta. Cairo may have a population of thirty-five million. The prospect is thrilling and alarming in the same measure. It is thrilling because Egypt has so much to offer. It has its huge educated middle class, a tradition of tolerance, energy, and, mixed with its chaos, great charm. It is and will continue to be by far the largest Arab nation by population, the anchor of the Arab world. But it is also alarming, thanks partly to its bumpy politics, and perhaps more importantly its economic vulnerability. Climate change is a huge threat, given that absolutely everything depends on the flow of that one river and that agricultural exports will continue to be vital for the foreseeable future.[5] Any sensitive observer of Egypt must wish it well, but its next thirty years will be a nail-biting ride.

For Egypt energy prices are not a huge issue, for it produces relatively little oil and its gas reserves, while very large, have yet to be fully exploited. For much of North Africa and for Algeria in particular the future of petrochemicals, both as fuel and as feedstock, is extremely important. And to the Middle East, where our story now moves, energy is absolutely central to the future.

THE MIDDLE EAST – THE QUEST FOR STABILITY

The Middle East is one of the most fragile regions of the planet. For the millions of people who have died in wars there, and the millions displaced and living in refugee camps, the past fifty and more years have been dreadful. Sadly, it is likely to remain fragile for the rest of this century and probably beyond. No one should rule out the possibility that by 2050 the region will be calmer and kinder. There is actually a decent chance that it will. But, equally, it would be unrealistic not to acknowledge that this is one of the places that might draw itself and the world into catastrophe. So what can sensibly be said?

There are three key issues: the relationship between Israel and its neighbours; the behaviour of Iran; and the importance of oil and gas in the region and the world. The first two will really be driven by geopolitics rather than economics, and given the unpredictability of those – witness Libya – all one can do is note the issues. But some thoughts on these might be helpful.

As far as Israel is concerned, two things stand out. One is that it is the most sophisticated economy in the Middle East. The other is that it does not play much of a regional economic role. In terms of its structure and competences it is a fully developed economy, akin to those of Western Europe, North America, Japan and so on. But it is not really integrated into the region. Its economy is plugged into Europe and North America, not the Middle East. The reasons are obvious. It is a Jewish state in an Arab region, with all the difficulties over the West Bank and Gaza, and with its neighbouring countries.

Leave aside the politics. It is not helpful for outsiders to opine on that. Let me instead quote this powerful passage from the last of his Reith Lectures by the Israeli-born pianist and conductor Daniel Barenboim, recorded in Jerusalem in 2006.[6]

> And therefore if Israel wants to have a permanent place it must become part of the Middle East, and it must be aware of the culture that already existed here, and not pretend, as has been done for a long time now, that it was a desert and an uncultured one at that. For the future of Israel it is necessary for Israelis to open their ears to the Arab culture. This is not an issue of Israel denying its European roots but instead a question of enriching and enhancing its European heritage by placing it side by side with its Middle Eastern heritage. Otherwise the State of Israel will remain forever a foreign body, and as such there is no possible perspective of future for its remaining here, because a foreign body can exist in a society, or in music, or in a human being, only for a limited amount of time.

Barenboim was essentially talking about culture, but his point could equally be applied to politics and economics. The political warning is chilling for all. But the economic message carries hope, for the fascinating question is whether Israel might play a much greater role in the region's economy: to become a core part of it rather than an implant. Israel could revolutionise the entire Middle East. It could help the region improve its export access to developed markets and in particular the United States. Its technologies could help make energy-poor countries rely less on imported fuels and energy-rich ones rely less on oil and gas exports. It could help rebuild the neighbouring countries devastated by civil war, and, of course, boost the wealth of the people on the West Bank and in Gaza. It could lift educational and managerial standards throughout.

Might any of this happen? To suggest such a seismic shift, given the attitudes and dissonance of the present, might seem strange. But economic cooperation can proceed irrespective of politics. A Middle East where there was closer economic integration would be in everyone's self-interest and mutual self-interest can sometimes prevail.

Self-interest would lead Iran, the other non-Arab regional power, to build a better relationship with its neighbours in the Middle East – as well as naturally with the rest of the world. Of course, the reverse has been true: a bloody war with Iraq, a stand-off with the West, hostilities with its Arab neighbours across the Gulf, economic sanctions imposed by the US – a long list of miserable events and outcomes. The list is all the more disheartening when set alongside Iran's deep civilisation and its cultured and sophisticated people. Anyone who has visited Iran, as we did in 2016, cannot but be charmed by the welcome from its young and be impressed by the culture of that huge country.

Yet it is difficult to have much confidence about the future direction for Iran. At one extreme it is certainly possible that there will be a counter-revolution, reversing the series of events that led to the overthrow of the Pahlavi dynasty in 1979. The current theocracy would be replaced by some other form of governance. However, revolutions are almost always destructive and since it is difficult to see this happening in any peaceful or orderly way, that outcome is not something that anyone should wish for. At the other extreme Iran may continue to try to cut itself off from Western culture, and carry on its vocal attacks on the US and its allies elsewhere in the Middle East. The result would be a string of confrontations any of which might slip into another regional war. The worst outcomes of that do not bear thinking about.

So we have to hope for some middle way, and fortunately that is the most likely path forward. Elements would include a retreat from international threats and from the current paranoia with which the country's leaders regard the rest of the world. There would be greater tolerance of foreign thoughts and social ideas, and an effort to engage with the millions of Iranian people who have left the country. There is so much about Iran that could, with quite small changes to its governance, blossom into the special place that it truly should be.

The third factor is the role of oil and gas. Parts of the region have little or none, while for some countries petrochemicals account for more than 90 per cent of export earnings. As we saw in Chapter 3 petrochemicals will continue to be a vital source of energy and chemical feedstock for the next thirty years and beyond. But while they will remain important, production levels are likely to plateau and then decline. It would seem likely, too, that prices will also plateau and then fall in real terms. The flow of money washing around the Middle East will become tighter.

For some countries this will mean little change. Gulf states with small populations such as Kuwait, Qatar and Abu Dhabi have such huge wealth that their people will be able to live in comfort for generations to come. Others, with more mouths to feed, will have to use their oil and gas revenues to invest in other industries, especially in services. Much depends on how Saudi Arabia manages this transition. Yes, it has huge natural resources which will drive it for another generation, but could it really become a big Dubai? Probably not, and if it were to fail in developing other sources of income it will struggle to give its people the standard of living they have become accustomed to enjoy. Iraq, with its troubled recent history and noisy current politics, needs money, too. For Iraq everyone has to hope that it will find the way to a more settled future for its people, that it will not be destabilised by being caught between a fractious Iran and its neighbours, and that the horrors of recent years will become a memory. We just have to hope.

Then for some parts of the Middle East lower oil prices might be a blessing. The region as a whole will in relative terms become less rich, but inequalities will fall. For plucky Jordan, the challenge will be to remain an island of calm. For Syria and in particular Lebanon, it will be to regain the modest prosperity that they once had before civil war savaged them. Better governance, such as Jordan has broadly enjoyed, could transform them. Lebanon was something of a paradise before the civil war that started in 1975 – the blend of French and Arab cultures, and a balanced constitution that respected the interests of both Muslim and Christian communities. We cannot undo history, but we can all learn from it.

That leads to a final thought. The region is fragile, but it also has huge human resources, and, as Daniel Barenboim noted, a culture that can enrich and enhance Israel's European heritage. One could take that point further. It is not simply Israel's heritage that it can enrich. It is that of the world. This is not a good time to be looking to the Middle East for universal values, and, among other issues, the treatment of the minority Christian communities there is deeply troubling. There is no point in trying to ascribe responsibility as to why that has happened. It has happened. What we might reasonably hope for over the next thirty years is that some of the region's traditional tolerance, built over many centuries, will gradually reassert itself. You can see it in Jordan now, coping as it does with millions of refugees, water shortages and other challenges. It would be silly to say that the Middle East needs a bigger Jordan. What is worth saying is that the region needs many of its embedded cultural traditions to be respected and supported, and its embedded tensions to be controlled and contained.

To be frank, this is one of the parts of the world where things can go horribly wrong over the next thirty years. We should all be troubled about that. But we should not allow our fears to blind us to the possibility that things could equally go rather right. The Middle East deserves a following wind instead of the headwinds it has faced for so many years. It is hard to be hopeful right now but some day that shift in the wind will come.

11

Australia, New Zealand and the Pacific Ocean

TWO LUCKY COUNTRIES, NOT ONE ...

The use of the word Oceania as the continent that encompasses Australia, New Zealand and the islands of the southern Pacific has rather slipped out of fashion. People use Australia or maybe Australasia instead. It is a pity because the Pacific may play a much bigger part in the future of our planet in the years ahead. It is nearly one-third of the world's surface, bigger than all the world's landmasses put together, and with half the world's water. Yet we know so little about it. We will, I am sure, know much more in thirty years' time.[1] We will come to that in a moment. Let's first think about the two English-speaking countries at its south-western corner, Australia and New Zealand.

Australia is the lucky country. In most regards it will remain so, for it will have a following wind over the next thirty years for many reasons. It has space. It has a culture that is envied in much of the world. It is in the East Asian time zone, currently the second fastest-growing economic region after Africa. It is part of the Anglosphere. It has all the other strengths noted in Chapter 1. There is one enormous issue. It is the driest continent and is threatened by climate change. Indeed, in that sense it is probably the most vulnerable country of the developed world.

Australia will continue to be a magnet for migrants, and migration will gradually pull it further away from its Anglo-Celtic roots. Its population will be heading towards forty million, and it will remain young and vibrant. It will be an economy that will be driven even more than now by education, information and entertainment rather than by mining and agriculture. It will, in short, continue to be a great success story – one of the places in the world where talented people will increasingly choose to live, work and play.

The shadow is that Australia will have to learn to cope with a warmer and probably even dryer climate.[2] This will not be a question of learning to manage its scarce water resources more carefully or of fitting homes and offices with more powerful air-conditioners. It is certainly all that. It is equally that the country will have to rethink both how to live with climate change, and also how to set about reversing it. Of course, no nation of forty million people can do much to change how the rest of the world tackles this. What it can do is to develop and apply best environmental practice. Australia will be perfectly habitable thirty years from now. But its leadership has to think far beyond that. What can Australia do to make sure it is a green and pleasant land through to 2100 and beyond?

It is easy to pose the question, but impossible to do more than sketch an approach. Obviously Australia should seek to apply best cost-effective environmental practice. How you cajole and nudge an independent society to do so is another matter, but really it will need a combination of science and common sense. How do you apply technology in a cost-effective way? To what extent can any democratic nation push people to change their behaviour if they don't want to? The less obvious approach, however, is to think of Australia as a sort of test bed as to how other developed societies might combat climate change, in much the same way as Japan is becoming a test bed for how to cope with an ageing population and Scandinavia a test bed for social policies. Australia will have a lot to learn, but it may also turn out to have a lot to teach.

There is one further set of decisions facing the country. It will be how fast it should grow – grow, that is, in population. A country that is geographically isolated and is inherently attractive for migrants can manage immigration more easily than one with land borders. If migrants don't want to come, well, you have a very different set of problems. The faster Australia grows, the more it will change. Those changes may be for the better, may be for the worse, or more likely a mix of the two. Only Australians can decide which way they want their country to head. They do, however, have a choice, and that in itself is a luxury denied to much of the rest of the world.

New Zealand has choices, too, but they are narrower. It will grow. It will remain a haven, a safe place in a turbulent world, as indeed it has been during the pandemic.[3] It will continue to influence the rest of the English-speaking world with its pioneering social and economic policies. Its physical isolation will become less of a defining feature as communications technologies become ever cheaper and ever more competent. For New Zealand – and unlike Australia – the direct impact of climate change seems likely to be neutral.

The rougher the world becomes, it would seem the more attractive the outlook for New Zealand. But no nation can cut itself off, except perhaps in the extreme circumstances of a pandemic, so the challenge will be to be more than an interesting and attractive community with a reasonable standard of wellbeing, but for ever in the shadow of its bigger brother to the west. It will in terms of its influence continue to punch above its weight. But it has to be able to retain, attract and welcome talent and to do that it may need more than the lifestyle that it offers. It is so much more than the bolt-hole for the uber-rich that it became during the pandemic.

Whatever happens over the next thirty years Australia and New Zealand will be fine. If one of the big ideas of this book is right, that this will be a strong period for the Anglosphere, then whatever they do they will be pulled along. They will be junior members of an elite premier league club. They have a fascinating hand of cards to play, perhaps the most interesting of any two countries in the world. Will they play them skilfully? Probably yes. So not one lucky country, but two.

... AND THE PACIFIC, THE GREATEST OCEAN

This book is mostly about people, about countries, about what happens on the world's continents. It has to be, for we are land creatures. Our future will be determined mostly by how we manage our custody of the 30 per cent of the planet on which we are able live, not the 70 per cent of its oceans. But it cannot be right not to acknowledge, however briefly and imperfectly, how our future as a species is also intertwined with whatever happens under the seas. Since more than half the world's water is in the Pacific it seems right to end this projection of how the world might look in 2050 with some thoughts about the oceans in general and the Pacific in particular.

We know so little about the Pacific. Exclude Australia, New Zealand and New Guinea and there are only a few millions of us living on its 25,000 islands. What we do on the little pinpricks of land does not have the capacity to change the world in the way that what we do on and under the Pacific does. Human beings have not been kind to the oceans and particularly the Pacific. With the possible exception of Antarctica, the Pacific is the most remote place on earth, yet parts of it are among the most polluted. There is a mass of discarded plastics the size of Texas between Hawaii and California. It is overfished, legally and illegally. It is suffering from acidification ... the list goes on.

Yet it also has the capacity to help the planet, for oceans absorb[4] at least a quarter, probably more, of the carbon human activity releases into the atmosphere. Understanding more about what the oceans might do could lead to a breakthrough in tackling climate change. The Pacific can't fix the problems we have helped to create, but the more we know about it the more likely we are to find solutions.

There is a wider point here, for this is not just about the specific concern, albeit a grave one, of climate change. The more we learn about the oceans and the creatures that live in them, the more sensitive we will be in balancing our own short-term objectives against our wider responsibilities to preserve the planet for future generations. The Pacific has the deepest place on earth, the Mariana Trench. It is encompassed by the Ring of Fire, the meeting point of several tectonic plates, so-called because 70 per cent of volcanic activity and 90 per cent of the world's earthquakes occur around the Pacific Rim. These events include the largest volcanic eruption ever recorded, Mount Tambora in Indonesia in 1815, and the world's strongest recorded earthquake, the Valdivia earthquake in Chile in 1960.

We do at least know quite a lot about the activity around the Pacific. We know much less about what goes on in it. Less than 20 per cent of the world's oceans, and a smaller proportion of the Pacific, have been surveyed.

We are already learning so much more. In 2017 only 6 per cent of the ocean floor had been surveyed. Then a project led by the Nippon Foundation set to work to create the General Bathymetric Chart of the Oceans.⁵ The target for completion is 2030. This is a mapping exercise, but other knowledge will inevitably flow from it. While it is pure speculation to guess at what we might learn about the Pacific, it is worth noting that the Ring of Fire could deliver a seismic blow – literally – to the world economy. It took six years for the population of Christchurch, New Zealand's second largest city, to recover to its previous level after the 2011 earthquake. If a similar or worse blow were to strike Los Angeles, the US's second largest city, or Tokyo, the world's largest city, then the consequences would be dreadful. We had a glimpse of the latter, also in 2011, when an earthquake and tidal wave set in train the events that led to the Fukushima nuclear disaster. With the possible exception of Vesuvius, which overlooks Naples, the greatest threat to human life from seismic or volcanic activity comes from the Ring of Fire.

So the Pacific basin holds great hope and great danger. The more we understand and respect it, the more likely it will be that we can deploy its potential value to humankind and the other species on our planet. The more likely it will also be that we can deal with those dangers and forestall catastrophe. And come 2050 we will know much, much more.

The Big Ideas of This Book

The Big Themes That Will Shape the World Ahead – Fears, Hopes, Judgements

BALANCING CERTAINTIES WITH UNCERTAINTIES

I should start this concluding chapter with a word of thanks to the reader for having travelled along with me so far. I have tried to look at the evidence and give my best shot as to how the world will develop over the next three decades. Of course I am worried that there is something huge that I am missing. I take some comfort from having spotted, nearly thirty years ago when writing *The World in 2020*, three of the features that have dominated the past few years: Brexit, political rupture in the US and a pandemic. But there will be things that will happen to the world a generation hence that I will have failed to spot. There will also be errors of judgement as to how important, or indeed unimportant, some of the forces I have identified really turn out to be. In any case, as the evidence accumulates we will need to modify our expectations. I see this book as a template against which people can fit their own ideas – to agree or disagree as they see fit. But more than that, I hope it helps all of us to assess the significance of events as they unfold. So this is really a journey into the future that we are making together.

Of course, the levels of certainty vary enormously. Some things we can be reasonably sure about: for example, that the world's population will be around ten billion people. Others we cannot be sure of at all. The best – or, I fear, worst – example of that will be whether the world has managed to cope effectively with climate change. My aim, however, is to give the overall feeling I have for the probability of particular outcomes. As events unfold or we learn more, those probabilities will inevitably change. I hope this gives a structure that will help all of us put the flow of events into perspective: what really matters and what is just noise.

One important objective, as I hope was clear from the Introduction, is to counter the negativity bias of so much of the commentary: to be realistic about the dangers and difficulties but also to be clear about the broadly positive outcomes for the welfare of our species and of our planet. I will in a moment set out the ten things that seem to me to matter most, ten things that will define the way the world develops over the next thirty years. They are on balance positive, some obviously so, some that require a certain amount of faith for them to turn out towards the favourable end of the spectrum. But it would be both dishonest and unconvincing not first to acknowledge my greatest fears. Here they are.

WHAT MIGHT GO WRONG?

1. The US political system fails to hold together

The US has to make its way through three difficult transitions. It has to share its wealth and opportunities more evenly. It has to move from being the world's largest economy to being the second largest after China. And it has to accept and indeed welcome becoming the world's first truly multiracial society.

All three have been bubbling away, and with the presidency of Donald Trump they burst out into the open. His support came from a wide variety of people, but if there was a common theme it was that many of them felt they had been denied the opportunities that were available to the liberal elite. My fear, when writing *The World in 2020* in the early 1990s, was that the revolt against elites might take place outside the political system, threatening democracy itself. As it turned out, the Constitution held. But if future US administrations fail to tackle the power of elites, there will be further challenges, probably led by someone more effective than Donald Trump. I am confident that US democracy will indeed pull through, more confident seeing the peaceful elevation of Donald Trump to the presidency, his chaotic departure from it and the election of Joe Biden. But I may be wrong. There has to be genuine equality of opportunity, and genuine respect for different shades of opinion. There may not be enough of either.

The second challenge is no longer being top dog. This will be very difficult for the American people, more difficult than it was for Britons, who could attribute their nation's loss of wealth and power to the exhausting effort the nation had to make in the fight against Hitler. The US has no such narrative for its citizens. The argument in this book is that by the middle of the century it will have become clear that, as China ages, the US is pulling ahead again, and the prospect will be for it to regain its status as the world's largest economy by the end of the century. But the US has first to get through several decades of relative decline without losing its self-confidence.

The transition to a truly multiracial society will be tough for all. It will require a deep commitment to making this work, not simply a virtue-signalling, box-ticking façade. The argument here is that the US will remain the great magnet for talent from all around the world and that this will be a key factor enabling it to retain its importance and authority. Becoming even more multiracial, and honouring the contribution of its African American citizens, will be a source of great strength. But the country has to accept that change at a deep level, for only then can it make such a society work for all its members. Writing against the background of the Black Lives Matter protests, building such a society seems an enormous challenge. But it has to be done. Maybe my confidence that it will be done is unfounded.

Behind these three specific challenges is a more general fear. Global leadership has to come from somewhere. The argument of this book is that we are moving to a more balanced world, where the emerging economies play a much more important role. That is welcome, inevitable and right. But the world still needs an anchor. A decent, self-confident United States can provide that leadership. It cannot come from anywhere else. This leadership will come as much by example as by anything else. It will remain the world's chief military power for the rest of this century, but its influence will be as much by what it is as what it does: soft power backed by hard power. Were the US to lose its self-confidence, then the world would become a much more dangerous place.

2. China, India and the US mismanage their relationship

Tensions between the US and China will inevitably mount, particularly so around the moment when China passes the US to become the world's largest economy. If the argument of this book is right, China will become calmer internally and less aggressive externally as its population ages. But it has to get from here to there, probably experiencing some disruptive political transformation in the 2030s or 2040s. China has also to accept the rise of India, a climb that will continue through the second half of the century. The flashpoints are obvious: a military takeover of Taiwan by China, border disputes with India, the status of the South China Sea and so on. It is so overwhelmingly in the self-interest of both nations, and indeed the rest of the world, to manage this transition in a calm and orderly way that it should be almost unthinkable that they will fail to do so. But miscalculations happen, and it is easy to envisage a series of events that would lead to catastrophe.

If, for example, it were to become clear that the Covid-19 virus did indeed escape from a laboratory in Wuhan and that the Chinese authorities deliberately concealed its origins, then any trust in the US towards China would evaporate. Or if an attempt by China to take control of Taiwan resulted in a large number of deaths, the US might react violently even though it would not be in its direct self-interest to do so. Or maybe there will be a confrontation not directly with the US but with India, and that then spills over into a tussle involving the US military forces, too. My worry is that deep down China has contempt for the US, and that deep down the US does not understand or respect China.[1] In any case the tensions will inevitably climb through the 2020s, making this a most dangerous period for the entire world.

3. Russia overplays its hand

Russia may suffer some sort of convulsion that damages both itself and its neighbours. Maybe it has: its invasion of Ukraine may be that convulsion. This is the world's largest landmass. Its current leadership is unpredictable, difficult for the rest of the world to deal with and probably more precarious than it seems. The judgement in this book is that Russia will play a smaller role in the world as its population ages and shrinks. However, to have 11 per cent of the world's land controlled by a regime that aggressively invades its neighbours is a danger to the entire globe. The danger is not so much that the Russian tanks will sweep across Poland as they have across Ukraine. The unified and powerful response of the West, and especially the Ukrainian people, to that invasion will transform the relationship between Russia and the rest of the world for a decade, maybe longer. It is impossible, writing in March 2022, to judge whether a new Iron Curtain has been drawn across Europe, but it seems likely that until there is a change of regime the West will be determined to contain Russia. And it will succeed in doing so.

The even greater danger for the rest of the world is that Russia might make some other mistake, perhaps some environmental experiment that goes wrong, that would have grave global consequences. Think of Chernobyl only much worse.

There are two things to remember here. One is that the Russian people deserve to be respected. The other is that the present regime will not be there for ever, and Russia will return at some stage to the ranks of the nations governed under the normal rules of acceptable behaviour. But we cannot be confident that this transition will be peaceful or orderly. Disorder in a nuclear-armed power rightly terrifies the entire world. That danger may be a temporary one, but it is a dreadful danger nonetheless.

4. Sub-Saharan Africa fails to escape from poverty

The relative optimism noted in the sections on Africa and
the Middle East may be wrong. The continent will continue
to be damaged by internal conflict, population growth and
environmental degradation. The balance of probability may
be that in general the nations of sub-Saharan Africa improve
governance, handle their divisions sensitively and successfully
improve their people's welfare. African people are, after all,
among the most entrepreneurial on earth. That is the mainstream
projection. But even if that general proposition is correct, there
will be instances of failure. Environmental degradation will add
to the pressures brought about by population growth. The most
troubling possibility of all would be if the youngest region of the
world were also to become the most volatile. The politics of the
Middle East add a further dimension to this instability but they
are at least a known factor. The world has lived with these for
many years. What it has not lived with will be Africa accounting
for a quarter of the world's population and rising, and with too
many of its young people being without a job.

What happens then? There is both a moral obligation for the rest
of the world to help, and a powerful self-interest in doing so. An
unstable African continent would be a catastrophe for humankind.
But quite apart from the practicalities – aside from emergency
relief, what can the rest of the world actually do? – outsiders have
to recognise that often in the past their interventions have made
matters worse rather than better. Notwithstanding the multitude
of problems they face, I am inclined to back the people of Africa.
But it will be very tough.

5. Religious conflict bursts out

Religion is not widely discussed in this book. That is not in any way
to downplay its importance to people of belief, or the influence
that religion has had over the centuries in shaping the world we live
in now. It is simply because people with an economics background

have less to contribute than those from other disciplines and competences. But it is impossible not to acknowledge the difficult relationship between the followers of the three largest religions of the world, the 2.5 billion Christians, the 1.8 billion Muslims and the 1.1 billion Hindus. There are inevitable flashpoints along the frontiers where dominant religions meet, such as India and Pakistan and the southern edge of the Sahara. Immigration, notably into Europe, has created new tensions, and the relationship between Israel and its neighbours remains one of the most controversial in the world.

On a long historical perspective such tensions have ebbed and flowed, and it seems sensible to expect periods of cooperative co-existence to be interspersed with periods of conflict. Alas, we seem now to be moving through a period of more tension, less tolerance and greater risk of open conflict. At best this is depressing; at worst, when tension leads to brutality, this can become a human tragedy. Reason would say that people of different beliefs should respect each other and work to the common good. The reality too often is they don't.

The modestly comforting way of looking at this is to see rising intolerance as a cycle that will reverse itself quite soon. I think that is the more likely outcome. The less comforting possibility is that the world is still in the very early stages of rising intolerance and that the pendulum will not swing back for many, many years. We cannot know, but if the latter view turns out to be true then religious conflict will continue to cast a dark shadow over us all.

6. Environmental degradation and climate change become irreversible

The next area where the positive conclusions may be wrong is the ability of the world to tackle environmental degradation. My argument is that technology will race to the rescue, slowing the damage that human beings are doing to the environment, and eventually reversing it. There are two ways in which this optimism might be misplaced.

One is that technology does not help enough. Yes, it can help reduce the damage, and, yes, it can help us to adapt in positive ways. But we may not be able to move fast enough and there may be irreversible changes to the climate that will make some parts of the planet difficult places for human beings to live. That might lead to migration on a scale that we have yet to contemplate, as hundreds of millions of people have to flee lands that have become uninhabitable and try to rebuild their lives elsewhere. On a thirty-year view this may be unlikely but in the second half of this century?

The other is that there is something big happening that we are missing. We know about the dangers of a tipping point in climate change and can work towards stopping the world reaching that moment. However, it would be arrogant for us to assume that, for all the work being done, we know enough about our planet not to be surprised and shocked by something beyond the limits of our imagination. Reason says that we will be sensible enough not to pass that tipping point for our planet's climate. Prudence says we should be on guard.

7. The long-term blow from Covid-19 – and pandemics that follow

The Covid-19 pandemic has warned us both of the fragility of our interconnected global economy and of the health challenges facing humankind. This pandemic itself was foreseeable. As noted earlier, *The World in 2020* warned of the dangers of a 'killer virus', though in the context of AIDS, the affliction that had burst out in the 1980s and early 1990s. SARS and MERS, two epidemics more closely associated with Covid-19, were still then in the future. What was almost impossible then to contemplate was the scale of the damage that a pandemic might do to the world economy. We know now better.

The world managed to contain, though not eliminate AIDS. It will contain Covid-19, and learn a great deal about how to tackle other similar viruses as and when they appear. But there will be other attacks on our health and wellbeing in ways that are impossible to predict. Our weapons are inevitably designed to fight the current war. We have to hope that they can be modified to fight the next ones, too. But even if they do, there will be long-term damage to us all. There are positive lessons, as already acknowledged, from the way global resources were marshalled to create the vaccines. But among the negative consequences will be that in the West at least people will be less confident of governments, now they have seen the limits of their competence. People will be more suspicious of other countries in general and China in particular. Perhaps my hopes are unfounded that the world will continue to gain the benefits of globalisation and tackle successfully its negative elements. Maybe the barriers to international cooperation will rise.

The comforting thought is that the world will learn the right lessons from this dreadful episode. For example, the effort to control Covid-19 will throw up other medical developments that will help control other diseases. The teams that developed the vaccines are already deploying what they have learned in other areas. Other great battles, such as coping with the waning effectiveness of existing antibiotics, and slow development of new ones, need to be fought. Now researchers may get the resources they need to fight them. But more than this, the world has learned a great deal about public health policy. There will be improvements in general hygiene and behaviour that will benefit all. The lifespan of people in most of the world will continue to increase.

The dispiriting thought – and this is my fear – is that the world may not learn these lessons and that the early years of the twenty-first century will seem to future generations a golden age of global cooperation.

8. The Middle East becomes truly unstable

The Middle East will always remain a flashpoint. It is where our civilisation began, the sites of the first cities, the lands of the first farmers and the birthplace of three of the world's great religions. But it is fragile and will remain so. It is easy to sketch a path towards a more harmonious future. This would include a just and permanent future for the West Bank and Gaza Palestinian territories; a rapprochement between the West and Iran; wise governance in Saudi Arabia and the Gulf states; greater economic prosperity in Egypt – the list goes on. It is, alas, equally easy to pick out the points of tension and predict disaster. Of those, obviously some sort of nuclear catastrophe must be at the top. But quite apart from that, recent history has been profoundly distressing. The so-called Arab Spring was a misnomer for uprisings that started in 2010 and which set off a series of bitter and bloody conflicts. These seem likely to continue in some form or other through the 2020s, maybe beyond.

The balance of probability is that, while tensions will remain, the Middle East will at some stage return to more comfortable co-existence between its kaleidoscope of cultures. But it has to build and share prosperity, for only that way can it find employment for its young people. If its young feel angry and dispossessed the Middle East can never be comfortable with itself.

9. The information revolution might have a malign impact, not a beneficial one

No journalist can call for less information. A world that is better educated and has wider access to knowledge must surely be preferred to one that is the reverse. Yet the great swathes of information now available, coupled with the rise of social media, seem to have undermined confidence in the veracity of what people read and see. Not only do people select views that support their own. They also select the news that chimes in with those views, thereby reinforcing their positions. Most worrying, there seems to be evidence that the higher people's education levels, the more adept they are at seeking out the evidence to support their views and the more likely they are to discount evidence that challenges their position.[2] This trait, confirmation bias, is not new at all. But it seems to have been encouraged by technology. More information has led to more disinformation. We simply do not know whether there is a technological fix that enables truth to fight its way to the top, or whether efforts to filter facts from opinions (and indeed from alternative facts) will fail. A Pew study[3] in 2017 on the future of truth and misinformation was, unsurprisingly, divided. The tussle over the 2020 US presidential election demonstrated that if people do not want to believe something is true, they won't do so, whatever the evidence.

In theory the more information there is, the more valuable are people with two sets of skills: sorters and boosters. The first are people who can sift through the mass, pick out the signals from the noise and help people understand what is true and important and what is neither. The other is people who can boost the signals, make people sit up and listen to their messages, whether constructive or destructive. In practice the sorters are often distrusted, witness the low reputation of journalists, or under pressure from their readership allow themselves to become advocates rather than judges. And the most effective boosters are those that peddle rubbish. The outcome has been confusion and distrust.

Maybe this is overly pessimistic. I hope that once people become accustomed to the vast availability of information and the perils of social media, gradually the benefits of widespread knowledge will shine through. Cults and conspiracy theories will continue to spring up as they always have, but there will be enough common sense around to enable humankind to keep pushing its understanding of the world forward.

10. The threat to democracy

That thought about the ways in which information can become corrupted leads to a final fear: that the entire principle of democracy will be undermined over the next thirty years. In a way, anyone who believes in democracy should be celebrating. A larger proportion of the world's population lives under some form of democracy than ever before in human history. Despots stand for election, even if their victory is made certain by rigging the ballots. But democracy is threatened.

The threat was well described by Barack Obama. In an interview in *The Atlantic*[4] in 2020 he said: 'If we do not have the capacity to distinguish what's true from what's false, then by definition the marketplace of ideas doesn't work. And by definition our democracy doesn't work.'

There is one obvious response to that, caught in the famous quotation of Winston Churchill: 'Many forms of Government have been tried, and will be tried in this world of sin and woe. No one pretends that democracy is perfect or all-wise. Indeed it has been said that democracy is the worst form of Government except for all those other forms that have been tried from time to time.'[5]

However, to say that every other system is worse will for some people at least sound less than convincing, given that China appears to be outperforming the West. It may turn out that the more serious threat to democracy is not the inability of the electorate to distinguish truth from falsehood, because most people have a common-sense scepticism of everything politicians of all colours say. Rather it is a wider loss of confidence about both the quality of governance that many democracies offer, and the entire market economic system of the West.

The two major crises of the twenty-first century have left a sense of unease that we are not running things well. The financial crisis of 2008/9 and the recession that followed undermined confidence in the financial system. Then the uneven response of the UK, Europe and the US to the Covid-19 crisis made their governments look inept. By contrast, China on both occasions seems to have performed better. It managed to avoid recession in 2009, thanks to a huge counter-cyclical investment programme. And then again in 2020 it became the only major economy to end the year with a larger economy than the year began. That is a remarkable achievement given that the virus originated in China. Actually, there are solid reasons to be confident about the long-term performance of the West in both crises, and some democracies in East Asia, including South Korea and Taiwan, achieved a response as effective as mainland China. But anyone who believes that democracy is the least bad form of government must acknowledge that it has to lift its game.

TEN BIG − MOSTLY POSITIVE − IDEAS

Anyone reading the book will have different takeaways: different ideas that seem important and different conclusions from the evidence set out. As a guide − and, remember, this is a template into which people must fit their own assessments − here are the ten big ideas that seem to me to be the most important shapers of the world over the next generation. Start with the biggest of all.

1. A middle-class world

In 2050 some two-thirds of the world's population will be middle class or rich. This has never happened before in the history of our species. There has never been a majority of humankind that has access to decent healthcare and education, has been able to travel, can eat good-quality food and for most has a reasonable range of work opportunities. Thanks to the communications revolution, this new great middle class has something else that previous generations did not have: immediate easy access to the pool of global knowledge.

We are accustomed to thinking of a world of rich and poor countries, the so-called advanced economies and the so-called emerging ones. It is useful shorthand, just as measuring a country's living standards by GDP is useful, too. In another thirty years there will still be highly developed countries, middle-income ones and poor ones, as there are now. But the balance will have shifted. There will be more wealthy and middle-income countries − and people − and fewer poor ones.

However, while we can be very sure that most people in the world will have broadly similar middle-class incomes, we cannot be at all sure of the extent to which they will have similar middle-class values. In any case those values themselves change over time. We may all live in similar homes and work in similar offices and factories, but we may spend our leisure hours quite differently. People also have different priorities in their spending patterns. Thus Japanese and Chinese people of similar earnings save a higher proportion of their income than Americans or Britons. Family attitudes are different: should young people marry before or after they start a family, or not marry at all?

Many of these differences are unimportant in the sense that countries can happily co-exist with different social norms and different legal frameworks. Eastern and Western Europe have rather different social attitudes and that has led to tension within the EU. Within the US there are big tensions between states. But both manage to get along well enough. True, the UK left the EU but that was not because middle-class Britons had different social attitudes from middle-class Germans or French. The issues were of identity and sovereignty, not values.

Looking ahead, there are two main questions. One is whether the new middle class will change the attitudes of the old middle class. The other is whether these attitudes will shift more generally, and, if so, how.

On the first, the shift of numbers will be important. It depends on the definition you take, but it is broadly true to say that at the moment there are more middle-class people living in developed economies than there are in emerging ones. But by 2050 that balance will have shifted. The new middle class will outnumber the old middle class by two or three to one. At the moment the flow of ideas is, again very broadly, from West to East. The lifestyles of Western Europe and the US are the ones emulated in China and India.

Go to one of the new executive housing estates on the outskirts of Bangalore or Shanghai and you are transported to an approximation of a housing estate for senior managers in California. The children will be dressed in the same outfits and be playing in the safe streets of the gated community with the same sports equipment. The homes will have similar household appliances. Maybe the new middle class will have a little less living space than their counterparts in more established economies, but from a distance at least their lifestyles look much the same.

These apparently similar lifestyles will continue to look much alike. But they already diverge under the surface. Take one example.

There is more desire in China for orderly schools that focus on the three 'Rs', reading, (w)riting and (a)rithmetic, than the self-expression and creativity favoured by many schools in the West. To oversimplify, China has followed the Japanese rather than the American pattern. Looking forward, if the children who have had a Chinese schooling (and, of course, there are many versions of that) start to do better in their careers than Americans and Europeans, then expect that to change education worldwide. Schooling is local, but the market for talent is global.

There are many other examples of possible ways in which Asia may come to have more influence over Europe and America. These include the idea of extended families that plan to support all their members, though, of course, with group obligations, rather than the extreme individualism of some societies of the West. They include less reliance on the state to provide welfare services, including pensions, and more personal responsibility. If the Western European welfare state model proves unable to cope adequately with the continent's ageing population, as seems likely, then the burden will shift to families to find ways of supporting their elderly members, as currently happens in Japan.

In short, the West is likely to realise that it can learn from the East. In financial terms a typical middle-class American family may in another thirty years' time have more resources than a typical Chinese one. But in aggregate buying capacity Chinese and Indian families will not only have more firepower; they may deploy their resources more judiciously. If that becomes apparent they will change the West.

What of more general shifts in this global middle-class society? That is a tough call. We know there is a pendulum: that ideas and values move over time. So we can be confident that the new middle-class world will feel different from that of today. There is obviously the vast area of social behaviour, the relationship between men and women, to inequalities of income and wealth, to race, and to religion. What is deemed normal and acceptable now will not be so in another generation, and vice versa. Different societies will continue to be startled, even shocked, by these shifting sands.

We can all make our guesses. Mine would be that there will be some movement towards more authoritarian society; that group identity and responsibility will become more emphasised vis-à-vis individual identity and rights. The way in which many Asian countries responded more effectively than Western ones to the Covid-19 crisis was thanks at least in part to the way in which their people accepted the loss of individual liberties for the greater good of society.

There is something else that may define the new middle-class world. That is whether the increased wealth of this older population will make people more peaceable. This is enormously important to the future of our species. On the face of it a prosperous global middle class should be able to contain aggressive nationalism. An older world should be a less aggressive one, or at least one that contains competition and directs it to positive ends. The most important investment for grandparents is the very future of their grandchildren. They will not want to wreck the world for them.

That is what should happen. The rising ranks of the middle class should make sure that their leaders get along. But the history of the twentieth century would seem to run counter to that comforting notion. In 1914 Europe was dominated by a rapidly growing, prosperous middle class, but it allowed its leaders to plunge it into catastrophe. It is impossible to ignore the surge of nationalism in China and India, and the rivalry between the US and China, without hearing a distant echo of those drumbeats that led to war. The First World War ended nearly a century of globalisation.

Maybe we should not make too much of that parallel, particularly since we still have the folk memory of the two world wars to help us remain grounded. However, we have to get through the next twenty years of rising global tensions before the ranks of the by then elderly middle class will assert control, calm us down and divert our energies to the many other challenges the world faces. Aggressive nationalism and intolerance of all kinds, including religious intolerance, will ebb away. But of this we can be sure. A middle-class world has never existed before in the history of our species. What is happening will have as big an impact on humankind as the

Industrial Revolution, the economic transformation that set this advance in motion.

2. A calmer, more comfortable, more self-confident United States

It might seem jarring to predict a calmer and more comfortable future for the US, writing in the aftermath of the tumultuous presidency of Donald Trump, and the evident serious political, racial and economic tensions across the land. Given the prospect of China overtaking the US in economic size sometime around 2030, it might seem strange to suggest that the country will become more self-confident. But the positive predictions for the US in this book are based on one almost certain outcome, one probable proposition and one reasonable, though more contentious, judgement. Together they suggest that by 2050 the US will be both happier with itself and more sure of its value to the world.

The near-certainty is that the country's population will carry on growing, one effect of which will be that it remains as the most youthful nation of the developed world. Population growth drives rising GDP, though not necessarily GDP per head; youthfulness drives dynamism. At the moment China does indeed pass the US in economic size, it will almost certainly have a falling population while the US will have a rising one.[6]

The probable proposition is that the US remains a magnet for talent. One of the big themes of this book is that countries that can attract energetic, talented people will thrive vis-à-vis those who lose their human capital through emigration. The US will naturally remain attractive for lower-skilled migrants because they will be able to do better there (and send money back) than they can in their home countries. It is not easy to be totally confident that the US will remain quite so powerful a magnet for top skills – except that if you ask where else those people might go, it is not easy to see alternatives. Maybe fewer Europeans will want to leave, depending on the relative success of the European economies. However, the greatest pool of such talent will be China and India. Some will go to Europe, if regulations allow. Some will choose the UK, particularly those who have studied there. But most will surely choose the US. If that is right, then US vibrancy is assured.

The third reason for confidence is mostly an intuitive judgement, but there is reason behind it. That judgement is that the US will tackle its current political, racial and economic tensions, and make a success of that effort.

Politics first. As noted in the Introduction it was possible to predict back in the early 1990s that there would be some rupture in US political life, probably in the second decade of this century. It has happened with the clash between the Obama, Trump and Biden administrations. The danger was that this break might happen outside the political system and result in the country losing control of itself. But the system has managed to hold together. The democracy that the Founding Fathers constructed has done what they designed it to do: it pulled back from chaos. To say that is not to take sides in the great American political tussle. I don't think it is right for non-Americans to so do. But a friendly Briton is allowed to observe that the US is coping with its political divisions with no more strain than many other democracies would have done, and less explosively than it did with many US fissures in the past. Democracy is and will remain a rough beast, but, if past experience is any guide, American politics will settle down to a less toxic level of trench warfare, a higher level of decency and greater respect for the truth.

Race. The idea developed earlier in this book is that, as the US population becomes even more diverse and non-Hispanic, white people become a minority, and the country will begin to become more comfortable with its diversity. That is not to pretend that racial tensions will disappear any more than it is to deny that many minorities have been put at a quite unfair disadvantage by their race. They won't; and they have. Rather, it is to hope that once it is clear that diversity is universal then it will be accepted and cherished. Remember that what is happening in America is paralleled by shifts across the world. Chinese people will be living in the world's largest economy. Indian people will be living in its most populous nation. African people will be living in the fastest-growing continent.

The world is becoming more balanced, with the advantages that Europeans and Americans gained by being the first nations to have an Industrial Revolution gradually eroding. In that better balanced world it would be natural for the US to become better balanced, too.

Race will remain an important and troubling issue everywhere: not only in the US, or even perhaps especially there. But all societies have always had to manage their divisions. Differences of wealth, class, age, opportunity and ability will always lead to deep unfairness. The task of decent people is to chisel away at these divisions, trying to nudge their societies towards more harmonious and cooperative outcomes. The US is at least trying to correct some of the imbalances in its societies, and another generation of effort should enable solid progress to be made.

And economics? Making that progress will be vastly easier if economic tensions are contained and channelled to positive ends. All countries have economic inequalities, so this is not about absolutes but, rather, of degrees. The US is towards the top end of inequalities among developed countries, and, however you measure them, the gaps have tended to widen. The middle class in particular has been squeezed. The result has been that, whereas in the 1950s and 1960s US middle-income earners were at the top of the global league table, now their living standards have stalled or declined. They are no longer clearly the best-paid workers in the world once healthcare and holiday allowances are taken into account. They may still have more living space than their counterparts in Western Europe, but they also have to cope with greater insecurities. The result has been understandable and huge frustration.

The US cannot be at ease with itself if this frustration is allowed to continue. Politicians of both sides have to tackle this. So far they have been only marginally successful, and on many measures not successful at all. Mercifully, the economic forces that have led to this great middle-class squeeze seem likely to go into reverse. One reason for thinking that is that the wages in industries that produce goods that are internationally traded have been squeezed down by the advent of China entering the world stage. Now

China's pay rates are rising, reducing its cost advantages. Another is demography. The US workforce will grow more slowly as it ages, and as the ready supply of labour tightens wages will be nudged upwards. Still another is technology. It is early days, but one of the side effects of the Covid-19 crisis seems to be an increase in labour productivity in service industries. The world is learning to use technology better. That should help increase real wages. And, finally, there is tax. There seems to be a general mood that the US tax system could become more progressive, helping middle-income earners.

Pull all this together and there is at least a reasonable chance that the next thirty years will come to be seen as a period of relative success for the US. The run-through to the 2040s will not be an easy ride, and internal and external tensions will tug away at its self-confidence. But the nation will probably emerge both more admired around the world and more at ease with itself by the middle of the century than appeared likely at the beginning of the 2020s.

3. The rise of the Anglosphere

One of the themes noted in the sections on the English-speaking countries was that they were members, whether they liked it or not, of an informal grouping that would become more important over the next thirty years. For a Briton to use the term the Anglosphere might seem to hark back to the days of the British Empire, a view that saw the independence of the American colonies as a family row between cousins. It is an image caught by Winston Churchill in his *A History of the English-speaking Peoples*, but one that might now seem at best nostalgic and at worst pretentious. True, the Commonwealth still exists and will continue, but does the idea of an Anglosphere make any sense?

Consider this. In 2050 the most populous country of the Americas will be the United States, English-speaking. That of Africa will be Nigeria, where English is the principal language. That of Asia will be India, where English is the unifying language despite the promotion of Hindi. Australia is the most populous part of Oceania. And Europe? Well, it looks likely that whatever political form the UK takes by then and whatever its relationship with Ireland, the combined population of the islands of Britain and Ireland will have passed that of Germany. And looking a little further ahead, by the 2070s the UK may well have become Europe's most populous nation.[7]

If you look in terms of the proportion of GDP accounted for by this wider English-speaking grouping, it is going to be something like 40 per cent of the world economy. What's more, it will be rising. The US is likely to grow faster than continental Europe, and India is almost certain to be growing faster than China.

The point here is that for a number of reasons the English-speaking world will become relatively more important both in headcount and in economic size. This has not yet been widely appreciated, partly because most people who happen to have English as their first or second language do not see themselves as sharing a common heritage. If they do, it is more an accident of history, and, what's more, a history aspects of which are sometimes resented. This is not simply a question of India promoting Hindi, or Hong Kong encouraging the use of Mandarin. Ireland has spent a century seeking to revitalise Irish Gaelic to reassert its heritage before the Norman invasions of the twelfth century onwards. Scotland is doing much the same with Scottish Gaelic.

The US is certainly ambivalent about its language determining its identity. George Washington famously made the point in his farewell address that for the United States, 'It is our true policy to steer clear of permanent alliances with any portion of the foreign world …'[8] The Republic of Ireland defines itself by stressing its European relations rather than its cultural and family links with the UK. Australia and New Zealand look to Asia for trade relations rather than to Europe or North America. Canada is in economic terms an offshoot of the US. These countries (minus Ireland) may cooperate on security in the Five Eyes alliance, but that is a practical group with a narrow purpose.

As for the wider Anglosphere, the countries of the emerging world and sometimes called the New Commonwealth, its members have such a wide range of political and economic differences that the idea that they should combine in anything more than ad hoc mutual interest is quite unrealistic. Politically they align with different blocs: Pakistan with China and India increasingly with the US, for example. If India does form a closer relationship with the US, stepping back from the non-aligned status it followed for most of the years since independence in 1947, it will be because of the threat from China, not because Americans speak English. The common language brings all sorts of advantages, linking countries together, even when they don't particularly want to be aligned.

The Commonwealth will continue and will do so because countries find it a useful identity. Countries are still joining, most recently Rwanda in 2009, and as of 2020 there are several applications pending. The only member to have left and not subsequently rejoined or applied to rejoin has been the Republic of Ireland. But it would be silly to see it as more than the loosest of clubs, with few rules or obligations, held together partly by shared history but mostly by the glue of mutual interest. The important point here is that the mutual interests of the Commonwealth and the US are likely to become stronger.

So see the Anglosphere not as a throwback to the British Empire but, rather, as a group of countries linked by language, but that also have common interests most of the time. Its members will certainly steer clear of any permanent alliances, as George Washington would have wished of the US, but they will find that circumstance keeps encouraging cooperation. It is the diametric opposite of the EU, with its ambition to create an ever-closer union. The Anglosphere will never be a union, or anything like it. It will simply be a group of nations, led often reluctantly by the US, that generally manage to get along with each other. That lack of ambition is a strength, not a weakness. The Anglosphere will become more important to the future of the world because its members will in aggregate become more important, not because some long-dead politician had a grandiose vision that it should be so.

4. China – the world's largest economy moves from aggression to cooperation

Part of what happens to the US depends on what happens to China, its main rival for global leadership. The big prediction of this book is that there will be some sort of transformation in China, most likely in the 2030s, when it turns away from aggressive expansionism and places more emphasis on a calm and more comfortable life for its elderly citizens. It is based on the premise that demography and politics will interact in a positive way to enable this shift to happen.

The facts of an ageing China, with the population falling quite swiftly by 2050, are not really in dispute. Its economy will slow down, rather in the same way that Japan's has done. The question really is how ageing will interact with social ideas and aspirations. An elderly China will feel quite different from the bouncing, relatively youthful one of today. The ideas and values of the old will gradually become much more evident and influential. That shift will change Chinese politics in one of two ways. There could be some sort of rupture and a move to a more democratic system. Or there could be a gradual adoption of the changed values without any change in the political system, replacing aggressive expansionism with a more settled effort to improve lifestyles in a sustainable way. I don't think it is possible to call which way the transformation will take place, but happen it will.

There is a temptation in the West to see this in ideological terms. Will China transition to some form of democracy or will it remain an autocracy under a charismatic leader? Surely it is more helpful to see it in practical terms. How will China define its self-interest? Will it want to cooperate with the rest of the world, accepting in a broad way the global norms of acceptable behaviour? Or will it want to impose its perception of national interest (or, rather, the perception of its leaders) whatever the rest of the world thinks?

Put the point this way. A single-party communist government that accepted global norms would be much easier for the US and the West to deal with than a democratic one that defied the opinion of the rest of the world and rejected those norms.

We cannot know which way Chinese politics will move, but we can have some feeling for how it will seek to relate to the rest of the world in the longer term. History helps a little, as there have been long periods in the past when the country looked inwards, running everything within its boundaries but not that interested in what happened beyond. The current period is an anomaly in that sense. Its Belt and Road Initiative, building infrastructure to speed trade around the globe, is seeking to establish Chinese influence far beyond its traditional territorial boundaries.

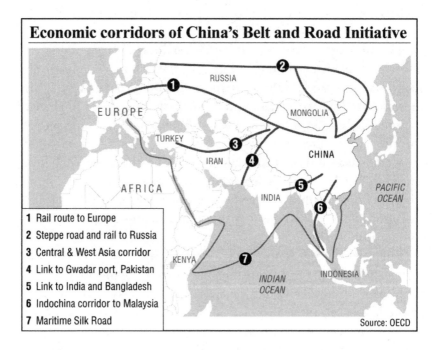

Economic corridors of China's Belt and Road Initiative

1 Rail route to Europe
2 Steppe road and rail to Russia
3 Central & West Asia corridor
4 Link to Gwadar port, Pakistan
5 Link to India and Bangladesh
6 Indochina corridor to Malaysia
7 Maritime Silk Road

Source: OECD

You could say this is payback for 'the century of humiliation'. But it would be consistent with the China of the past were the China of the future to retreat into its own area of influence. It would also be consistent with the experience of Japan over the past half-century.

At some stage China's global ambitions will fall away. Until they do, the country will be a difficult partner. This is an immediate issue for the US, but actually an issue for everyone. My hope is that once it is clear that China is the world's largest economy and is respected for that, it will step back and become less threatening. The hostile language and commercial tactics that it deploys against nations that appear to thwart it will fade. True, there is no evidence of this at the moment, but it is too early to expect this theme to manifest itself. If this is right, while the next two or three decades will be difficult, the second half of the century will be easier for all.

There is, however, a period of profound danger ahead. There will be flashpoints. China will not be comfortable until it regains control of Taiwan, and this may not happen peacefully. Relations with Russia could break down. The South China Sea is an obvious source of tension. The rise of India and its own fractious relationship with Pakistan could spark open conflict with China, a conflict that could get out of control. We all have to hope that the world navigates its way through these dangers to the calmer and more cooperative second half of the century.

5. The European Union diverges into a core and a periphery

Any Briton writing that they expect the European Union to break up into a looser federation is liable to the jibe that 'they would say that, wouldn't they?'

After all, the UK has been only the second country to leave the EU and its predecessor organisation the Treaty of Rome, formed in 1957. The other country, Greenland, remains an associate member as an Overseas Country and Territory and its citizens keep the right to move to and live in the EU.[9] The UK's rupture is of a different league. While there are many discordant voices within the EU member states, there is as yet no significant force suggesting that another member will leave in the next few years. The big difference, aside from scale, is that most countries facing calls to exit are net recipients of funds from the EU, whereas the UK was the second largest net contributor.

However, if the experience of the UK is anything, it is how a small dissident group within a country can become the mainstream driving force in less than twenty years. The challenge for the EU will be to persuade its members that the net benefits they receive from membership exceed the costs they have to bear. The argument of this book is that, as Europe becomes a smaller part of the world economy, that balance of advantage will shift. Instead of being members of the world's largest trading bloc, they will find they are members of a league representing perhaps 12 per cent of the world economy, and one losing ground in relative terms with every year that passes. For core Europe – Germany, the Benelux, France and perhaps Italy – the benefits of easy access to each other's markets will probably outweigh the costs. For outer Europe, and especially the newer joiners, membership will appear increasingly irksome. If the financial transfers remain substantial the EU can probably buy their continued allegiance, but that will become irksome in its turn to the net contributors. This will not be a stable relationship.

The argument of this book is that there will be some set of events that will turn the EU from its aim of becoming an ever-closer union to a more utilitarian association of very different cultures even though their history happens to have land borders with each other. Something called the European Union will survive, but, to do so, the EU will have to reverse its efforts to force countries to converge and instead focus on managing a looser club.

Will the euro survive? Within the EU it is thought to be almost inconceivable that it might not. The argument in this book is that if it does it will be as a smaller currency zone centred on Germany. The longer weaker member states keep it the more their economies will struggle, and the most likely outcome will be to split it into two zones, with the outer zone devaluing against the core. It is impossible to see the detail or the timing, but it is easy to see that there will be some kind of currency crisis that will test the entire basis on which the EU is founded. That crisis will be the moment of decision as to what form the looser union should take.

What the EU leadership does then will, for Europeans, seem a seminal moment in the continent's history. It could create the circumstances where the UK, Russia and Turkey become part of the outer group, though that outcome currently looks most unlikely. The UK will explore its other options, Russia will seek to destabilise the EU and Turkey will be looking towards Asia. Or the EU could simply shed a number of its members and pull inwards to something like the original signatories of the Treaty of Rome. Viewed from the outside, however, it will not matter that much what Europe decides to do. It will be a comfortable corner of a much bigger world. The action – the forces that will shape the future of humankind – will be taking place elsewhere. One of those places will be India.

6. India and the Indian subcontinent – the prize within its grasp

India will be both the world's most populous country and its third largest economy. What will it do with the authority that this status inevitably and properly gives it?

The argument in this book is that whatever happens India will move towards its rightful place as one of the great powers of the world. But it also faces massive challenges. These include the need to improve the quality of its education system as well as broadening its reach. There will inevitably be grave environmental pressures. And India has to learn to live with the rest of the subcontinent, particularly Pakistan, but also Bangladesh, as well as finding a way of turning China into a friendly partner rather than a spiky rival.

The next thirty years will be very dangerous. India has moved away from accommodating its Muslim population as enterprising participants in a non-sectarian state, and focused instead on the identity of its Hindu majority. It has made some progress in economic and educational reform, but inequalities are increasing. Its infrastructure is improving, but only slowly. The environmental challenges have yet to be tackled adequately. So, lots of problems. But looming over everything is the relationship with China, and its ally Pakistan.

You have to assume that there will be no war with these three countries, or at least that the skirmishes that will continue to flare up will be contained. It goes without saying that war between three nuclear-armed powers would be a catastrophe for the entire world. It does not bear thinking about, so let's not do so. Instead, let's think about what might go right.

There has to be a political change in India, so that it sees itself as a partner with Pakistan and Bangladesh in promoting the role of the subcontinent as a global leader. There also have to be corresponding changes in Pakistan and Bangladesh. They do not need to be friends or political allies and they won't be. But there is a powerful case for closer economic cooperation and at some stage in the future the potential benefits from such cooperation will lead to that happening. Maybe this will not happen by 2050. Maybe there has to be some searing political or environmental event that drives the leaders of each country into appreciating that it is in the self-interest of all that the people of the subcontinent should work more closely together.

On a very long view it is easy to predict that this will happen, and impossible to say when. Maybe history has some clues, perhaps looking back far beyond the British or the Mughal empires to the classical age of the Gupta Empire and earlier. It is for scholars of Indian history to comment on that. Maybe the subcontinent could move towards a region of economic cooperation, the original form of Europe's Common Market, though without any objective at all of political union. Maybe it will simply be better trade links on an ad hoc basis. But in a way the detail does not matter. There will in any case be no final form for the political relationships between the peoples of the subcontinent. What is inevitable is that the voice of those peoples will be louder, their importance greater and their ability to shape the future of the world one of the vital themes of the second half of this century.

7. Africa becomes more important to the world

It will be a nail-biting ride, but the judgement here is that Africa will manage the journey towards its bigger role in the world economy with more success than many outside commentators expect. It will, in the jargon of financial markets, surprise on the upside. That success will not be universal. It would be unrealistic to expect that. Religious tensions will continue in Africa, as elsewhere. Some countries will stumble from one economic crisis to the next, partly as a consequence of poor governance, partly because of rising environmental pressures. Just about everywhere populations will climb, and the argument of this book is that finding jobs for this mass of young people is the continent's greatest single challenge.

It is absurd to generalise about such a vast and diverse continent. But I think it is important to recognise that the positive story about its future – that it will tackle many of the problems it faces with reasonable success – is just as likely an outcome as the negative one – that it will be struck by environmental and human disasters and be unable to cope. More than this, I suggest that instead of the view of many people in the developed world who see Africa in a dismal light, it will be more realistic to recognise its strengths and accept that its values will always be different from those of the West.

Put it this way. Nigeria will never be a big Sweden. If it manages to hold together, it will become over the next thirty years a bigger, even more vibrant and somewhat better organised version of itself. It certainly has the huge engine of its entrepreneurs to power it along. That will be a beacon. The world will, I suggest, be surprised by the success stories that come out of Africa: examples of real progress in lifting living standards and opportunities for its people. The gap between success and failure is a narrow one. Above all, Africa will have the resource of youth, a resource that will become increasingly scarce in our ageing world. If the majority of its nations can educate enough of its young people, they become the solution to so many problems. If not, well, it will be troubling indeed. But what is overwhelmingly likely is that Africa in 2050 will be just as boisterous, just as unruly as it is today, but also rather better at channelling that teenage energy into positive outcomes. We should all hope that will be the case.

8. Globalisation changes its direction – from moving goods to moving ideas and money

It had become pretty clear before Covid-19 struck that the form of globalisation that had run from the end of the Second World War had stalled. Physical trade as a proportion of global GDP had reached a plateau around 2008, as the push-back against offshoring jobs and managing complex supply chains gathered impetus. But invisible trade, that is trade in services, continued to climb. These trends seem to have been intensified by the response to the virus. Manufacturers became more aware of their vulnerability to interruptions to supplies and sought to buy local where they could, whereas at least one important part of trade in services, cross-border financial flows, boomed.

The last great period of globalisation, that of the Victorian and Edwardian eras, was brought to a halt by the First World War. The spectre of that catastrophe looms over all of us. As Jack Ma, founder of the Alibaba online retail giant, puts it, 'Globalisation is good ... when trade stops war comes'. Since China in general and Alibaba in particular have been great beneficiaries of China's incorporation into the rest of the world economy, you could argue that he would say that. You could equally argue that the relationship is at least partially the other way round: when war comes, trade stops.[10] But the idea that if countries retreat from trading with each other it signifies a potentially dangerous shift in geopolitics is surely right. All great economic movements come to an end and it seems pretty well inevitable that the next thirty years will see rising nationalism and at least some retreat from globalisation. Indeed, that trend has already begun. In 2020 Jack Ma found himself in conflict with the authorities for some outspoken remarks about financial regulation, and his own future is unclear.[11]

Many people would see a retreat from globalism as a disaster, a rerun of the protectionism of the 1930s. It need not be. More likely, trade will change its nature. Raw materials will continue to be transported about the globe, though trade in fuels will top out and start to decline as energy use switches away from coal, oil and gas. Trade in agricultural produce will continue, for there will always be some parts of the world where there is a competitive advantage in food production. But trade in manufactured goods will decline.

The money will be in design and marketing; manufacture will be local.

So we will move towards a world where globalisation will take the form of cross-border flows of money and know-how rather than flows of goods and people. This will be less contentious, less obvious. Jobs will not be seen to be lost because production moves offshore. Things will be made locally instead. There will still be great international competition for skills, but often the people will not need to move to deploy those skills; they will work remotely instead.

We caught glimpses of this new form of globalisation in the emergency measures taken to combat the pandemic. If you can do your job from home, that home does not need to be in the same country as your employer or client. There will be practical limits to this new version of offshoring, and those limits will slowly become apparent. But in a generation's time the world will have figured out how best to exploit the possibilities created by the communications revolution: what needs human contact and what does not. The consequence of that will be a less aggressive, less socially destructive, and accordingly more acceptable version of globalisation.

There will still be trade tensions and certainly still huge rivalry between the major economic powers, notably the US and China. Protectionism won't go away. But there is not likely to be any return to the destructive trade restrictions of the 1930s. A middle-class world would lean against it, for it would be the group whose living standards and general wellbeing would be most at risk. And to go back to the first theme outlined above, it will be the global middle class who will be running the show.

9. Technology to the rescue

One of the great sources of tension over the past thirty years has been the way in which inequalities have shrunk between countries but have widened within them. The narrowing between the developed and emerging worlds is easy to explain. It is catch-up: China has deployed the technology developed in the

West. It is harder to explain why inequalities have grown within most developed countries, but part of the explanation has been that the benefits from technological advantage have been slow to flow through into general living standards. Even allowing for the under-measurement of the benefits from the communications revolution, living standards in most developed countries have at best climbed slowly. The principal challenge has been to achieve as rapid gains in productivity in services as we have been able to generate in manufacturing.

That now seems almost certain to change, partly as a result of the new business practices that have been introduced to cope with the Covid-19 pandemic. The emergency has forced companies the world over to think of new and more efficient ways of creating and delivering their services. This is as important as Henry Ford's moving production line. The combination of big data and artificial intelligence was already leading to huge improvements in both quality and efficiency, but it always takes time for new practices to spread. Now the world has had several years of normal competitive development crammed into a few months. What would have happened slowly and steadily has happened at lightning speed.

One of the challenges that anyone predicting the advance of technology has to face has been the failure of such predictions in the past. Some technologies leap forward; others get stuck. As we saw with the iPhone and the iPad, there are some technologies that we only know we want when we get them. Until Covid-19 we did not know how much we needed Zoom. There will be products and services that will be commonplace in thirty years that we cannot really envisage now. However, if you stand back and think about what people ideally would want from technology there are some signposts as to how the future will unfold. For example, there is a universal demand for better and cheaper healthcare. That will grow as the population ages. It is possible to envisage massive advances in medical technology, diagnostics and treatments that will both cut health bills and enable people to live longer and healthier lives.

It is a straightforward idea but an enormously important one: too often we see technology in terms of what it might be able to do, and not enough in terms of what we might want or need it to do. So it may be that by 2050 people will be able to fly to Mars, but that will have zero impact on most people's lives. What will change our lives will be the ways in which technology can help tackle practical global problems. The two most important of these will be productivity in the service industries and degradation of the environment. The first is noted above; the second is the final of the ten big ideas the book seeks to highlight.

10. A more harmonious relationship between humankind and our planet

We have nowhere else to go. So we have to make sure that our planet remains a habitable and decent home for ourselves and all the other species with which we share the earth. This is not just about climate change and the extent to which human activity has speeded up global warming. It is about the vast range of ways in which human activity has had an impact on the world over the past several thousand years, and the ways in which this impact has intensified after the Industrial Revolution.

The spread of economic development over the past half-century, welcome in so many ways, has increased the burden we place on the planet. That has forced most developed countries to think about how their economies might be reshaped to cut that burden. The switch to low-carbon sources of energy is one headline aspect of that, but there are many others. These include increasing crop yields, reducing freshwater use, preserving and extending forests – and so on. The effort to combine sustainability with higher living standards will dominate the next thirty years and beyond.

There will be unavoidable trade-offs. However, the argument outlined in Chapter 3 is that there will be technical breakthroughs that will enable these trade-offs to be made at a much lower cost on both sides. As far as climate change is concerned there is likely to be some moment when the world suddenly decides to throw everything it has at tackling the problem. The race to create effective vaccines against Covid-19 in 2020 has been a wonderful example of what the combination of governments, multinational enterprises and academic institutions can achieve when they absolutely have to. The response was not planned centrally, for there was no single point where decisions were taken. Instead, it happened through a mixture of competition and cooperation. And in a rough and ready way it worked.

See that as a dry run for humankind's efforts to contain the damage we have done to the planet. At the moment, at the beginning of the 2020s, the will is not there. There is an awareness among the elites in Western Europe and North America of the scale of the problem, but the response has been incoherent, hypocritical and unsatisfactory. That will change, particularly since global capitalism is aware that investors will put increasing pressure on both private and public sectors to rethink their policies. Put bluntly, if there is money to be made in pursuing green growth, market capitalism will figure out a way of doing so. And if voters call for more regulation, governments will bring that in.

What is difficult to see is the process and the timing of change. My instinct is that there will be a sudden lurch, triggered by some catastrophic event or some charismatic leader. Take the switch to electric cars. That is happening with astounding speed. But it took a maverick South African working in California to produce the car that led to the landslide. The switch would probably have happened anyway, but without Elon Musk and Tesla it would have happened twenty years later.

Conversely, it is quite possible that there will simply be incremental mounting pressure for change, and that some set of technical innovations will trigger sudden economic transformation. If the economics change, everything becomes much easier. But we don't need to know, indeed we cannot know, how technology will race to the rescue of the environment. We just need to be confident and alert, and to be realistic about what can be achieved in the timescale necessary.

As far as climate change is concerned this is partly, as argued earlier, a matter of insurance. Because the uncertainties are so great and the time lags so uncertain there is the case for acting earlier rather than delaying until the evidence piles up. But environmental good practice is really also a matter of morality. We are custodians of the planet and must strive to be good stewards of its resources. If that sounds prim, consider this. As societies age and wealth and living standards climb, people are able to pay less attention to their day-to-day needs and more to the long-term interests of their children and grandchildren. Economic growth does put a greater burden on resources, as indeed does population growth. But there is already some shift in values taking place, and that shift is likely to broaden and deepen in the years ahead. Thanks to the combination of this shift in values and advances in technology we will be able to lighten the footprint human beings place on our planet – as indeed we must.

THE WORLD IN 2050 ... AND BEYOND

What will the world really feel like a generation hence? I have tried to explain my fears and hopes, but it is time to give my best judgements as to how those fears and hopes will pan out. These are based on the evidence, but also on a sense of history and my own intuition.

I am reasonably confident that humankind will manage to navigate its way through a difficult period without some catastrophe that would make everything in this book quite irrelevant. There is the obvious tussle between the two economic giants, the US and China, and that will get worse before it gets better. There are tensions from the rise of India as it marches towards becoming the world's third largest economy. Sadly, there will also be continuing difficulties in the Middle East and other flashpoints. Russia will continue to be an awkward partner and will try to destabilise the EU. Africa must curb its internal conflicts if it is to push on to greater prosperity. But will any of these tensions be allowed to burst out into a world war, or even a new cold war akin to the period between the end of the Second World War in 1945 and the fall of the Berlin Wall in 1989? My answer is: no, they won't. The world's main powers will have grumpy co-existence, not armed conflict.

THE WORLD IN 2050

My prime reason for believing this is that there is still the fading folk memory of the catastrophic first half of the twentieth century. That experience has inoculated the world for a while yet. Global leaders will not be so stupid or so arrogant as to go there again.

I believe that the world will also manage the huge transfer of power to the emerging nations, and the developed countries will accept that. They have no alternative but to do so. But this should not simply be a question of acceptance. I think people in Europe and North America will come to respect the optimism of the two Asian giants, China and India. I expect, too, they will come to acknowledge that some characteristics of Western societies, in particular the excessive attention paid to individual rights rather than collective harmony, do not make people happier. The West has still many things to teach the East, including the drivers behind technological advance and legal systems that will sometimes curb the power of the executive. But it also has much to learn, more perhaps than most Britons, Europeans and Americans find easy to accept.

Technology will race on. Most of the advances will be incremental but there may well be some step change in our knowledge that puts everything we think we know into a different perspective. Could there be something akin to the way in which Charles Darwin explained how human beings evolved in his book *On the Origin of Species*?[12] Or maybe a technical discovery of a similar order of magnitude to antibiotics, or, I am afraid, the atom bomb? Both are certainly plausible, even likely. Less likely would be the discovery of a new physics – something that overturns the laws that we regard as bedrock. I don't think it is for economists to speculate about this. My point is simply that there will be technological advances that will transform our day-to-day lives over the next thirty years in much the same way as the iPhone and social media have done over the past thirty years. Most of those advances already exist in some prototype form in a lab or a research department somewhere in the world. A tiny handful will burst out and change some aspect of our lives. But they won't change everything. In 2050 people will still be living in the same homes, eating much the same food, dressing in more or less the same clothes, travelling using refined versions of present-day technology, and in the main part doing jobs that would be recognisable today. What will change is that there will be a general increase in global living standards, with many more of us living what in shorthand we call middle-class lives.

Here is a huge prize to be grasped. When most people are leading middle-class lives the world will be dominated by their ideas and aspirations. The challenge will be to give a decent lifestyle to those who will not yet have joined the middle classes, for if poorer people feel they cannot surmount the barriers and share in prosperity, they will rebel and threaten progress for all. This is about differences in wealth in the various regions, but it is also about differences in age. Thus Africa will remain the poorest continent, partly because of its history but also because its age structure means it is the youngest continent. It takes time to build wealth. Young people will inevitably be poorer than older people. But an elderly, rich world cannot erect walls around it to keep the young and the poor out. It has to help spread the wealth if it is indeed to grasp the prize.

That leads to a final thought. The next thirty years are of profound importance. They are important to us personally, obviously, because this is the world we are living in and we cannot choose the moment to be born. But not only is it objectively the best time to be alive – that Barack Obama quotation on page 31 – it is also a time of special importance for humankind. It is a period where humanity could make grave mistakes, over the environment, over technology and over harmonious or not so harmonious international relations. It is equally a period where we could get things right, laying the ground for a calmer and more settled second half to the century. We have to try to manage as best we can, squabbling with each other, of course – that's allowed – but also being aware of the common strands that bind us. We are so lucky to be living through this time. For all the evident troubles this is the most peaceful and prosperous time the world has ever known.

History does not end. To take 2050 as a date to focus on is simply to give a helpful snapshot of a familiar period of time: one generation ahead. Our children will be the age we are now. They will be peering into the second half of the century, to a time when the numbers of human beings on the planet will start to decline. That will shift our perspective of ourselves and our relationship with the planet. We will not change. Our ideas about how societies should be organised will shift a bit, but our hopes, aspirations, fears – and flaws – will be much the same. Our task then, as now, will be to keep and nurture the best of what we have, and do a little better where and when we can manage to do so. For our children and grandchildren, that is the challenging but ultimately thrilling journey ahead.

Notes and Sources

INTRODUCTION: THE JOURNEY FROM 2020

1 CERN, the European Organization for Nuclear Research, based just outside Geneva, gives an excellent brief record of how one of its researchers, Tim (now Sir Tim) Berners-Lee, invented the World Wide Web: https://home.cern/science/computing/birth-web/short-history-web. There are many histories of the development of the early browsers, with the Wikipedia entry https://en.wikipedia.org/wiki/History_of_the_web_browser one of the best.

2 After Angus Maddison died in 2010, his work has been kept up to date and modified where there is new data by former colleagues at the University of Groningen, the Netherlands, as the Maddison Project: https://www.rug.nl/ggdc/historicaldevelopment/maddison/releases/maddison-project-database-2018?lang=en. His book *The World Economy: A Millennial Perspective* is available in a number of languages from the OECD: https://www.oecd.org/dev/development centrestudiestheworldeconomyamillennialperspective.htm

3 Robert Solow wrote a biographical note when awarded his Nobel Prize in 1987: https://www.nobelprize.org/prizes/economic-sciences/1987/solow/biographical/ and there is an assessment of his work in the *MIT Technology Review*, December 2019: https://www.technologyreview.com/2019/12/27/131259/the-productive-career-of-robert-solow/. The UK economic study group tutor2u gives a simple explanation of the Solow Growth Model: https://www.tutor2u.net/economics/reference/economic-growth-neo-classical-growth-the-solow-model,

and Harvard Web Publishing has a clear presentation on the model for scholars: https://scholar.harvard.edu/files/nbairoliya/files/lec10.pdf

4 Jim O'Neill's *Building Better Global Economic BRICs* is available on the Goldman Sachs archive: https://www.goldmansachs.com/insights/archive/building-better.html

5 Dominic Wilson and Roopa Purushothaman, with Jim O'Neill, Paulo Leme, Sandra Lawson, Warren Pearson, and Goldman Sachs colleagues, *Dreaming with the BRICs*. This, too, is available on the GS archive: https://www.goldmansachs.com/insights/archive/brics-dream.html#:~:text=Over%20the%20next%2050%20years,The%20results%20are%20startling

6 The original projections by the HSBC economics team were called *The World in 2050* and covered just the top thirty countries. These were published in 2011. The next year the exercise was extended to cover the top 100 countries, and called *From the Top 30 to the Top 100*. The original report is available here: https://warwick.ac.uk/fac/soc/pais/research/researchcentres/csgr/green/foresight/economy/2011_hsbc_the_world_in_2050_-_quantifying_the_shift_in_the_global_economy.pdf, and the second exercise here: https://books.google.co.uk/books/about/The_World_in_2050.html?id=sGONnQAACAAJ&redir_esc=y. In 2018 the HSBC team did a further run of the model for the top thirty, correcting some of the inputs – though the broad conclusions were similar to the earlier exercises: https://enterprise.press/wp-content/uploads/2018/10/HSBC-The-World-in-2030-Report.pdf

7 Robert J. Gordon, *The Rise and Fall of American Growth: The U.S. Standard of Living Since the Civil War* (Princeton University Press, 2017), https://press.princeton.edu/books/paperback/9780691175805/the-rise-and-fall-of-american-growth

8 The *Wall Street Journal* dubbed Hal Varian as 'the Adam Smith of Googlenomics'. He has set out his view on the measurement problem in a number of places, including this interview with the American Enterprise Institute: https://www.aei.org/economics/googlenomics-a-long-read-qa-with-chief-economist-hal-varian/. His photography example comes from a presentation to a Brookings Panel, September 2016: *A microeconomist looks at productivity: A view from the Valley*, https://www.brookings.edu/wp-content/uploads/2016/08/varian.pdf.

9 The Brookings Institution carried a good summary of what was known about assortative mating in 2014: Richard V. Reeves and

Joanna Venator, *Opposites Don't Attract – Assortative Mating and Social Mobility*: https://www.brookings.edu/blog/social-mobility-memos/2014/02/10/opposites-dont-attract-assortative-mating-and-social-mobility/. A 2019 study, Branko Milanovic, *Rich Like Me: How Assortative Mating is Driving Income Inequality*, published on the *Quillette* platform, examines subsequent data and concludes the trend is getting even stronger: https://quillette.com/2019/10/18/rich-like-me-how-assortative-mating-is-driving-income-inequality/

10 Francis Fukuyama's essay 'The End of History?' was published in *The National Interest*, Summer 1989. The book *The End of History and the Last Man* (The Free Press, 1992), dropped the question mark from the extended title.

11 Car production fell back after 2017 and in 2020 was just under twenty million: https://www.oica.net/category/production-statistics/2020-statistics/

12 The Belt and Road Initiative, launched in 2013, pulls together China's effort to build global communications infrastructure, with a network of ports, railways, airports, energy projects and other investments around the world. An OECD study in 2018 concluded that there were considerable benefits from greater global connectivity, but noted that host countries needed to make sure they got the best value for money from their investments: https://www.oecd.org/finance/Chinas-Belt-and-Road-Initiative-in-the-global-trade-investment-and-finance-landscape.pdf. Since then it has become clear that many projects have not been proved to be good value for the recipients.

13 Britain had invaded Hong Kong in 1841, and it was ceded by China in 1842 in the Treaty of Nanjing. The Convention of Peking added part of the Kowloon peninsula to the British territories. There is a host of accounts of Britain's dishonourable behaviour towards China in the nineteenth century, but, for a short factual timeline of the seizure of Hong Kong and its subsequent return to China, the BBC is as fair and dispassionate a source as any: https://www.bbc.co.uk/newsround/52907269

14 Steven Pinker's website https://stevenpinker.com/publications/better-angels-our-nature gives access to his work, including future writings.

15 Hans Rosling's TED Talks are online: https://www.ted.com/speakers/hans_rosling. Bill Gates, who is a great enthusiast of his work,

has a fine explanation of why he believes '*Factfulness* is one of the most educational books I've ever read': https://www.gatesnotes.com/books/factfulness

16 The link to Barack Obama's talk to the students in Laos is at https://www.youtube.com/watch?v=nK7AbxTGDSU

I THE WORLD WE LIVE IN NOW

1 The US lead over Saudi Arabia and Russia, the next two largest oil producers, increased through to 2020, with the US then producing 20 per cent of global output. The government agency the US Energy Information Administration is a good source of output data: https://www.eia.gov/tools/faqs/faq.php?id=709&t=6

2 Ranking world universities was pioneered by the Jiao Tong University in 2003: http://www.shanghairanking.com/ARWU2020.html. Other well-regarded rankings include that done by two UK-based organisations, QS: https://www.topuniversities.com/qs-world-university-rankings, and *Times Higher Education*: https://www.timeshighereducat ion.com/world-university-rankings. Round University Ranking, based in Moscow, produces broadly similar outcomes: https://roundranking. com/ranking/world-university-rankings.html#world-2021, as does the US News and World Report: https://www.usnews.com/education/best-global-universities/rankings. The actual ranking depends on methodology and perhaps the nationality of the organisation carrying out the survey, but the differences between the different exercises are much less marked than the similarities.

3 One way of measuring US commercial dominance is to look at the market value of all its quoted companies vis-à-vis those of other large economies. Thanks largely to the valuation put on its high-tech giants, the German data group Statista calculated that in early 2021 US firms accounted for 56 per cent of the world total: https://www.statista.com/statistics/710680/global-stock-markets-by-country/

4 The fun way of catching a feeling for both the creation of Facebook and the privileged, driving Harvard University ethos that led to its birth is the 2010 film *The Social Network*. Inevitably the detail has been fictionalised, so the story should be taken with a pinch of salt. https://www.youtube.com/watch?v=lB95KLmpLR

5 The PISA (Programme for International Student Assessment) study was started by the OECD in 2000 and 'measures 15-year-olds' ability

to use their reading, mathematics and science knowledge and skills to meet real-life challenges': https://www.oecd.org/pisa/

6 The National Bureau of Economic Research explains why Canada, unlike the US, avoided not only the 2008 banking crash but also previous crises in the nineteenth century and in 1907 and 1930. Thanks to a concentrated banking system and a single strong regulator, no Canadian bank had to be bailed out. https://www.nber.org/digest/dec11/why-canada-didnt-have-banking-crisis-2008

7 The puzzle is that the country ranked highest in the world by its citizens should also come so close to breaking up. The issue is well explained in Harold D. Clark and Allan Kornberg, *Choosing Canada? The 1995 Quebec Sovereignty Referendum*, published online by Cambridge University Press in 2013.

8 https://www.wsj.com/articles/400-murders-a-day-the-crisis-of-latin-america-1537455390

9 *The Economist* explains what went wrong in a briefing in its edition of 15 February 2014, 'The tragedy of Argentina: A century of decline': https://www.economist.com/briefing/2014/02/17/a-century-of-decline

10 The Covid-19 crisis will almost certainly further increase the gap in economic performance in Europe that became evident since the euro was adopted. See: Dirk Ehnts and Michael Paetz, 'COVID-19 and its consequences for the Euro Area', *Eurasian Economic Review* (2021): https://link.springer.com/article/10.1007/s40822-020-00159-w

11 See http://www.shanghairanking.com/ARWU2020.html, https://www.topuniversities.com/qs-world-university-rankings, https://www.times highereducation.com/world-university-rankings, https://round ranking.com/ranking/world-university-rankings.html#world-2021 and https://www.usnews.com/education/best-global-universities/rankings

12 Andrew Haldane, then chief economist at the Bank of England, explained the UK's productivity problem in the Annual Lecture of the Academy of Social Sciences in 2018, *The UK's Productivity Problem: Hub No Spokes*: https://www.bankofengland.co.uk/-/media/boe/files/speech/2018/the-uks-productivity-problem-hub-no-spokes-speech-by-andy-haldane

13 Calculations on start-ups depend on whether you take amounts raised or numbers of businesses founded per head of population. As a rough indication, between 2015 and 2019 the UK raised more funds for start-ups than Germany and France put together. https://www.seedtable.com/european-tech-statistics

14 The only country in Europe with a higher proportion of services in national income than the UK in 2020 was Luxembourg, with its very large financial sector. In Germany services were 70 per cent of national income. https://data.oecd.org/natincome/value-added-by-activity.htm

15 The differences between Inner London and the rest of the country are particularly stark: https://vividmaps.com/the-top-ten-richest-and-poorest-areas/

16 The Office for National Statistics does regular reports presenting the most recent data on health state life expectancies: https://www.ons.gov.uk/peoplepopulationandcommunity/healthandsocialcare/healthandlifeexpectancies/bulletins/healthstatelifeexpectanciesuk/2017to2019

17 PISA study: https://www.oecd.org/pisa/

18 Haldane, *The UK's Productivity Problem.*

19 Ibid.

20 This study, published by the National Bureau of Economic Research, is here: https://gabriel-zucman.eu/files/TWZ2018.pdf. In 2021 President Joe Biden proposed that there should be a global minimum corporate tax rate to counter the practices that led to the loss of revenue from companies exploiting international tax loopholes.

21 These are 2020 figures. In 2021 the position of the US may be topped by China, which looks almost certain to become Germany's largest export market. It was number two, ahead of France, number three. Number four was the Netherlands and five the UK. So three of Germany's top five markets were outside the EU. https://tradingeconomics.com/germany/exports-by-country

22 The World's Top Exports keep a useful tally of export rankings: http://www.worldstopexports.com/car-exports-country

23 World's Top Exports: http://www.worldstopexports.com/drugs-medicine-exports-country/

24 World Bank: https://data.worldbank.org/indicator/NV.IND.MANF.ZS

25 The Netherlands and Mexico fight it out for top tomato exporter, with the Dutch ahead in 2018 and Mexico gaining top slot in 2019. https://www.worldstopexports.com/tomatoes-exports-country/

26 Ranking of luxury brands is a contested issue – is Porsche a luxury brand or a car manufacturer? – but if you focus on fashion and accessories, France clearly leads the way with Louis Vuitton

right out in front. https://www.businessupturn.com/companies/
here-are-the-top-10-luxury-brands-of-the-year-2020/

27 There are some coloured and remastered clips of the Exposition on
YouTube, which capture the atmosphere of the modernity of the
age, such as the moving pavement here: https://www.youtube.com/
watch?v=a-c28UwMAnc

28 Published by Princeton University Press: https://press.princeton.
edu/books/paperback/9780691037387/making-democracy-work

29 Between 2008 and 2016 Greece lost more than a quarter of its GDP.
Yannis Stournaras, governor of the Bank of Greece, gave a thorough
and balanced assessment of the impact of the recession on the
economy to the European Court of Auditors in 2018: https://www.
bis.org/review/r190816e.htm

30 Evidence for an upswing in the fertility rate is mixed. It has risen a
little since the early 2000s, though still well below replacement rate.
Official projections are here: http://www.ine.es/prensa/np994.pdf

31 Statista keeps a running tally of the size of these wealth funds. In
2021 Norway retained the top position. https://www.statista.com/
statistics/276617/sovereign-wealth-funds-worldwide-based-on-
assets-under-management/

32 The World Happiness Report analyses the happiness of people
in 156 countries. *The Conversation* carried an explanation of why
Denmark ranks at the top here: http://theconversation.com/why-
denmark-dominates-the-world-happiness-report-rankings-year-after-
year-93542

33 Russian education has been deeply affected by the decline in the
numbers of young people, but the government has pushed ahead in
trying to attract foreign students as well as sending its own people
abroad – with incentives to return. https://wenr.wes.org/2017/06/
education-in-the-russian-federation

34 There has been so much analysis of the achievements of Deng
Xiaoping that it is hard to know which to pick out. Two good
studies are a special report by the London School of Economics,
From Deng to Xi: https://www.lse.ac.uk/ideas/Assets/Documents/
reports/LSE-IDEAS-From-Deng-to-Xi.pdf in 2017, and *The charts
that show how Deng Xiaoping unleashed China's pent-up capitalist
energy in 1978*, published by *Quartz* in 2018: https://qz.com/1498654/
the-astonishing-impact-of-chinas-1978-reforms-in-charts/

35 In January 2021 the top five social networks ranked by number of users were American, led by Facebook and YouTube, but the next five were all Chinese. https://www.statista.com/statistics/272014/global-social-networks-ranked-by-number-of-users/

36 In 1997, when Hong Kong reverted to Chinese rule under the 'one country, two systems' agreement, it accounted for nearly 20 per cent of China's GDP. By 2020, thanks to the far faster growth on the mainland, Hong Kong was less than 3 per cent of China's GDP. https://www.ejinsight.com/eji/article/id/1580225/20170609-hk-versus-china-gdp-a-sobering-reality

37 Until Covid-19 struck, more forecasters, including HSBC, expected India to have passed Japan in the late 2020s. However, the damage brought about by the pandemic may delay that by two or three years, with Bank of America projecting that this will now occur in 2031. https://www.cnbc.com/2021/03/24/india-to-overtake-japan-as-third-largest-economy-in-2031-bofa-securities.html

38 The performance of Sri Lanka is particularly impressive, but Bangladesh has done well to close the gap with Pakistan. Indeed, by 2019 it had pulled level with Pakistan in terms of GDP per head. The biggest disappointment in relative terms has been Pakistan. In 1998 it was richer than China, but by 2019 its income per head was less than one-third that of China. https://data.worldbank.org/indicator/NY.GDP.PCAP.PP.CD?locations=IN-PK-BD-LK-CN

39 Countries count crime in different ways but it is clear Japan has the lowest murder rate in the world: https://worldpopulationreview.com/country-rankings/murder-rate-by-country. For overall crimes, Switzerland, New Zealand and Norway also report very low crime levels, on some measures lower than Japan: https://www.encyclopedia.com/articles/countries-with-the-lowest-crime-rate-in-the-world/

40 South Korea has become deeply worried about its low birth rate, still falling in 2019: https://data.worldbank.org/indicator/SP.DYN.TFRT.IN?locations=KR. In 2020 it declined even further as a result of the pandemic.

41 An excellent study by McKinsey Global Institute, *South East Asia at the crossroads: Three paths to prosperity*, argues that South East Asia will continue to be one of the most vibrant regions of the world in the period to 2030: https://www.mckinsey.com/~/media/McKinsey/Featured%20Insights/Asia%20Pacific/Three%20paths%20to%20sustained%20

economic%20growth%20in%20Southeast%20Asia/MGI%20SE%20
Asia_Executive%20summary_November%202014.ashx

42 The country studies by *Encyclopedia Britannica* give a straightforward assessment of the different countries' economic performance and challenges: https://www.britannica.com/place/Nigeria/Economy

43 Ghana is also one of Africa's most successful democracies, with fair elections and orderly transfers of power. https://www.nytimes.com/2018/03/10/world/africa/ghana-worlds-fastest-growing-economy.html

44 I became aware of this barrier to growth from a private conversation with Kofi Annan over lunch in Oxford. He told me that to travel from one African country to another the most convenient way was often to fly via London or Paris.

45 World Bank data: https://www.worldbank.org/en/country/ethiopia/overview

46 *Quartz Africa* is a good source for an assessment of both the progress and the challenges: https://www.oecd.org/pisa/, https://qz.com/africa/1109739/ethiopia-is-one-of-the-fastest-growing-economies-in-the-world/

47 The Oxford University Press Handbooks are also useful sources: https://global.oup.com/academic/product/the-oxford-handbook-of-the-ethiopian-economy-9780198814986?cc=gb&lang=en&

48 World Bank data: https://data.worldbank.org/indicator/SL.UEM.TOTL.ZS?locations=ZA

49 China's Belt and Road Initiative, linking China and Europe by improved ports (the belt) and better road and rail facilities (the road) is hugely controversial. Some projects have failed, leaving the country concerned with high debts and/or losing control over parts of its transport infrastructure. But the investment has produced massive visible results. https://www.the-american-interest.com/2019/04/04/misdiagnosing-the-chinese-infrastructure-push/

50 See http://www.shanghairanking.com/ARWU2020.html, https://www.topuniversities.com/qs-world-university-rankings, https://www.timeshighereducation.com/world-university-rankings, https://roundranking.com/ranking/world-university-rankings.html#world-2021 and https://www.usnews.com/education/best-global-universities/rankings

51 There are many commentaries on Adam Smith's real meaning when he wrote that. The full interchange between himself and

his friend Sir John Sinclair is: Sir John: '*If we go on at this rate, the nation must be ruined.*' Smith replied: '*Be assured young friend, that there is a great deal of ruin in a nation.*' There is a thoughtful note on the way the quotation is often misinterpreted here: http://adamsmithslostlegacy.blogspot.com/2008/08/is-this-correct-use-of-quotation.html

2 DEMOGRAPHY — AN AGEING WORLD AND A YOUTHFUL ONE

1 The *2019 Revision of World Population Prospects* is the twenty-sixth round of official United Nations population estimates and projections: https://population.un.org/wpp/. It is the most thorough study of population trends in the world and, given its long experience, the best base for thinking how demography will shape the world economy. Another interesting piece of analysis is that published in *The Lancet* in 2020, which also looks at the impact on the economic size of the various countries. The primary source for this book is UN data, but there are references to *The Lancet* research, where it suggests different outcomes. https://www.thelancet.com/article/S0140-6736(20)30677-2/fulltext

2 A record 13.6 per cent of all properties in Japan were registered as 'akaya', homes that had been abandoned without heirs or tenants, in 2018. https://www.bbc.com/worklife/article/20191023-what-will-japan-do-with-all-of-its-empty-ghost-homes

3 The National Institute of Population and Social Security Research (IPSS) is a national research institute in Japan, established in 1996 and affiliated to the Ministry of Health, Labour and Welfare. https://www.g20-insights.org/think_tanks/national-institute-for-population-and-social-security-research/

4 See the paper from Brookings Institution, Giovanna di Maio, *Italy and Immigration: Europe's Achilles heel*: https://www.brookings.edu/blog/order-from-chaos/2019/01/14/italy-and-immigration-europes-achilles-heel/

5 The authors note: 'we are fulfilling our duty as whistle blowers, even though we will no longer be around to say (sadly) "told you so".' https://www.robert-schuman.eu/en/european-issues/0462-europe-2050-demographic-suicide

6 Brookings published a simple summary of the census findings, noting that the country would become 'minority white' by

2045: https://www.brookings.edu/blog/the-avenue/2018/03/14/the-us-will-become-minority-white-in-2045-census-projects/

7 The Pew Research Center is a good source of unbiased analytical information about global economic and social data. https://www.pewresearch.org/fact-tank/2019/05/22/u-s-fertility-rate-explained/

8 President Putin has made it a priority to try to attract more immigrants. https://www.rferl.org/a/migrants-welcome-is-russia-trying-to-solve-its-demographic-crisis-by-attracting-foreigners-/30677952.html

9 There is a big debate in Russia as to whether its migration trends have reversed: https://www.rbth.com/lifestyle/329990-has-russia-migration-crisis

10 A handy way of catching these long-term trends in the relationship between China and India (and for the other major blocs) are the Angus Maddison Historical Statistics, which give estimates for both GDP and population, and hence also GDP per head: https://www.rug.nl/ggdc/historicaldevelopment/maddison/?lang=en

11 In 2019, just before the pandemic, India's unemployment rate was the highest since the 1970s. https://www.bbc.co.uk/news/world-asia-india-47068223

12 See *2019 Revision of World Population Prospects*: https://population.un.org/wpp/ and https://www.thelancet.com/article/S0140-6736(20)30677-2/fulltext.

13 See the paper published by the Hoover Institution, Jack A. Goldstone, 2019, *Africa 2050: Demographic Truth and Consequences*: https://www.hoover.org/research/africa-2050-demographic-truth-and-consequences

14 The origins of the phrase 'demography is destiny' have been tracked down by Professor John Weeks, San Diego State University: it was probably first used in the book by Richard Scammon and Ben Wattenberg, *The Real Majority* (New York: Coward-McCann, 1970). https://weekspopulation.blogspot.com/2013/11/the-origins-of-demography-is-destiny.html

15 In this paper the European Commission takes a relatively optimistic view of Europe's demographic challenges, looking through to 2060. Though it was published in 2019 it bases its calculations in the EU-28 – as though the UK were still a member. https://publications.jrc.ec.europa.eu/repository/handle/JRC116398

16 The Center for Immigration Studies, a Washington DC think-tank that describes itself as 'Low-immigration, Pro-immigrant', keeps a running total of US sanctuary cities, counties and states: https://cis. org/Map-Sanctuary-Cities-Counties-and-States

17 There have been many studies of how Ireland transformed both its population trends and its economic performance from the 1950s onwards. A good summary of the arguments by academics from Queen's University Belfast and University College Dublin was published by Economics Observatory in 2021: https://www. economicsobservatory.com/irelands-economy-since-independence- what-lessons-from-the-past-100-years

18 The *New York Times* looked at the data and outlook here: https://www. nytimes.com/interactive/2019/01/17/world/asia/china-population- crisis.html

19 World By Map publishes detailed information on a wealth of economic and population areas. The calculations on median age in 2020 range from Monaco at 55.4 years and Japan at 48.6, to Uganda at 15.7 and Niger at 14.8. In 2020 the median age of the world's population was estimated to be 31. https://www.citypopulation.de/ en/world/bymap/medianage/

3 RESOURCES AND THE ENVIRONMENT – DECARBONISING THE WORLD ECONOMY

1 *The Stern Review* is published by Cambridge University Press: https://www.cambridge.org/us/academic/subjects/earth-and- environmental-science/climatology-and-climate-change/ economics-climate-change-stern-review?format=PB

2 The United Nations Framework Convention on Climate Change explains what the Paris Agreement is about here: https://unfccc.int/ process-and-meetings/the-paris-agreement/the-paris-agreement

3 In 2006, Kofi Annan's initiative resulted in the Principles for Responsible Investment, an agreement signed by the heads of leading investment institutions from sixteen countries. https://www.un.org/ press/en/2006/sg2111.doc.htm

4 There has been a vast number of accounts about the Tesla story. *Business Insider* carried a clear summary in 2014 of the ups and downs of its early years, reminding readers that Elon Musk was not one of the original founders of the company. It was launched by Marc

Tarpenning and Martin Eberhard in 2003 and Elon Musk joined in 2004. https://www.businessinsider.com/the-complete-tesla-story-2014-7?r=US&IR=T#tesla-motors-was-founded-in-2003-by-five-silicon-valley-entrepreneurs-1. The company went public in 2010.

5 The World Resources Institute reckons that a quarter of the world's population faces extremely high stresses from lack of water supplies. https://www.wri.org/blog/2019/08/17-countries-home-one-quarter-world-population-face-extremely-high-water-stress

6 The Aral Sea began shrinking in the 1960s and in 2014 its eastern basin became dry for the first time in 600 years. https://www.nationalgeographic.com/science/article/141001-aral-sea-shrinking-drought-water-environment. Since then its northern part has started to refill and efforts continue to restore more of it. https://www.usaid.gov/central-asia-regional/success-stories/jun-2021-regional-efforts-restore-aral-sea-ecosystem

7 Since 1970 fewer people have died in famines than in any previous period of recorded history. https://ourworldindata.org/why-do-far-fewer-people-die-in-famines-today

8 Amartya Sen, *Poverty and Famines: An Essay on Entitlement and Deprivation*, 1983, available from Oxford Scholarship Online, November 2003: https://www.oxfordscholarship.com/view/10.1093/0198284632.001.0001/acprof-9780198284635

9 Palm oil production, much of it for biofuels, has been one of the key drivers of environmental destruction in South East Asia and increasingly in South America. https://www.transportenvironment.org/what-we-do/biofuels/why-palm-oil-biodiesel-bad

10 The UK government publishes a detailed annual report on the country's energy use and performance since 1970, including consumption by fuel and by sector: https://assets.publishing.service.gov.uk/government/uploads/system/uploads/attachment_data/file/928350/2020_Energy_Consumption_in_the_UK__ECUK_.pdf

11 The UK has been increasing the proportion of food it produces since the decision to leave the EU. In 2017 it produced 50 per cent, the rest being imported. By 2019 that proportion had risen to 55 per cent. https://www.gov.uk/government/statistics/food-statistics-pocketbook/food-statistics-in-your-pocket-global-and-uk-supply

12 The falling costs of renewable sources of energy and legislation to curb the use of fossil fuels may make BP's most optimistic scenario

the most likely outcome. https://www.bp.com/content/dam/bp/
business-sites/en/global/corporate/pdfs/energy-economics/energy-
outlook/bp-energy-outlook-2019.pdf

13 The source is the Union of Concerned Scientists, founded in 1969 by
scientists and students at the Massachusetts Institute of Technology.
https://www.ucsusa.org/resources/environmental-impacts-natural-gas

14 In 1989 there were 420 reactors operating in the world, according to a
tally kept by the World Nuclear Association. By 2020 there were 441.
https://www.world-nuclear.org/information-library/current-and-
future-generation/nuclear-power-in-the-world-today.aspx

15 There are fears that large parts of Jakarta may be under water by 2050,
but moving the capital to Kalimantan will not solve that problem
and will extend urbanisation to previously undeveloped territory.
https://www.bbc.co.uk/news/world-asia-49481090

16 A study by the WWF and the Zoological Society of London (ZSL)
in 2015 concluded that the number of fish in the oceans was on
'the brink of collapse': https://www.scientificamerican.com/article/
ocean-fish-numbers-cut-in-half-since-1970/

17 The Census for Marine Life, a group of global researchers, produced
the first tally of global species in 2011: https://www.sciencedaily.com/
releases/2011/08/110823180459.htm

18 The EU argued that 'the promotion of biofuels offers clear benefits
both for security of energy supply and for mitigating climate change'
in a 2009 directive: https://ec.europa.eu/transport/themes/urban/
vehicles/road/biofuels_en

19 In 2018 the European Parliament called for a ban on using plant oil
for transport. https://www.reuters.com/article/us-eu-climatechange-
palmoil/eu-to-phase-out-palm-oil-from-transport-fuel-by-2030-
idUSKBN1JA21F

20 The Orangutan Foundation has been scathing about the massive
expansion of palm oil plantations and their threat to the survival of
orangutan populations in the wild: https://orangutan.org/rainforest/
the-effects-of-palm-oil/

21 Cobalt is one of several bottlenecks in the minerals needed for
battery production: https://ec.europa.eu/jrc/en/news/cobalt-potential-
bottle neck-transition-electric-mobility

22 The World Economic Forum's Global Battery Alliance in 2019
noted two key issues: the environmental and human costs of mining

scarce minerals, and recycling challenge as batteries come to the end of their life cycle: https://www.weforum.org/agenda/2019/03/the-dirty-secret-of-electric-vehicles/

23 In 2019 the BBC reported: 'The future of electric cars may depend on mining critically important metals on the ocean floor.' https://www.bbc.co.uk/news/science-environment-49759626

24 A story in *Newsweek* in 1975 prompted fears that there had been a sudden shift in the global climate, with a colder world leading to a slump in food production. https://yaleclimateconnections.org/2007/11/common-climate-misconceptions-1970s-global-cooling-concerns-lacked-todays-scientific-rigor-and-relevance/

25 The Intergovernmental Panel on Climate Change published a special report on the impact of a 1.5° increase in global temperatures above pre-Industrial Revolution levels in 2018: https://www.ipcc.ch/sr15/about/

4 TRADE AND FINANCE — GLOBALISATION CHANGES DIRECTION

1 The central idea supporting the proposition that trade benefits both sides is the concept of comparative advantage. This was developed by David Ricardo, the British economist, in his book *On the Principles of Political Economy and Taxation* (John Murray, 1817). Investopedia has a clear explanation of the concept here: https://www.investopedia.com/terms/c/comparativeadvantage.asp

2 There has been a string of books about the collapse of Lehman Brothers, and the debate continues as to whether there would have been less damage to the financial system and the world economy had the authorities decided to rescue it. One of the best analytical studies of the financial crisis is Alan S. Blinder's *After the Music Stopped* (Penguin Random House, 2013): https://www.penguinrandomhouse.com/books/312602/after-the-music-stopped-by-alan-s-blinder/. However, the most enjoyable way of catching a feeling for the story of the family that built up the financial empire was Stefano Massini's *The Lehman Trilogy*, which played in London in 2018 and in New York in 2019. https://www.nationaltheatre.org.uk/shows/the-lehman-trilogy

3 The pivotal event in the nineteenth century that pushed central banks to accept the role as lender of last resort to the banking system was the collapse of London's largest discount house, Overend Gurney,

in 1866. The Bank of England allowed it to fail, but then was forced to spend much more on supplying liquidity to the other banks. The bank published an analysis of the crisis on its 150th anniversary in its *Quarterly Bulletin*, in July 2016: https://www.bankofengland.co.uk/-/media/boe/files/quarterly-bulletin/2016/the-demise-of-overend-gurney.pdf?la=en&hash=04B001A02BD5ED7B35D4FB3CF1DDC2 33A1D271BD

4 The trend towards bringing jobs back to the US started around 2010, when manufacturing employment, which had been falling, started to climb. *Industry Week* carried an analysis of this transformation in July 2019: https://www.industryweek.com/the-economy/article/22027880/reshoring-was-at-record-levels-in-2018-is-it-enough

5 The Reserve Bank of Australia's *Bulletin* examined the shift to trade in services in its March 2019 issue: https://www.rba.gov.au/publications/bulletin/2019/mar/the-international-trade-in-services.html

6 The strongest argument against exchange controls is that they don't work. The Bank of England carried a short history of exchange controls around the world in its *Quarterly Bulletin*, September 1967. Though the UK was able to prevent British investors moving their money into other currencies, there was nothing to stop foreign holders doing so. A run on the pound led to sterling being devalued two months later, on 18 November. https://www.bankofengland.co.uk/quarterly-bulletin/1967/q3/the-uk-exchange-control-a-short-history

7 The corresponding figure for foreign-owned condominiums in Toronto was only 6 per cent. https://www.cmhc-schl.gc.ca/en/media-newsroom/news-releases/2019/new-insights-non-resident-ownership-and-participation-bc-on-ns-housing-markets

8 By the middle of 2021 the value of both Apple and Microsoft had risen above $2 trillion. https://www.cnet.com/news/microsoft-joins-apple-in-2-trillion-market-cap-club/

9 Negative real interest rates are historically extremely unusual. Before the twentieth century, which saw negative rates after the First World War and the Second World War, and briefly during the great inflation of the 1970s, the only period in the past 700 years of negative real rates was after the Black Death in the 1340s. Paul Schmelzing, *Eight centuries of global real interest rates, R-G, and the 'suprasecular' decline, 1311–2018*, Bank of England Staff Working Paper No. 845, 2020: https://www.bankofengland.co.uk/-/media/boe/files/

working-paper/2020/eight-centuries-of-global-real-interest-rates-r-g-and-the-suprasecular-decline-1311-2018

10 Eswar Prasad, *Has the dollar lost ground as the dominant international currency?* Brookings Institution, September 2019: https://www.brookings.edu/research/has-the-dollar-lost-ground-as-the-dominant-international-currency/

11 The sorry tale of Argentina as a serial defaulter is told in a Bloomberg column: Ben Bartenstein, Sydney Maki and Marisa Gertz, 'One Country, Nine Defaults: Argentina Is Caught in a Vicious Circle', updated May 2020: https://www.bloomberg.com/news/photo-essays/2019-09-11/one-country-eight-defaults-the-argentine-debacles?sref=IVPqAjWt

12 The insight that half the world's population was middle class for the first time in the history of humankind was highlighted in an article by Homi Kharas and Kristofer Hamel, 'A global tipping point: Half the world's population is now middle class or wealthier', published by Brookings Institution in September 2018. It starts: 'Something of enormous global significance is happening almost without notice. For the first time since agriculture-based civilisation began 10,000 years ago, the majority of humankind is no longer poor or vulnerable to falling into poverty.' The authors projected forward to 2030. In this book assumptions about the scale of the middle-class revolution are based on the HSBC calculations of GDP per head referred to in the Introduction. https://www.brookings.edu/blog/future-development/2018/09/27/a-global-tipping-point-half-the-world-is-now-middle-class-or-wealthier/

13 The blow to the world economy from the Covid-19 pandemic, while large and unevenly distributed, is small by comparison to the damage brought about by the wars of the twentieth century. The IMF estimates that for the world as a whole all the ground lost in 2020 will have been recovered by the end of 2021. *World Economic Outlook*, April 2021: https://www.imf.org/en/Publications/WEO/Issues/2021/03/23/world-economic-outlook-april-2021

5 TECHNOLOGY RACES ONWARDS

1 There are many clips of Steve Jobs's introduction of the iPhone in 2007 and they bear watching again and again for the simplicity of the explanation of why the iPhone did indeed 'change everything'. One clip is here: https://www.youtube.com/watch?v=x7qPAY9JqE4

2 The cost of higher education in the US rose by 497 per cent between the academic years of 1985-6 and 2017-18, more than twice the overall rate of inflation. https://www.forbes.com/sites/ zengernews/2020/08/31/college-tuition-is-rising-at-twice-the-inflation-rate-while-students-learn-at-home/?sh=38e7c2652f98

3 Jordan's water supplies were tight in the early 2000s when the population was just over five million. By 2020 it had risen to more than ten million. https://millenniumindicators.un.org/unsd/ ENVIRONMENT/envpdf/pap_wasess4a3jordan.pdf

4 In Jordan the average amount of water available annually per person is less than 150 cubic metres – one-sixtieth of the amount that is available to a person in the United States. https://www.nature.com/ articles/549142a

5 The UK's Office for National Statistics keeps a monthly tally of the proportion of retail sales (excluding motor fuel) that are online. This rose from 19 per cent to more than 36 per cent at the peak of the pandemic, and the proportion fell back to 26 per cent in the middle of 2021 when all shops were permitted to reopen. https://www.ons.gov.uk/businessindustryandtrade/retailindustry/ timeseries/j4mc/drsi

6 One of the many lessons from the Covid-19 pandemic was that it is impossible to teach children effectively online. Children may be unwilling to go to school, as Jacques's soliloquy, https://www. poetryfoundation.org/poems/56966/speech-all-the-worlds-a-stage in *As You Like It* tells us, but there are serious concerns that young people who lose time at school may be at a lasting disadvantage in later life.

7 *Popular Mechanics*, founded in 1902, has a long track record in predicting future technological developments. It surveys some of its predictions here: https://www.popularmechanics.com/flight/g462/ future-that-never-was-next-gen-tech-concepts/

8 The ONS has published some long-term data on changes in the UK economy, including trends in self-employment. Arguably, the unusual period was between 1945 and 1980, when self-employment was relatively low, rather than the present period when it has been climbing. https:// www.ons.gov.uk/economy/nationalaccounts/uksectoraccounts/ compendium/economicreview/april2019/longtermtrendsinukemploy ment1861to2018#employees-and-self-employed-workers

9 The Pew Research Center monitors social and economic attitudes in the US and internationally. It summarised its recent work on US personal satisfaction in an article: Patrick Van Kessel, 'How Americans feel about the satisfactions and stresses of modern life' in February 2020: https://www.pewresearch.org/fact-tank/2020/02/05/how-americans-feel-about-the-satisfactions-and-stresses-of-modern-life/

10 The OECD did a detailed study, *The Labour Share in G20 Economies*, in 2015: https://www.oecd.org/g20/topics/employment-and-social-policy/The-Labour-Share-in-G20-Economies.pdf

11 Charles Goodhart and Manoj Pradhan, *The Great Demographic Reversal: Ageing Societies, Waning Inequality, and an Inflation Revival* (Palgrave Macmillan, 2020).

12 It is quite possible that the shrinking share of labour in GNP may be about to change. The case for this was made in a paper: Charles Goodhart and Manoj Pradhan, *Demographics will reverse three multi-decade global trends*, BIS Working Papers No. 656, published by the Bank for International Settlements in 2017. This was subsequently developed into the book cited in note 11 above.

13 The story is put in clear perspective in a paper, Chris Smith, Brian McGuire, Ting Huang and Gary Yang, *The History of Artificial Intelligence* (University of Washington, 2006): https://courses.cs.washington.edu/courses/csep590/06au/projects/history-ai.pdf

14 Moorfields Eye Hospital, with the UCL Institute of Ophthalmology, was the highest ranked site in the world for eye research and teaching by the Centre for World University Rankings, 2017. https://www.moorfields.nhs.uk/content/breakthrough-ai-technology-improve-care-patients

15 The worries about the impact that widespread application of AI might have were summarised in a paper in *The Harvard Gazette* in October 2020, Christina Pazzanase, 'Great promise but potential for peril': https://news.harvard.edu/gazette/story/2020/10/ethical-concerns-mount-as-ai-takes-bigger-decision-making-role/

16 'The Zeta fiasco began with a triumphant claim and ended in utter embarrassment.' The story is told in a newsletter by ITER, an international project in the South of France to develop a fusion device to produce net energy: https://www.iter.org/newsline/-/2905

17 See John Horgan, 'Brilliant Scientists are Open-Minded about Paranormal Stuff, So Why Not You?', *Scientific American*, July 2012:

https://blogs.scientificamerican.com/cross-check/brilliant-scientists-
are-open-minded-about-paranormal-stuff-so-why-not-you/

18 Pew Research Center, October 2015: https://www.pewresearch.org/
fact-tank/2015/10/30/18-of-americans-say-theyve-seen-a-ghost/

6 HOW GOVERNMENTS – AND
GOVERNANCE – WILL SHIFT

1 Pew Research runs regular surveys of support for democracy around the
world. A thirty-four-nation survey in February 2020 (i.e. ahead of the
pandemic) reported that 'Democracy remains a popular idea among
average citizens, but commitment to democratic ideals is not always
strong. And many are unhappy with how democracy is working':
https://www.pewresearch.org/global/2020/02/27/democratic-rights-
popular-globally-but-commitment-to-them-not-always-strong/

2 A good source for data comparing the performance of the world
economy over different time periods, and that of developed countries
vis-à-vis the emerging world, is the series of *World Economic Outlook*
reports from the IMF: https://www.imf.org/en/Publications/WEO/
Issues/2021/03/23/world-economic-outlook-april-2021

3 See Hal Varian, https://www.aei.org/economics/googlenomics-a-
long- read-qa-with-chief-economist-hal-varian/, and *A microeconomist
looks at productivity.*

4 Hillary Clinton is far from alone as an example of a politician
disparaging voters who did not support them. National Public
Radio gave an apolitical explanation of why this phrase led to such a
strong reaction: https://www.npr.org/2016/09/10/493427601/hillary-
clintons-basket-of-deplorables-in-full-context-of-this-ugly-campaign

5 The Nobel Peace Prize was awarded to the European Union by
the Norwegian Nobel Committee, despite, or perhaps because of,
Norway not being a member of the EU. https://www.nobelprize.org/
prizes/peace/2012/summary/

6 The Berlin Wall was indeed torn down two years later. The Reagan
Foundation carries a recording of this speech here: https://www.
youtube.com/watch?v=5MDFX-dNtsM

7 According to OECD data one of the most trusted democracies is
Finland.   https://www.oecd.org/gov/understanding-the-drivers-of-
trust-in-government-institutions-in-finland-52600c9e-en.htm

8 There is a case to be made that voters will reward politicians who are prepared to make unpopular decisions. This was argued in an EC paper on the European economy: Marco Buti, Alessandro Turrini, Paul Van den Noord and Pietro Biroli, *Defying the 'Juncker Curse': Can Reformist Governments Be Re-elected?*, European Commission, Rodolfo Debenedetti Foundation, May 2008: https://ec.europa.eu/economy_finance/publications/pages/publication12586_en.pdf

9 The WHO set up an independent panel to review its performance. The panel concluded that the WHO should have declared a pandemic earlier than it did and that the combined response of the WHO and national governments was a 'toxic cocktail'. https://theindependentpanel.org/wp-content/uploads/2021/05/COVID-19-Make-it-the-Last-Pandemic_final.pdf

10 See Ben Bartenstein, Sydney Maki and Marisa Gertz, *One Country, Nine Defaults*, https://www.bloomberg.com/news/photo-essays/2019-09-11/one-country-eight-defaults-the-argentine-debacles?sref=IVPqAjWt.

11 See *ESG Reports and Ratings: What They Are, Why They Matter*, The Harvard Law School Forum on Corporate Governance, July 2017: https://corpgov.law.harvard.edu/2017/07/27/esg-reports-and-ratings-what-they-are-why-they-matter/

12 The 'no platform' movement in the UK dates back to the 1970s. See: Dr Evan Smith, 'A Policy Widely Abused: The Origins of the "No Platform" Policy of the National Union of Students', *History & Policy*, 2016. https://www.historyandpolicy.org/opinion-articles/articles/a-policy-widely-abused

13 See Homi Kharas and Kristofer Hamel, *A global tipping point:* https://www.brookings.edu/blog/future-development/2018/09/27/a-global-tipping-point-half-theworld-is-now-middle-class-or-wealthier/.

14 Samuel Huntington's essay 'The Clash of Civilizations' was first published in *Foreign Affairs* in 1993, and then developed in a book in 1995. It was enormously influential, catching the mood of concern about the pressures on the West. In 2013 *Foreign Affairs* carried a retrospective study, explaining how the essay came to be commissioned, and looking at what it got right and what it had got wrong: https://www.foreignaffairs.com/system/files/c0007.pdf

15 *The Future of World Religions: Population Growth Projections,*
   2010–2050: Why Muslims Are Rising Fastest and the Unaffiliated Are
   Shrinking as a Share of the World's Population: https://www.pewforum.
   org/2015/04/02/religious-projections-2010-2050/

7 THE AMERICAS

1 The Covid-19 pandemic seems to have cut fertility rates in much of
  the world, but it is probably most helpful to stick to the UN 2019
  projections until its impact is clearer. https://population.un.org/
  wpp/Publications/Files/WPP2019_Highlights.pdf

2 If the Pew projections prove right, the proportion of the US
  population of working age would decline only slightly, which would
  suggest that the US economy's size would be relatively larger than
  it would be under the UN numbers. https://www.pewresearch.org/
  hispanic/2008/02/11/us-population-projections-2005-2050/

3 Growth in the share of GDP accounted for by healthcare may have
  started to level off from about 2010 onwards. In 2018 it accounted for
  24 per cent of government spending. Ryan Nunn, Jana Parsons and
  Jay Shambaugh, *A dozen facts about the economics of the US healthcare system*, Brookings, 2020: https://www.brookings.edu/research/a-
  dozen-facts-about-the-economics-of-the-u-s-health-care-system/

4 See Patrick T. Ryan and Thomas H. Lee, 'Patients Are Giving High
  Marks to U.S. Health Care Providers During the Crisis', *Harvard
  Business Review*, May 2020: https://hbr.org/2020/05/patients-are-
  giving-high-marks-to-u-s-health-care-providers-during-the-crisis

5 The word 'meritocracy' was coined by Michael Young, later Lord
  Young of Dartington, in his satirical book *The Rise of the Meritocracy
  1870–2033*, published in 1958. He intended it to be used in a pejorative
  sense, but subsequently it came to be presented as a political ideal,
  notably by Tony Blair: 'I want a meritocracy, not survival of the fittest.'
  https://www.independent.co.uk/voices/commentators/i-want-
  meritocracy-not-survival-fittest-5365602.html

6 Daniel Markovits, *The Meritocracy Trap: How America's Foundational
  Myth Feeds Inequality, Dismantles the Middle Class* and *Devours the Elite*
  (Penguin Random House, 2020): https://www.penguinrandomhouse.
  com/books/548174/the-meritocracy-trap-by-daniel-markovits/

7 Anne Case and Angus Deaton, *Deaths of Despair and the Future of
  Capitalism* (Princeton University Press, 2020).

8 The US response to the pandemic may become a catalyst pushing the country towards collective responsibility and away from individual choice. Vaccination is a key indicator. The relatively successful vaccination programme of the US suggests that there is considerable underlying collective responsibility on that issue. https://www.cnbc.com/2021/07/30/us-covid-vaccine-rates-delta-variant.html

9 Los Cabos was the highest, with more than 110 murders per 100,000 people. Other Mexican cities in the top ten were Acapulco, Tijuana, La Paz and Ciudad Victoria. https://www.statista.com/statistics/243797/ranking-of-the-most-dangerous-cities-in-the-world-by-murder-rate-per-capita/

10 During the 1960s and early 1970s GDP per head in Venezuela fluctuated around 80 per cent of the US level. Data from the Maddison Historical Statistics Project, discussed in Diego Restuccia, *The Case of Venezuela*, Working Paper, Becker Friedman Institute, University of Chicago, 2019: https://bfi.uchicago.edu/wp-content/uploads/The-Case-of-Venezuela_2.pdf

8 EUROPE

1 Transparency International does an annual tally of perceived corruption. In 2020 New Zealand and Denmark had the lowest levels, followed by Finland, Singapore, Switzerland and Sweden. Out of 179 countries surveyed, Spain ranked 32nd, Italy 52nd and Greece 59th. https://www.transparency.org/en/cpi/2020/index/nzl

2 In 2020 the European Commission announced a €750 billion recovery plan designed to help members repair their economy from the damage done by the pandemic, NextGenerationEU. There has been no agreement as to whether this plan involves some mutualisation of Europe's debts, as claimed by some observers. This has been denied by the Commission. As of mid-2021 the plan was moving ahead. https://ec.europa.eu/commission/presscorner/detail/en/AC_21_3028

3 The authors of the Bruegel paper 'argue that none of the existing models of partnership with the EU would be suitable for the UK. They propose a new form of collaboration, a continental partnership, which is considerably less deep than EU membership but rather closer than a simple free-trade agreement.' Jean Pisani-Ferry, Norbert Röttgen, André Sapir, Paul Tucker and Guntram Wolff, *Europe after Brexit: A proposal for a continental partnership*,

Bruegel, August 2016: https://www.bruegel.org/2016/08/europe-after- brexit-a-proposal-for-a-continental-partnership/

4 The Atlantic Charter was signed by Winston Churchill and Franklin D. Roosevelt on 14 August 1941 and started formal military cooperation between the UK and US: https://www.nato.int/cps/en/natohq/official_texts_16912.htm. Discussions about intelligence cooperation had begun in February, when the head of Bletchley Park, Alastair Dennison, welcomed four US intelligence officials. This was the first of a series of meetings, which developed into the Five Eyes alliance: https://www.bbc.co.uk/news/uk-56284453. The alliance continues to develop. In 2019 it discussed cooperation beyond intelligence-sharing, including on critical technology, Hong Kong, supply chains and the Covid-19 pandemic, according to a statement by Australia's foreign minister Marise Payne in 2020. New Zealand resisted this expansion of the role of Five Eyes: https://www.reuters.com/world/china/new-zealand-says-uncomfortable-with-expanding-five-eyes-2021-04-19/

5 *New Statesman*, 29 January 2020: https://www.newstatesman.com/politics/uk/2020/01/over-next-decade-existential-questions-about-monarchy-will-have-be-answered

6 The Irish government has a clear description of the different elements of the Good Friday Agreement. The passage relating to a future referendum is: 'Before the Agreement, the Irish Constitution maintained a territorial claim to Northern Ireland. The new provisions approved by referendum state that, while it is the firm will of the Irish nation to unite the island, such changes can only be brought about by consent of a majority of the people, democratically expressed, in both jurisdictions in the island.' https://www.citizensinformation.ie/en/government_in_ireland/ireland_and_the_uk/good_friday_agreement.html

7 Ray Bassett, *Ireland and the EU Post Brexit* (Grangeland Ventures, 2020): https://www.waterstones.com/book/ireland-and-the-eu-post-brexit/ray-bassett/9781838039707

8 The phrase became the title of his pamphlet, *Ancestral Voices: Religion and Nationalism in Ireland* (University of Chicago Press, 1994): https://press.uchicago.edu/ucp/books/book/chicago/A/bo3623618.html

9 When, in 2015, Angela Merkel, the German Chancellor, famously said 'Wir schaffen das' – 'We can do it' – in response to the large numbers of immigrants seeking to enter the country, she acknowledged that

integrating the migrants would be a task for a long time. The Harvard Kennedy School uses this as a case programme here: https://case. hks.harvard.edu/wir-schaffen-das-angela-merkel-and-germanys-response-to-the-refugee-crisis-in-europe/

10 La Francophonie is both a description of the 300 million people who speak French across five continents, and an organisation dedicated since 1970 to promoting the language, and political, educational, economic and cultural cooperation among French speakers. https://www.francophonie.org/francophonie-brief-1763

11 It may seem curious to non-French speakers that thirty years of huge political disruption should be called 'Les Trente Glorieuses'. But along with the so-called economic miracles of Germany and France, it caught the sense of relief as Western Europe recovered from the Second World War. See Nicholas Crafts and Gianni Toniolo, *'Les Trente Glorieuses': From the Marshall Plan to the Oil Crisis* (Oxford University Press, 2012): https://www.oxfordhandbooks.com/view/10.1093/oxfordhb/9780199560981.001.0001/oxfordhb-9780199560981-e-18

12 Talks between Switzerland and the EU about their future relationship broke down in May 2021. https://www.bruegel.org/2021/05/what-swiss-voters-expect-to-happen-next-after-eu-talks-fail/

13 East Thrace, the part of Turkey that is in Europe, accounts for 3 per cent of the country's land area and 14 per cent of its population. https://en.wikipedia.org/wiki/East_Thrace#:~:text=East%20Thrace%20has%20an%20area,2%20for%20Asiatic%20Turkey%2C%20which

9 ASIA

1 For a good explanation of why China is so determined to redress the wrongs of the century of humiliation, see: Matt Shiavenza, 'How Humiliation Drove Modern Chinese History', *The Atlantic*, October 2013: https://www.theatlantic.com/china/archive/2013/10/how-humiliation-drove-modern-chinese-history/280878/

2 The UN central projection for China's population shows it still above one billion in 2100. This may be too high. *The Lancet* has carried a new study of global population trends and their economic implications through to 2100. All its projections for China's population show it falling below one billion in the 2070s. 'Fertility, mortality, migration, and population scenarios for 195 countries and territories from 2017

to 2100: a forecasting analysis for the Global Burden of Disease Study', Prof Stein Emil Vollset, DrPH et al., *The Lancet*, July 2020: https://www.thelancet.com/article/S0140-6736(20)30677-2/ fulltext

3 The commitment to reach carbon neutrality by 2060 was made by President Xi Jinping in September 2020. https://www.bbc.co.uk/ news/science-environment-54256826

4 Christian Nordqvist, 'The Origins of The Black Death Traced Back To China, Gene Sequencing Has Revealed', *Medical News Today*, November 2010: https://www.medicalnewstoday.com/ articles/206309#1

5 *The Lancet* population study (see note 2 above) projected that by 2100 the US would have recovered its position as the world's largest economy, passing China towards the end of the century.

6 Lev Nachman, Nathan Kar Ming Chan and Chit Wai John Mok, 'Hong Kongers Say Taiwan Is Their First Choice As Exile Looms', *Foreign Policy*, July 2020: https://foreignpolicy.com/2020/07/08/ hong-kong-exile-taiwan-first-choice/

7 The share of pre-tax income of both the top 1 per cent and the top 10 per cent of Indians rose sharply from 1990 through to 2010, but seem to have not risen much further since then. https://wid.world/ country/india/

8 One measure of Japan turning inwards has been the decline in the number of students studying abroad. This reached a peak of 83,000 in 2004, but since then has fallen to below 60,000. https:// thediplomat.com/2021/06/japans-youth-lack-interest-in-studying-abroad-thats-a-problem-for-japanese-businesses/

9 The Human Capital Project was launched in 2018 by the World Bank to measure the skill levels of the workforce, and help find ways of improving these by, among other things, better education and healthcare: https:// www.worldbank.org/en/publication/human-capital

10 The World Bank's country studies give a balanced and candid assessment of their economic progress: https://www.worldbank.org/ en/country/vietnam/overview

11 In 2016 the International Court of Arbitration in The Hague ruled that China's claims of sovereignty over the South China Sea had no legal basis. https://www.nytimes.com/2016/07/13/world/asia/south-china-sea-hague-ruling-philippines.html

10 AFRICA AND THE MIDDLE EAST

1 Source: World Population Review. Niger, Nigeria's northern neighbour, in 2020 had an even lower median age, 14.8 years, the lowest in the world. https://worldpopulationreview.com/country-rankings/median-age

2 In 1960 median life expectancy for sub-Saharan Africa was just over forty, according to World Bank data. By 1989 it was over fifty. It then fell slightly before recovering from 2001 onwards. By 2019 it was just under sixty-two. https://data.worldbank.org/indicator/SP.DYN.LE00.IN?locations=ZG

3 The symbolic handshake between Tony Blair and Colonel Muammar Gaddafi ended thirty years of non-communication between the West and Libya. https://www.theguardian.com/world/2004/mar/25/libya.politics

4 Saif al-Islam Gaddafi gave the Ralph Miliband Lecture at the LSE in May 2010. The lecture series was named after the father of David and Ed Miliband, David being former foreign secretary under Gordon Brown and Ed former leader of the Labour Party. https://www.bbc.co.uk/news/uk-england-london-12659391

5 The most recent subject of tension between Egypt, Sudan and Ethiopia is the Grand Ethiopian Renaissance Dam. A dispute over the filling of the dam, which will generate power from the waters of the Blue Nile, was discussed at the UN Security Council in July 2021. https://www.bbc.co.uk/news/world-africa-53432948

6 The BBC has a transcript of the Reith Lectures of Daniel Barenboim here: http://downloads.bbc.co.uk/rmhttp/radio4/transcripts/20060428_reith.pdf

11 AUSTRALIA, NEW ZEALAND AND THE PACIFIC OCEAN

1 Technically the continent of Oceania only refers to the landmasses of the south-western quadrant of the Pacific Ocean, not the Pacific itself. Continents are land, not sea. But the Pacific is so important to the future of the world that one cannot ignore it. https://www.britannica.com/place/Oceania-region-Pacific-Ocean

2 The Australian government has a website that carries information 'to support the planning needs of Australia's natural resource management sector, and to provide information to assist climate

adaptation processes': https://www.climatechangeinaustralia.gov.au/en/overview/about-site/

3 For an analysis of New Zealand's approach to the pandemic see: Alexis Robert, 'Lessons from New Zealand's COVID-19 Outbreak Response', *The Lancet*, October 2020.

4 See Dr Jamie Schutler and Professor Andy Watson, Guest post: 'The oceans are absorbing more carbon than previously thought', *Carbon Brief*, September 2020: https://www.carbonbrief.org/guest-post-the-oceans-are-absorbing-more-carbon-than-previously-thought

5 The General Bathymetric Chart of the Oceans publishes an up-to-date record of the progress of the project: https://www.gebco.net/

12 THE BIG THEMES THAT WILL SHAPE THE WORLD AHEAD – FEARS, HOPES, JUDGEMENTS

1 Writing in 2021 it is too early to gauge the long-term impact of the pandemic on US/China relations, particularly since the origins of the virus are still unclear. But it cannot be positive. The question is whether it will be somewhat negative, or profoundly so.

2 Cognitive bias may be particularly evident in higher education, at least in troubled academic units. See: Sebastian Wraight, C. K. Gunsalus and Nicholas Burbules, 'Understanding and Navigating Cognitive Biases', *Inside Higher Ed*, September 2018: https://www.insidehighered.com/advice/2018/09/26/cognitive-biases-are-work-many-troubled-academic-departments-opinion

3 Janna Anderson and Lee Rainie, 'The Future of Truth and Misinformation Online', Pew Research Center, October 2017: https://www.pewresearch.org/internet/2017/10/19/the-future-of-truth-and-misinformation-online/

4 'Why Obama Fears for Our Democracy'. Interview in *The Atlantic*, November 2020: https://www.theatlantic.com/ideas/archive/2020/11/why-obama-fears-for-our-democracy/617087/

5 Sometimes the quote is concertinaed into 'democracy is the worst form of government – except for all the others ...' omitting the qualifying 'it has been said'. The speech was made in November 1947. https://winstonchurchill.org/resources/quotes/the-worst-form-of-government/

6 The Chinese government expects the population to start falling in 2029. But it may be sooner. https://www.reuters.com/article/us-china-population-idUSKCN1OZ08A

7 The central estimate in the population study published in *The Lancet* suggests that the UK will be the most populous country in Europe in 2100 with 71.45 million people, followed by France at 67.15 million and Germany at 66.42 million. See 'Fertility, mortality, migration, and population scenarios', Vollset et al., *The Lancet*: https://www.thelancet.com/article/S0140-6736 (20)30677-2/fulltext

8 George Washington's *Farewell Address* was a collaborative effort, with an initial draft by James Madison, a substantial rewrite by Alexander Hamilton and a final edit by Washington. https://www.mountvernon.org/library/digitalhistory/digital-encyclopedia/article/george-washington-s-farewell-address/

9 The population of Greenland in 2021 was 57,000, so the practical impact of its leaving the EU in 1982 was minimal. https://www.thenewfederalist.eu/23rd-february-1982-the-day-greenland-left-the-european-union?lang=fr#:~:text=On%2023rd%20February%201982%2C%20Greenland,times%20the%20size%20of%20Germany.

10 Jack Ma called for a total rethink of how globalisation should work to make it more inclusive at the World Economic Forum at Davos in January 2019. https://www.weforum.org/agenda/2019/01/jack-mas-plans-to-reform-globalization-from-the-bottom-up-heres-how/

11 A helpful BBC report on Jack Ma's disappearance at the end of 2020 is here: https://www.bbc.co.uk/news/technology-56448688

12 Charles Darwin's *On the Origin of Species* is available in eBook form on the Project Gutenberg website: https://www.gutenberg.org/files/1228/1228-h/1228-h.htm

ACKNOWLEDGEMENTS

1 Julian Gewirtz, *Unlikely Partners: Chinese Reformers, Western Economists, and the Making of Global China* (Cambridge: Harvard University Press, 2017). https://www. hup.harvard.edu/catalog.php?isbn=9780674971134.

Acknowledgements

This book has truly been a group effort, and it is impossible to name everyone who has shaped my ideas about the way the future of the world economy has been unfolding. But quite aside from being able to thank some of the people who have contributed in one way or another, I should try to explain how my thinking developed.

First, my background and education. My interest in trying to understand how the world economy will evolve goes back to my upbringing in Ireland, where my father Donald McRae, after service in the RAF in the Second World War, set up a small textile agency. Going round with him to the clothing manufacturers in Dublin gave me a feeling for the business world. Visiting his German suppliers near Düsseldorf, who were still rebuilding after the devastation of the war, taught me about the resilience of the country's medium-sized enterprises, the Mittelstand. In the 1950s and early 1960s Ireland was still struggling to establish its clothing exports, and the German economy was still rebuilding after the destruction of the war. Both faced a tough haul. But the quality of German goods was excellent and I became aware how Germany was displacing Britain in that area of manufacturing. I could also see how the Irish economy could do so much better, and how exports would be the key to success.

The further advantage in being brought up in Ireland was that, as in all small countries, you are forced to think global. The noise of the domestic economy is not loud enough to drown out the signals from the rest of the world. Prior to joining the European Union, Ireland inevitably looked to the UK, where so many of its people were going to find work, but also to the US and to Europe. This was long before investment by the American high-tech giants helped transform the economy, and payments from the EU helped transform its infrastructure, but culturally Ireland already was beginning to feel like both a mid-Atlantic nation and a continental European one. I remember the wave of warmth that swept over the country when John F. Kennedy visited in 1963 – and also that unlike in Britain, the roads were full of French and German cars.

I was also fortunate to be taught my economics in Ireland, at Trinity College Dublin. That is partly because the course was exceptionally broad, ranging from politics and economic history through to statistics and econometrics. But it was also because our tutors were directly involved in real-life economic policy. I remember a seminar with Professor Louden Ryan about incomes policy and inflation. Ireland had a system of national collective bargaining, and with wage costs pushing up inflation it was seeking to try to talk down pay increases. We students were arguing that in the long run incomes policies would fail, and that supply and demand for labour would determine real pay rates. Louden looked at his watch, and said that in an hour's time he would be advising the government on setting a pay norm for the coming year. If they managed to hold down pay settlements by a half a percentage point there would be a few thousand more people in work in a year's time. Was that not something worth trying to do?

Of course we had to agree. For students it was a lesson about the interplay between politics and economics. Looking at China now you can see similar issues about the relationship between government policies, private enterprise and working people, as we saw in Ireland more than half a century ago.

My next debt is to journalism, and to my many colleagues with whom I have worked over the years, particularly at the *Independent* but also at the *Guardian* and most recently the *Mail on Sunday*. The phrase popularised by Philip Graham, co-owner of the *Washington Post*, is that journalism is 'the first rough draft of history'. I think that is right. If you spend your time writing about what is happening to your area of interest, in my case the world economy, you become aware that you will make judgements that turn out to be wrong. You know that what you are producing is a very rough draft. But you do catch a sense of what is truly important and what is just noise. You are guided both by your colleagues and by your competitors, and you can see in print where you have been right and where you have not. Having written *The World in 2020* of course helps, but as I acknowledged then, I relied a great deal on the interaction with other journalists, sometimes in ways that I was not really aware of at the time. I can hardly scratch the surface, but I would particularly like to acknowledge a debt to three people who taught me the basics, in particular the need for a mixture of scepticism and judgement, and that ultimately the person who truly matters is your reader. These are William Clarke and Richard Fry, both of whom I worked with at *The Banker*, and Sir Patrick Sergeant, the City Editor at the *Daily Mail* who founded *Euromoney*.

At the *Guardian* I was fortunate to work with Alastair Hetherington, the editor who hired me, and Sir Peter Gibbings, managing director and then chairman, who together had saved the paper from being taken over by *The Times* in 1966. They helped me understand the fragile base on which independent journalism rested. It was a joy to work with the team of outstanding journalists there and to see the paper gradually achieve a sound financial position.

At the *Independent*, my first debt is to its founders, Andreas Whittam Smith, Stephen Glover and Matthew Symonds, for having created a newspaper that gave huge freedom to its writers. I am also grateful to the people I have worked with there for many years, and particularly for the unfailing support from its editors, including Andrew Marr, Simon Kelner and Amol Rajan. I should also thank Sir Anthony O'Reilly, who controlled the group from 1998 to 2009, for his enthusiasm for the global view I have tried to project. Finally, my thanks to my colleagues on the *Daily Mail* and the *Mail on Sunday* for helping me craft my words for the huge readership those papers bring.

The other massive benefit of being a journalist is that you talk with vast numbers of people all around the world and in all walks of life. The success of *The World in 2020* led me to spend much of the past quarter-century travelling the globe, talking about its economic future. That was a huge privilege. You learn as much as you give, probably more, from a dinner overlooking the Bosphorus in Istanbul, or a breakfast in Monaco with the clients of a US corporation, or a tour of Australian cities with a fund management group. Sometimes it is the chance remark that helps frame a judgement. I remember being told by the head of the largest industrial group in a middle-income country that he saw 'no light at the end of the tunnel'. Since then that country, despite its huge potential, has had a very bumpy ride. Of course given the breadth of the subject matter of this book, many judgements here are second-hand. Where I haven't detailed knowledge myself, I have relied on the views of people whose judgement I would trust. I am grateful to my craft of journalism. I am even more grateful to the hundreds of people who, either in conversations or in their writings, have shaped my understanding of how the world economy works. But while I have been influenced by many people, the big ideas of the final chapter, in particular, really are my own best effort to reach the right balance between the forces that are pulling against each other. The errors are all my own.

For the economic core of the book, the vision of the late Angus Maddison was extraordinarily helpful, as I acknowledge in the Introduction. I should also thank the economists at the OECD for introducing me to his work, though sadly I never met him. As I also stress in the Introduction, it was the pioneering calculations of the Goldman Sachs team that developed the BRICs report, which really changed everyone's perceptions of the importance of the emerging economies. Lord O'Neill deserves the credit he has received for leading that team. I have used the more recent work by HSBC and thank Stephen King, senior economic adviser to the bank, and Karen Ward, now at J. P. Morgan Asset Management. I should also pay tribute to the thousands of statisticians in governments and international agencies. They are the unsung heroes who collect, sift and evaluate the data – almost always without political spin – on which the rest us depend.

Some parts of the world have been straightforward to assess. I was born in England during the Second World War, but growing up on the other side of the Irish Sea has given me a more detached perspective on the future of these islands. Continental Europe has been familiar territory, both for work and for holidays. And I have been most fortunate in getting to know the United States, with many visits since spending a summer in the north suburbs of Chicago in the 1960s – and meeting my many cousins right across the country. I have long felt that I can get a truer fix on the country from a few days chatting with family in Montana than from any number of interviews in Washington DC or New York. I now have a further direct interest in the future of the US: American grandchildren.

Other parts of the world have been more difficult to assess, and though I have visited nearly all the places I have written about, sometimes I have relied on others. I am grateful to my hosts and hope I have fairly reflected the range of views I have encountered. I hope my cautious optimism about Latin America, sub-Saharan Africa and the Middle East will be justified and thank the scores of people I have spoken with about these areas over many years.

My world view has been much shaped by witnessing the economic take-off, first of China, and then of India. For China my interest was sharpened by my father-in-law, Sir Alec Cairncross, who made several visits to China in the 1980s, met with Deng Xiaoping, and was one of the foreign advisers on the famous cruise on the SS *Bashan* on the Yangtze River in 1985. He urged China to move cautiously in liberalising its economy, in sharp contrast to the 'big bang' approach subsequently taken by Russia. The role of western advisers is told in *Unlikely Partners: Chinese Reformers, Western Economists, and the Making of Global China* by Julian Gewirtz.[1] Many years later, Guo Shuqing, then chairman of China Construction Bank, who had met Sir Alec when studying at Oxford University, helped my wife, Frances Cairncross, and me to organise a visit to several cities in China.

He is currently chairman of the China Banking and Insurance Regulatory Commission. While he had no role in this book and our conversations took place before Xi Jinping became President of the People's Republic, I am grateful to him for the feeling he gave me of the longer-term aims of the Chinese leadership, and the mixture of caution and self-confidence with which it is seeking to achieve those aims. For a different perspective on China, I have been guided by several friends who have made their careers in Hong Kong, and particularly by David Webb, an activist investor and former investment banker, who runs a website that aims to improve corporate and financial governance.

I have come to know and I hope understand India thanks to many family friends there. In particular I would like to thank Sathi and Mithu Alur – a connection that goes back more than fifty years. Sathi has been, among other activities, a consultant for the World Bank, while Mithu founded ADAPT, a charity that provides education and skills development for people with cerebral palsy, based in Mumbai. They and their family have helped me understand many aspects of India's economic and social progression. Thanks also to Mohan and Nina Bopiah, architects in Bangalore, who gave me a window onto the high-tech boom of the region.

I also thank a noted Japanese economist and a friend of long standing, Tadashi Nakamae, for his insights into both the economy of Japan and its society. We have cooperated on several projects, including co-writing a book, and thanks to his insights I feel I understand much more about the country and its ideas.

A number of people have been directly involved with the book. First of all my thanks to Michael Fishwick, my editor at Bloomsbury, who commissioned it and has encouraged and supported me from the start – just as he did with *The World in 2020* all those years ago. Michael, it has been great to work with you again. It has been edited by four people. My daughter Alex Dimsdale has helped shape the whole project from the very beginning, encouraging me to get on and write it, commenting on the direction and tone, and then copy-editing the draft. Many of the best phrases come from her. It was further edited by Adrian Baker, a colleague on the *Mail on Sunday*, who saw a way of fixing a serious structural flaw in the final chapter. Thank you so much for that. It was then polished by Richard Collins, who was also a wise sounding-board as to the best way of putting something to make the point I was trying to get over. And finally it was beautifully proofread by Catherine Best, who not only caught some embarrassing errors and made those small changes that make reading the book more pleasurable, but also inspired one crucial sentence that I am really pleased to have got on board. Many thanks also go to Michael Roscoe, who I have worked with for many years, who prepared the excellent graphs, and to David Atkinson, who has done the index. Thank you all so very much. It has been a joy to work with you.

At Bloomsbury, I feel I have been really well served. Alongside Michael Fishwick have been Amanda Waters and Kieron Connolly. Lauren Whybrow and Elisabeth Denison have ushered the book through production with efficiency and grace. Greg Heinimann designed the beautiful cover. Sophie Davidson took the author photo. The rights team, led by Stephanie Purcell, have been most professional. My thanks, too, to Anna Massardi and Genista Tate-Alexander for their work in publicity and marketing.

However, my greatest debt is to my family. I have noted above the huge role my daughter Alex played in creating this book. I also owe thanks to her American husband Taylor Dimsdale, an environmental analyst, for important reshaping of the chapter on resources and the environment. My other daughter Izzy and her husband Jamie Aitkenhead have helped more generally by being a sounding-board for my ideas on geopolitics and economics. Finally, my deepest gratitude goes to Frances Cairncross, my spouse, partner and best friend for more than half a century. All of you will recognise thoughts, ideas and judgements that I have taken from you and dropped into the book. For this, and for so much more, I am profoundly grateful.

Hamish McRae
London, March 2022

Index

A Note on the Author

Hamish McRae is an economic commentator for the *Independent*, and writes weekly columns on economics and finance in the *Mail on Sunday* and the *i* newspaper. He has been financial editor of the *Guardian* and the *Independent*, and has won numerous awards, including Business and Finance Journalist of the Year at the British Press Awards. He is an Orwell Fellow. His other books include *The World in 2020: Power, Culture and Prosperity – A Vision of the Future; What Works: Success in Stressful Times*; and, written with Frances Cairncross, *Capital City: London as a Financial Centre.*

A Note on the Type

The text of this book is set Adobe Garamond. It is one of several versions of Garamond based on the designs of Claude Garamond. It is thought that Garamond based his font on Bembo, cut in 1495 by Francesco Griffo in collaboration with the Italian printer Aldus Manutius. Garamond types were first used in books printed in Paris around 1532. Many of the present-day versions of this type are based on the Typi Academiae of Jean Jannon cut in Sedan in 1615.

Claude Garamond was born in Paris in 1480. He learned how to cut type from his father and by the age of fifteen he was able to fashion steel punches the size of a pica with great precision. At the age of sixty he was commissioned by King Francis I to design a Greek alphabet, and for this he was given the honourable title of royal type founder. He died in 1561.